How RTI Works in Secondary Schools

Building a Framework for Success

Holly Windram

Kerry Bollman

Sara Johnson

Solution Tree | Press

a division of

Solution Tree

555 North Morton Street
Bloomington, IN 47404
800.733.6786 (toll free) / 812.336.7700
FAX: 812.336.7790
email: info@solution-tree.com
solution-tree.com

Visit **go.solution-tree.com/rti** to download the reproducibles in this book.

Printed in the United States of America

15 14 13 12 11   1 2 3 4 5

FSC
www.fsc.org
MIX
Paper from
responsible sources
FSC® C011935

Library of Congress Cataloging-in-Publication Data

Windram, Holly.
  How RTI works in secondary schools : building a framework for success / Holly Windram, Kerry Bollman, Sara Johnson.
       p. cm.
  Includes bibliographical references and index.
  ISBN 978-1-935542-87-2 (perfect bound) -- ISBN 978-1-935542-88-9 (library edition)
  1. Remedial teaching--United States. 2. Education, Secondary--United States. 3. Response to intervention (Learning disabled children) I. Bollman, Kerry. II. Johnson, Sara. III. Title.
  LB1029.R4W56 2012
  371.9'043--dc23
                                 2011037661

Solution Tree
Jeffrey C. Jones, CEO & President

Solution Tree Press
President: Douglas M. Rife
Publisher: Robert D. Clouse
Vice President of Production: Gretchen Knapp
Managing Production Editor: Caroline Wise
Senior Production Editor: Edward M. Levy
Proofreader: Sarah Payne-Mills
Text Designer: Raven Bongiani
Cover Designer: Orlando Angel

Acknowledgments

We are grateful to our amazing husbands, Luke, Alex, and Casey, for their patience, love, and support. We also thank our children, Sophia, Elinor, Zachary, Ingrid, Ben, Sam, and Allie for their love, honesty, and constant reminders of what is really important.

Many thanks to all our colleagues at the St. Croix River Education District. The thoughtful work of the Instructional Services Team, in particular, is well represented in this text. We are appreciative of the staff in SCRED member districts, who work tirelessly to make the ideals of RTI a reality, and to serve all children with excellence. We continue to learn from your work.

We thank Dave Ertl, Chisago Lakes High School principal for challenging us to refine and improve our ideas, saying "no" until those ideas were really ready, and then giving his full support. We thank our students for having taught us at least as much as we have taught them.

Finally, thank you to the staff of Solution Tree for the opportunity to share the excellent work of numerous educators who are fully committed to kids.

Solution Tree Press would like to thank the following reviewers:

Barbara Criss
Coordinator, Response to Intervention
Lexington County School District One
Lexington, South Carolina

Susan Gingras Fitzell
Educational Consultant
AimHi Educational Programs
Manchester, New Hampshire

Carole Marcotte
Director of Curriculum
Regional School Unit #23
Saco, Maine

Sara Prewett
Program Associate, Center for Research on Learning
The University of Kansas
Lawrence, Kansas

Wendy Robinson
Regional Director
Heartland Area Education Agency 11
Johnston, Iowa

Suzanne Shumock
Intervention Coach
Sumrall Middle School
Sumrall, Mississippi

Dolly Thomas
Eighth-Grade Inclusion Teacher
Western Oaks Middle School
Bethany, Oklahoma

Teresa Weightman-Moore
Special Education Department Coordinator
Hononegah High School
Rockton, Illinois

Karen Wendorf-Heldt
Director of Education
Wausau School District
Wausau, Wisconsin

Table of Contents

Reproducible pages are in italics.
Visit **go.solution-tree.com/rti** to download the reproducibles in this book.

Chapter 4

Tier 1 Assessment: Screening for Secondary Students 47

Chapter 5

Tier 1 Core Instruction: Academics 63

Chapter 6

Tier 1 Core Instruction: Schoolwide Positive Behavior Supports . . . 77

Chapter 7

Tier 1 Problem Solving: The Systems Level 89

Chapter 8

Tier 2 Assessment: Progress Monitoring Options 109

Chapter 14

RTI and Special Education Entitlement Under SLD 189

Epilogue 197

References and Resources 203

Index 223

About the Authors

Holly Windram, PhD, is the chief education officer for the Grand Rapids Christian Schools in Grand Rapids, Michigan. In this role, she manages and evaluates all curriculum and instructional programming preK–12, with an emphasis on data-based decision making, problem-solving, and research-based instruction that is well matched to student needs. Previously, she was a school psychologist, assistant director of special education, and director of special education at the St. Croix River Education District. She consults and presents nationally on how to establish, scale up, and sustain a response to intervention (RTI) framework in secondary settings with regard to assessment, instruction, and problem solving for both academics and positive behavior supports.

Holly has given dozens of presentations on implementation of an intensive five-step problem-solving process, secondary classroom management, roles for school psychologists within an RTI framework, implementing a Tier 2 "check and connect" intervention for secondary learners, action planning for RTI implementation, and implementation integrity within an RTI framework. She is a member of the Association for Supervision and Curriculum Development, the Council for Exceptional Children, the National Association of School Psychologists, and Phi Beta Kappa.

Holly completed bachelor's degrees in psychology and English at Michigan State University and earned a doctorate in educational psychology from the University of Minnesota.

Kerry Bollman is instructional services coordinator and reading center director for St. Croix River Education District. She consults regularly with general and special education staff on research-based and data-driven assessment and instruction, as well as on developing schoolwide organizational frameworks around problem-solving teams to address the needs of all students. The district has received national recognition for its use of these response to intervention systems.

Previously, as an intervention specialist in the suburban Chicago area, Kerry supported implementation of behavioral and academic programming for students with significant disabilities and provided coaching for and later coordinated a statewide grant to support problem-solving teams in elementary and secondary schools. Her areas of expertise include curriculum-based assessment and evaluation, early literacy, designing and evaluating academic interventions, and data-based decision making within an RTI framework.

Kerry was instrumental in the original design of the Minnesota Reading Corps, a tutoring program that harnesses the power of volunteers to provide one-on-one and small-group reading practice to students from the age of three through grade 3, and currently supports statewide training and evaluation of the program. She has published several articles on RTI topics and provides training and consultation locally and nationally. She earned a bachelor's degree from Northwestern University and completed the Specialist in School Psychology program at Illinois State University.

Sara Johnson is the principal at Lakeside Elementary School in the Chisago Lakes School District. She had previously served as the associate principal at Chisago Lakes High School in Lindstrom, Minnesota. She is also an adjunct professor, teaching graduate classes on implementing response to intervention at St. Cloud State University. Sara was a school counselor and dean before becoming an administrator in 2003. At Chisago Lakes, her focus has been on establishing an effective RTI system for the school of approximately 1,200 students in grades 9 through 12. Her presentations provide real-life, hands-on experiences for educators working to implement an RTI system in their school. In addition to numerous presentations on RTI-related topics, she has written several journal articles.

Sara received a bachelor's degree from Moorhead State University and a master's and K–12 administrative license from St. Cloud State University in St. Cloud, Minnesota.

The three authors are practitioners who have worked in school districts that have lengthy, hands-on experience with RTI implementation across multiple secondary settings. These schools are in member districts of the St. Croix River Education District, based in Rush City, Minnesota, which has a thirty-year history of research-based, data-driven practices leading to increased student achievement (Bollman, Silberglitt, & Gibbons, 2007; Burns & Gibbons, 2008). In addition, they have worked and provided consultation in secondary settings across the United States. Also included are the voices of diverse secondary practitioners who have all been directly involved with putting research into practice at various points in the RTI continuum in progressive secondary buildings across the nation.

To book Holly, Kerry, or Sara for professional development, contact pd@solution-tree.com.

Introduction

It might seem like too bold an undertaking to write a book proclaiming to know how something works, as if there could possibly be one answer—especially something as complex and multifaceted as response to intervention. Perhaps a more accurate (though far less elegant) title would have been *RTI in Secondary Schools: What We Have Found the Crucial Elements to Be, and Ideas and Resources We Have Tested Out for Implementing These Elements Successfully.* It should be clear why we didn't use it; however, we feel confident that that is what you will learn in this book.

Although there is not any one way that RTI works, we believe there are a few non-negotiable tenets that permeate any quality implementation. Among these are (1) quality assessment practices for all, some, and few students; (2) a cascade of instructional options designed to meet the needs of the full continuum of students in the building; and (3) systems for ongoing decision making aimed at using the data to determine how to best allocate the instructional resources to maximize student outcomes.

In this book, we will share what we have learned about making these systems a reality in secondary settings. In this respect, the phrase *How RTI Works* in the title is especially apt. This book is designed for readers interested in actual implementation of RTI. This is because, in our view, RTI is more than a highfalutin theoretical construct about allocation of resources. It is a collection of actions set in place by educators who believe that if we work together to share the load, we really can reach every student.

How This Book Is Organized

The goal of chapters 1 and 2 is to lay the groundwork for why RTI should be implemented in secondary settings and to describe the critical constructs in practice. Chapter 3 describes the innovative RTI practices at Chisago Lakes High School, a midsized, midwestern 9–12 building. RTI is conceptualized within a multitiered model (Batchse et al., 2005). Chapters 3 through 6 focus on Tier 1, or core practices that are applied to every student. Chapters 7 through 9 focuses on Tier 2, or supplemental practices applied to some, but not all students. Chapters 10 through 13 focus on Tier 3, or intensive practices applied to a few students. In chapter 14, we discuss RTI as it relates to special education eligibility for specific learning disabilities. In the epilogue, we share some final thoughts.

At the end of certain chapters, you will find reproducible forms and checklists, as well as sample schedules and agendas, that you can use to ensure that your implementation has a high degree of integrity. At **go.solution-tree.com/rti**, you will find these same reproducibles available for downloading. Also online, you will find an extensive list of resources, keyed to the chapter topics.

Let's begin with the most basic question, What is RTI, and what does it look like for secondary schools?

CHAPTER 1

What Is RTI, and What Does It Look Like for Secondary Schools?

The persistence of these educational [achievement] gaps imposes on the United States the economic equivalent of a permanent national recession.

—McKinsey

If a child can't learn the way we teach, maybe we should teach the way they learn.

—Ignacio Estrada

Advance Organizer

✓ While response to intervention, or RTI, is a relatively new term in education, the constructs and practices involved in implementing RTI are not.

✓ The starting point for implementing RTI is the belief that we educate all our children.

✓ The rationale for implementing an RTI framework is legal, social, and financial. We cannot afford not to do it.

✓ Secondary settings have unique features that warrant special consideration for RTI implementation.

If you are a secondary educator who has attended any educational conference or workshop in recent years, or if you have been listening to current trends in education, you have heard the phrase *response to intervention,* or *RTI*. Chances are you have noticed vendors for educational products or publications attaching the acronym RTI to their product, whether or not it was there five or ten years ago, and presenters adding it to presentation titles. Chances are also that when you did hear this term, it was embedded in an elementary school context.

If you are a secondary educator, it is likely that you have anywhere from a vague to well-developed understanding of RTI as an organizational framework to meet the needs of all learners across a multitiered model (most often three tiers) that includes data-driven decision making and empirically supported instruction. However, you have probably picked up this book because you have a more urgent question no one has been able to answer thus far, How does RTI work in secondary schools? This book is designed to answer that question.

Nothing New Under the Sun

Let's get straight to the heart of RTI and what this book is about: effective instruction leads to successful outcomes for kids. *Instruction* means everything we do, say, or teach every minute of the school day related to academics and social behavior, and *kids* refers to every child who walks through our schools' doors. RTI is not about adding something new to an already full plate. While there has been a proliferation of rhetoric around RTI as the new gold standard for educating all our children, any educator, nontenured or veteran, will find that the fundamental constructs of RTI are the same as those of effective instructional practices that have been known for decades—that is, high-quality, research-supported instruction; frequent monitoring of learning using data; teachers working in teams to plan how to teach, what to teach, and when to teach; and a schoolwide infrastructure to support it all. Frankly, the core principles and practices of RTI are nothing new under the sun when it comes to what we know about good, effective instruction.

So why has RTI generated so much conversation and interest even among secondary educators?

RTI has generated interest because it helps us work smarter to accelerate the learning of all students. But RTI should not be viewed as another passing education fad. It is not a product, intervention, or program. RTI is a way to bring structure and a common language to practices that already exist in our schools and to eliminate the ineffective, unnecessary ones. The power of an RTI framework is its ability to create cohesion among all the various initiatives designed to support student outcomes at a system level.

Throughout this book, we will share many experiences of diverse stakeholders—teachers, counselors, school psychologists, principals, students, and parents—who have found that RTI enhances, validates, and makes more efficient and effective the way secondary students are served. You will hear those stakeholders tell you, in their own words, that once they saw how implementing this framework with integrity affected outcomes for kids, they could not go back to educating them the way they did before.

Asking the Really Tough Question

We argue that three components—assessment, team decision-making processes, and effective instruction—are of primary importance to implementing RTI. However, underlying those three basic components is a fundamental question, the answer to which will dictate whether RTI really has a chance in a particular building. That question is, Do we believe that all kids can learn? In secondary schools, this question is often the elephant in the room regarding change. Every staff member, whether certified or noncertified, who has contact with our kids, must confront it.

Let's ask it in an even more direct way: do we believe that it is our job to educate all kids who come to our buildings and our classrooms? Sadly, some public educators would answer no. They would say that they signed up to teach algebra, or physical education, or family and consumer science. They did not sign up to teach basic reading or math, or to implement behavior interventions for kids who just don't care. Some secondary educators believe that by the time students have reached this level of schooling, it is up to each student whether or not he or she chooses to learn. According to this reasoning, if kids don't show up, pay attention, or do the work, they are choosing not to participate in their learning. Moreover, these educators ask, why are students with learning disabilities, students for whom English is not their native tongue, students who are homeless, whose parents are incarcerated, who suffer with depression and anxiety (the list goes on) . . . , why are these students in our classrooms? Why should we have to teach them when they might not even be able to read the textbooks or complete the assigned work on time?

When we signed up to teach in public education, our contracts did not specify that we would have to teach only the kids we wanted to teach. Thankfully, we don't have the right to decide who gets the opportunity to learn in our schools. We educate all our kids. Secondary school staff must understand that:

▶ Students are in the process of learning acceptable behavior. Student knowledge of and capacity to perform appropriate social, behavioral, or academic skills should not be assumed.

▶ Natural consequences (for example, not graduating, not getting senior privileges) will be sufficient for behavior change for some but not all students.

▶ Not all students are self-motivated by academic and social success. (Sugai, Flannery, & Bohanon-Edmonson, 2004)

Engaging learning environments for today's students are digital-rich, transactional, socially driven, and globally conscious. In order to effectively teach all our kids, a schoolwide, coordinated continuum of services must be in place to support educators. We must acknowledge that mediocre instruction or the failure of even a few of our kids is completely and totally unacceptable. We need to embark on a mission of relentless problem solving and action steps to avoid those outcomes.

Isn't RTI Already Happening?

In most buildings, the answer is yes, to some degree, but not often fully. All schools have a continuum of strengths and weaknesses in practices, roles, organization, and so on. All buildings have expert teachers and assessment, instruction, and organizational decision-making practices for academics and social behaviors that are effective for kids—some more, some less. Why then isn't this framework implemented fully in our secondary schools? Or, put another way, what is getting in the way of being able to implement an RTI framework fully and with integrity? To answer this, we have to examine our actual practices, and we start by finding answers to questions like these:

- ▶ Is the expected behavior not happening because it is a skill deficit, meaning we (practitioners) do not know how to do it?

- ▶ Is it a performance deficit, meaning we do know how to do it but are not motivated to perform the task?

- ▶ Is it some combination of both?

If we are unsure about the answer, research directs us to treat the problem as a skill deficit first to ensure the tools are in the toolbox to get the job done (Duhon et al., 2004; Noell, Witt, & Gansle, 2001).

Of all the skills that secondary teachers need in order to implement RTI, most critical is the ability to use assessment data to drive decision making about instruction (Schmoker, 2006). That is, teachers need to be comfortable using data that are reliable, valid, and instructionally relevant in order to know whether or not students are attaining the critical learning objectives. These data are not used to evaluate teachers, but rather to make instructional practices transparent so that teachers can be open and objective about what is and is not working for kids. In sharing data, we build courage to stop doing things that are not working and start using practices that are meaningful and different instead (DuFour & Eaker, 1998).

Data analysis skills alone will not be sufficient, however. Teachers also need to know how to work efficiently and effectively in teams. We're not referring to having meetings to talk about the upcoming class field trip, what the parent newsletter will say, or how many textbooks need to be ordered (although these have their place to be sure). The team meetings we're referring to are data-driven discussions with a targeted focus on how instruction is leading to achieving identified learning objectives—and if that is not happening, then the meetings must be dedicated to developing a plan well matched to specific needs. A problem-solving process, a structure to drive decision making, is key. Utilizing this process keeps a team's discussion focused on specific problems, instructional variables, measurable outcomes, and concrete tasks. At the end of such a meeting, teachers feel that not a minute has been wasted. Instead, the team is energized by the rich conversation and progress.

Finally, teachers need the instructional tools that will enable them to get their job done. They need access to solid, research-based curricula and interventions. They must precisely communicate the content learning objectives to students. In particular, secondary teachers need to know how to teach reading in their content area, even if they teach physical education, family and consumer science, or (especially) industrial tech; how to create and maintain effective classroom structures and routines that will maximize student engagement; how to design and use formative assessment so they can immediately know whether students are meeting their content-area standards.

You get the picture. If teachers don't have these tools, they need administrators who will advocate strongly on their behalf to provide them with highly relevant, ongoing, job-embedded professional development opportunities. And professional development doesn't always mean bringing in a speaker or going to a workshop, although there are many valuable and practical opportunities out there. High-quality professional development also happens through collaboration with colleagues within our own buildings or districts.

Why Should I Care?

Mike Schmoker (2006), in his book *Results Now*, writes, "Educators are also in the life-saving business" (p. 5). We know that we get a greater return on our investments when we act early and with sufficient intensity to make a meaningful difference (Sherman et al., 1998). Prevention and early intervention are keys to fostering resiliency, increasing graduation rates, and ensuring the integrity of the diplomas our kids will receive. They are also the keys to mitigating the negative effects of all the complex variables that can be barriers to school success for our adolescent learners. Furthermore, the kids that come to our doorsteps today learn differently than we did when we were in middle or high school (Sousa & Tomlinson, 2011). An RTI framework supplies our secondary buildings, staff, and students with a system for attaining those outcomes. We care about implementing it because we care about improving the outcomes for our kids.

Now let's review the federal mandates that drive our practices and see how they assist in promoting the practices we talk about when we refer to RTI.

Federal Mandates

In the United States, current educational practices for all learners originated out of legal mandates, such as the Civil Rights Act of 1964 and the Education for All Handicapped Children Act of 1975. The most recent reauthorization of the Elementary and Secondary Schools Act of 1965, renamed in 2001 as No Child Left Behind (NCLB), has become the dominant—and controversial—force driving education practices. For example, there are over a hundred references to "scientific research-based instruction" in NCLB. In addition, NCLB mandates that all educators be "highly qualified" (section 1119), that academic standards be challenging and rigorous, and that schools maintain adequate yearly progress (AYP) toward these standards (section 1111). These kinds of mandates put considerable pressure on schools to measurably demonstrate achievement, and they are held accountable for a lack thereof.

In 2004, the Individuals With Disabilities Education Act (IDEA or IDEIA) was reauthorized. This law was originally called the Education for All Handicapped Children Act of 1975. A notable change in the IDEA in 2004 was the option to utilize a "process that determines if the child responds to scientific, research-based intervention" in identifying students with learning disabilities (IDEA, 2004, §300.307). This was in response to a preponderance of research showing an overidentification of students with learning disabilities, when in fact the problem was that they weren't getting effective instruction, particularly in the area of reading (see, for example, Gresham, 2002; National Reading Panel, 2000; Vellutino et al. 1996). Taken together, NCLB and the IDEA direct educators to provide effective, research-based instruction through general education in order to prevent students from experiencing school failure or being misidentified as learning disabled.

Because RTI was codified in special education law (IDEA, 2004), some debate exists as to whether it should be seen as an instructional framework that is reactive or preventative in nature. Some view RTI as strictly a special education initiative to identify, in a new manner, students with a learning disability. Others view RTI as a systems-level initiative to prevent academic difficulties by offering a multitiered continuum of service (including special education eligibility). We (and many others) view RTI as a proactive, preventive, general education framework transcending reading, writing, math, and social and behavioral instruction. In chapter 3 (page 21), we share data on the preventive benefits of an RTI framework for both academics and social and behavioral skills in elementary and secondary settings. We should, first and foremost, care about implementing RTI preventatively in our secondary schools because its well-established, research-supported practices use our resources most efficiently to maximize student achievement.

The Other Costly Outcomes

National longitudinal studies show that about 75 percent of students with reading problems in third grade will have them in ninth grade (Shaywitz et al., 1999, as cited in Diamond, 2004). Marian Wright Edelman (2009) uses the phrase "cradle-to-prison pipeline" in her critique of school policies and procedures that punish and reject students rather than proactively intervene to teach needed skills. Teaching practices that are ineffective and reactive are also associated with increased low achievement, poor mental health, drug use, poorer overall physical health, and incarceration (Moretti, 2007). In addition, students with reading problems suffer additional emotional and psychological consequences, including low motivation, anxiety, and lack of self-efficacy (Wigfield & Eccles, 1994, as cited in Diamond, 2004).

The 2003 National Assessment of Adult Literacy in Prison reports that only 43 percent of prison inmates had earned a high school diploma or equivalent (Greenberg, Dunleavy, & Kutner, 2007). In addition, 78 percent of prison inmates scored at a basic or below basic level on three literacy scales (prose, document, and quantitative), compared to only 54 percent of the general household population. About 17 percent were diagnosed with a learning disability. These are the other costly outcomes that are fostered when our students can't read or do not have appropriate social skills.

Achievement in eighth grade is highly correlated with attending college (Bui, (2005), and earning a bachelor's degree translates into being in the top 70 percent of income earners in the United States (McKinsey Global Institute, 2009). This means less reliance on public resources and an increase in the number of thoughtful, literate members of our communities. Consider that enrolling juvenile offenders in quality reading instruction reduces recidivism by 20 percent or more (Brunner, 1993)—far better than boot camp (Sherman et al., 1998). Fewer kids in legal detention means more kids available to be in school, learn skills, earn diplomas, go to college, and join the workforce. Imagine if all incarcerated young people received highly effective literacy programs in conjunction with highly effective instruction in all content areas as well social skills. We'd depopulate our prisons and increase the population of literate, civil, and productive citizens in our society. Better yet, what if we could intervene well before the cradle-to-prison pathway gets even remotely close to prison?

In his State of the Union address in 2005, President Bush stated:

> My budget substantially reduces or eliminates more than 150 government programs that are not getting results, or duplicate current efforts, or do not fulfill essential priorities. The principle here is clear: a taxpayer dollar must be spent wisely, or not at all. (Bush, 2005)

The trend toward accountability continued with President Obama's inaugural address (2009): "Those of us who manage the public's dollars will be held to account—to spend wisely, reform bad habits, and do our business in the light of day." These statements resonate with educators for good reason. We have known for decades that it is vastly more expensive to rehabilitate or "close the gap" than it is to do it right in the first place, or at least catch kids before the gap becomes too wide.

While research supports investments in prevention and intervention practices that start at birth and continue into early childhood (National Institute for Literacy, 2008), these same efforts can and will work effectively in secondary settings (Alliance for Excellence in Education, 2008; Snow, 2002; Sugai et al., 2004). A schoolwide commitment must be made to live up to promises of prevention and intervention. These practices must be predominant in the daily instruction of all students (both general and special education) for academics and social and behavioral skills.

What Is So Unique About RTI in Secondary Settings?

In terms of the core features of RTI, frankly, there is nothing unique about implementation in secondary settings. Remember the big idea: effective instruction leads to successful outcomes for kids. RTI is about using psychometrically sound assessment, research-based instruction, and a formal decision-making procedure across a multitiered model of service delivery. These foundational constructs are the same across any preK–12 educational setting.

However, ask anyone who works in a secondary school, and he or she will tell you that secondary staff, students, and curriculum issues are a whole other beast.

Here is a summary of unique considerations for implementing RTI in secondary settings (Allain, 2008; Sugai et al., 2004):

▶ **More staff and more kids**—The challenge here is building consistency as capacity increases across more people and within a larger organizational structure. Secondary staff generally spend more time working within departments or enclaves than in schoolwide staff meetings or discussions.

▶ **Multiple feeder schools**—Not only are there more kids in secondary school, many districts have students flowing from multiple elementary schools into one or more larger secondary configurations (middle school, junior high, or high school). When these transitions occur, new buildingwide norms must be established.

▶ **Larger numbers and more diversity**—This means that individual differentiation to meet unique learner needs is more challenging. More importantly, there are fewer opportunities to build critical relationships with struggling or disengaged students.

▶ **Curriculum specialization**—Traditionally, as students progress through the secondary grades, academics become increasingly focused on knowledge dissemination and independent skill application in specific content areas. Basic reading, math, writing, and prosocial behavior skills are increasingly assumed, and not taught or reinforced.

▶ **Increased student responsibilities**—Secondary students are expected to independently self-monitor, self-motivate, organize, and assume responsibility for their own learning, as well as accommodate new personal responsibilities such as driving, dating, and so on. As with basic academic skills, we must not assume these skills have been sufficiently acquired, and explicit instruction and positive reinforcement may be needed.

▶ **Decreased parental involvement**—Parental involvement is equally, if not more, important at this stage. Unfortunately, research continually shows that just at the time when students need parents to be increasingly present and involved, parental involvement declines (Patrikakou, 2004).

▶ **Larger gaps**—Student skill and performance discrepancies are greater at the secondary level then they are at the elementary (Deshler & Kovaleski, 2007; Diamond, 2004).

▶ **Higher stakes**—When students are in sixth grade, we can predict who will graduate with a diploma and who will and will not attend a postsecondary training institution (Balfonz, 2009; Deshler & Kovaleski, 2007). While early intervention in preschool and elementary school is far more economical and effective for closing achievement gaps, the lifelong effects of poor achievement are too great to not continue intervening and problem solving at the secondary level.

Why Should I Read This Book?

This book is intended to be a handbook for secondary RTI practices, with an emphasis on action steps and specific examples of how to put those steps into practice. We describe how students can be identified as having a special learning disability through an RTI process and cite specific secondary-level case examples. More importantly, we describe specific cases of students for whom special education would have been the only option in a traditional model, who instead find success in general education as a result of targeted, research-based, data- and team-driven instruction. Specific tasks for ensuring fidelity of implementation across all levels of practice are also detailed.

While there has been a targeted focus on secondary-setting systems change directed at reading instruction (Allain, 2008; Burns & Gibbons, 2008; Johnson, Smith, & Harris, 2009), we describe implementation practices for the whole breadth of an RTI framework, which includes reading, writing, math, and social and behavioral issues (the latter through School-Wide Positive Behavior Intervention Supports, SWPBIS). We present testimony and data to show that, when done with fidelity, RTI practices can reach all learners, even our most challenging, and lead to very rewarding success.

Conclusion

In order to find a solution to the issues facing secondary students and staff that prevent us from implementing the most effective instruction we can, we must examine the problem together, and we must do it now. Implementing RTI is a schoolwide effort. It's hard work, and sometimes it feels more frustrating than rewarding. But we must persevere. We need to make some hard decisions about how we will invest the precious financial resources and human capital of our school districts and buildings. Being a secondary educator can be brutally hard at times, especially when it feels as if our efforts are not paying off. However, we find that most often, being a secondary educator is exceptionally rewarding and fun. We stay in this business because of the small successes we witness every day. Those small successes add up, and we should celebrate them.

Let's continue, now, to pull apart the many layers of RTI implementation in secondary settings.

CHAPTER 2

Getting Started: What Does It All Mean?

If you want to build a ship, don't drum up people to collect wood and don't assign them tasks and work, but rather teach them to long for the endless immensity of the sea.

—Antoine de Saint-Exupéry

Someone in the district office went to a conference, and now we have to do RTI.

—Anonymous

Advance Organizer

✓ *RTI helps to provides a common language to our practices once we decide what language we will speak.*

✓ *There are often numerous definitions for common terms associated with the RTI framework. Deciding what definitions your building and teams will use make the implementation process easier.*

✓ *The RTI triangle or pyramid has its origins in public health and helps us conceptualize a multitiered model of RTI.*

The basic principles of response to intervention sound *so* good: effective, efficient screening so no student falls through the cracks; strong curriculum and instruction with a cascade of options designed to meet the needs of all kids; and a systematic and strategic process for making data-based decisions to accelerate student growth. Those principles sound great! Why wouldn't schools want to jump right in? And many do. We commonly receive inquiries from secondary practitioners who are in the early stages of implementing RTI in their buildings and want to know what to do when they have hit a wall. Often they find that after a few months or even a year of attempting to get things off the ground to "do" RTI, there is an overwhelming sense of confusion, frustration, or in the worst cases, near mutiny of school staff against this new initiative. They have teams that are meeting, they have data they are collecting, and they have kids receiving some interventions. But now, they feel uncertain of their next steps and are revisiting their intentions for doing RTI in the first place. In a word, they feel stuck.

After some questioning and discussion, we tend to find that these secondary schools did not spend enough time laying the groundwork for the adjustment to practices the RTI framework requires. Time taken to build consensus around the basic tenets and desired outcomes of an RTI framework and to develop a common vision to achieve these is time very well spent. A second common problem is that buildings do not have a well-established leadership team at the helm of this work. It is wise for secondary schools to take a few months, or even a full school year, to develop their plan for implementation, while simultaneously implementing small pilot tests of each construct to work out some of the initial bugs. Doing this work requires a team of committed administration and staff who can manage and adjust work on an ongoing basis. Any system change will at times inevitably experience taking two steps forward and one step back; however, in order to maintain positive momentum, how the process gets started makes a substantial difference. In the next two chapters, we share guidance for setting up systems for a successful launch of RTI that is based on research, data, and lessons learned.

Speaking a Common Language

One significant benefit of an RTI framework is that it provides structure and a common language or vocabulary to build shared knowledge among all staff in our schools. That said, RTI brings with it terminology that is often defined differently depending on which website you visit, article you read, or practitioner you talk to. For this book, we chose to use definitions that seemed to make the most sense to the everyday secondary practitioner and be the most succinct. Let's look at some of these terms.

Response to intervention (RTI): RTI refers to the daily practice of providing research-supported instruction for academics and social and behavior skills across multiple tiers of increasingly intense instruction, along with frequent progress monitoring to make changes to instruction as needed, and the application of a problem-solving process within teams to student data to make educational decisions (Johnson, Mellard, Fuchs, & McKnight, 2006; NASDE, 2005).

Schoolwide positive behavior interventions and supports (SWPBS): This is the decision-making framework that guides selection, integration, and implementation of the best evidence-based practices for improving important academic and behavioral outcomes for all students. Core features include data-based decision making, measurable and achievable outcomes, evidence-based practices, and systems to support these practices (OSEP Technical Assistance Center on Positive Behavioral Interventions and Supports, n.d.).

Note that there really isn't much difference between the core features of RTI and SWPBS other than in name. For purposes of this book, we will refer to practices as occurring within an RTI framework, because we feel this more appropriately captures all instruction rather than emphasizing a particular area of content. *Professional learning communities* (PLCs; DuFour & Eaker, 1998) and *data-based decision-making model* (DBDM) are other terms you may hear that also have elements of RTI and similar features and practices.

Don't let your school or team get hung up on terminology. Remember: effective instruction leads to successful outcomes for kids. Regardless of what you call it, the keys to effective instruction are data-based decision making within a team and research-supported instruction that is well matched to students' needs (DuFour & Eaker, 1998; Johnson et al., 2006). When schools stay focused on these basic practices, effective instruction occurs more frequently than not.

Assessment: Assessment is the practice of evaluating educational outcomes. Within an RTI framework there are four terms to designate types of assessment—*universal screening, progress monitoring, diagnostic assessment*, and *summative assessment.*

- ▶ **Universal screening**—Typically conducted three times per school year (for example, fall, winter, and spring), universal screening measures consist of brief, practical assessments focused on target skills that are highly predictive of future outcomes. Universal screening is for the purpose of identifying students who may be at risk for not meeting these outcomes (Johnson et al., 2006).

- ▶ **Progress monitoring**—This is the practice of collecting student performance data frequently (for example, once per week) using brief, sensitive measures to see if classroom instruction is working, as referenced in the work of Stan Deno (n.d.) and Lynn S. Fuchs (n.d.). Progress monitoring may consist of formative assessment, common formative assessment, or curriculum based measures (CBMs).

  - ▷ **Formative assessment**. A process that uses numerous kinds of data and data sources to provide ongoing feedback to teachers and students so teachers can adjust their practices to improve students' achievement of the intended instructional outcomes (Ainsworth, 2007; McManus, 2008).

  - ▷ **Common formative assessments**. A category of formative assessments that is collaboratively designed, administered, scored, and analyzed by a team of practitioners, usually for a specific content area (Ainsworth, 2007).

  - ▷ **Curriculum-based measures**. A category of formative assessment, also referred to as *general outcomes measures* (GOMs) or *probes,* that provides brief standardized monitoring of students' progress through a curriculum in either basic skills or content knowledge (Deno, 1985; Fuchs & Deno, 1991).

Some sources define progress monitoring as formative measures developed over the course of several years that have demonstrated technical adequacy, meaning they are reliable and valid from a statistical standpoint (Johnson et al., 2006). CBM is an example of such a measure. This is different from how others define formative or common formative assessments (Ainsworth, 2007; Salvia, Ysseldyke, & Bolt, 2010), that is, as assessments that are teacher developed and have tremendous face validity and instructional utility, but are often not designed to meet the technical standards of being statistically reliable and valid. In practice, the key is to be clear within your building and teams about what you mean by these terms. Assessment practices for secondary settings are described in more detail in chapters 4 (page 47), 8 (page 109), and 11 (page 149).

▶ **Diagnostic assessment**—Diagnostic assessment practices serve to identify particular characteristics or features of an identified problem. Diagnostic testing can help us answer questions about why a particular problem might be occurring or what specific aspects of a particular topic may be problematic for students—for example, curriculum-based evaluation (Howell & Nolet, 2000), or the Autism Diagnostic Observation Schedule (ADOS).

▶ **Summative assessment**—Also known as *outcomes evaluation*, these are assessments that occur infrequently to evaluate the cumulative progress of students toward learning outcome. If formative assessment is the cook tasting the soup, summative assessment is the dinner guests tasting the soup. Examples of summative assessments include grades, state tests, or intelligence tests.

Instruction: Instruction includes what is taught, how it is taught, and when it is taught. This book describes a three-tiered model of instruction or educational service delivery (Johnson et al., 2006; Vaughn, 2003), defined as Tier 1, Tier 2, and Tier 3.

▶ **Tier 1 (also referred to as universal or primary)**—This is the core academic and social and behaviorial instruction that every learner in a school building is taught. The goal is that at least 80 percent of learners will make a year's growth in a year's time through core instruction alone. In addition, at least 95 percent of learners achieving at grade level will maintain progress from year to year through core instruction.

▶ **Tier 2 (also referred to as secondary or strategic)**—Tier 2 refers to the instruction that is delivered *in addition to* (supplemental to) the core instruction for some learners. The *standard treatment protocol (STP)* is a common set of research-based instructional approaches that are implemented in addition to Tier 1 instruction to prevent and mediate educational problems. As with Tier 1, there may be differentiation within Tier 2. Perhaps 10 to 15 percent of learners will need this additional instruction (short or long term) in an area of relative weakness to close the achievement gap between them and their peers.

▶ **Tier 3 (also referred to as tertiary or intensive)**—Tier 3 is the instruction that is delivered to a few students (about 5 percent) for a short or long term in addition to the core. Such instruction is of greater intensity and more individualized in order to address a unique area of relative weakness. Tier 3 may include special education services, but it is not necessarily or commonly synonymous with special education.

The concept behind having multiple tiers of instruction is that you need the right tools at the right time to meet the different learning needs of the kids. The phrases *multiple tiers of instruction* or *cascade of services* refer to a system with a robust cadre of instructional options for the diverse and changing needs of students.

The RTI pyramid: A graphic (fig. 2.1), often depicted in red, yellow, and green, the RTI pyramid has become synonymous with the term *response to intervention*.

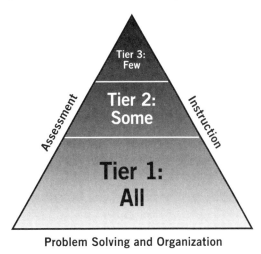

Figure 2.1: Visual summary of an RTI framework for academics and social and behaviorial problems.

The RTI pyramid was at first commonly associated with public health (Commission on Chronic Illness, 1957), and then with mental health (Caplan, 1964). Consider how our health system fits in this model. First, we have preventive services such as education about healthy diet and the importance of exercise. Healthcare providers offer screenings in the form of well-child checkups and annual exams on a regular basis. Think of this as core instruction, or Tier 1. Next, we have doctor's offices and other clinics that provide healthcare when people have short- or long-term health conditions requiring additional support (asthma, for example). This is supplemental intervention, or Tier 2. Finally, hospitals and medical specialists are available to support people with significant health concerns. This is Tier 3. We have hospital services in the United States to reasonably meet the needs of about 5 percent of our population at any given time and doctors' offices with appointments available to support another 15–20 percent. Therefore, we need about 80 percent of our population to be healthy, without need of medical assistance, at any given time, so that our healthcare resources are not stretched too thin.

Consider what happens when the threat of a flu pandemic arises. In public health, we strengthen our core instruction to keep as many people healthy as possible. Signs are posted with hand-washing steps. Public places offer hand wipes and sanitizers. Children (and adults) are taught to sneeze into their elbows. Notice that just as we do not rush to build more hospitals when an epidemic threatens, we should not rush to build more supplemental interventions when we have too many students performing below expectation. Core instruction must be strengthened in order to avoid student failure. Researchers began discussing this model in relation to students with behavioral needs in the mid-1990s (Walker et al., 1996).

It is important to note that while the three-tiered model is most common in practice and has research support (O'Connor, Fulmer, & Harty, 2003; Vaughn, 2003), some states and districts have chosen four, five, or even eight tiers to represent their continuum of service options. We find that the more complex systems become, the more difficult it is to implement the practices. That is why three tiers is appealing; however, it really doesn't matter how many tiers are in your building. What matters is that all practitioners know what is meant by Tier 1, Tier 2, Tier 3, and so on, and that there is a continuum of service options of increasing intensity to meet diverse instructional needs. Instructional practices for secondary schools at Tier 1, Tier 2, and Tier 3 are discussed in detail in chapters 4 (page 47), 5 (page 63), 8 (page 109), 11 (page 149), and 12 (page 159) of this book.

Problem solving: *Problem solving* is a general term that describes any set of activities designed to "eliminate the difference between 'what is' and 'what should be' with respect to student development" (Deno, 2002, p. 38). It involves both organization and process.

▶ **Problem-solving organization**—This refers to how buildings allocate or organize their fiscal, institutional (for example, the master or daily schedule), and human resources to drive decision making. The amount of resources are allocated with increasing explicitness or quantity across tiers of service delivery as the needs of students become more intensive.

▶ **Problem-solving process**—This is the sequential set of steps, questions, and practices to foster data-based decision making for designing and evaluating interventions that are well matched to student needs. This book describes in detail (chapter 7, page 89) a five-step problem-solving model (Batsche & Knoff, 1995; Bergen & Kratochwill, 1990; Knoff, 2002) used at the St. Croix River Education District (Bollman et al., 2007). The five steps of the model are:

1. Problem identification

2. Problem analysis

3. Plan development

4. Plan implementation

5. Plan evaluation

All of these terms and the tasks and roles associated with them are summarized in chapters 10 and 13. Note that because the RTI framework is primarily carried out through general education, special education is not specifically included. Special education does, however, continue to be one of the continuum of service options for students as the framework develops. Chapter 14 (page 189) provides more details.

Conclusion

Building a sustainable RTI system at any level requires a shared understanding of the concepts, as well as a shared vocabulary for discussing their implementation. In short, our words matter. They matter because, if we can speak clearly to each other about our vision for a school that uses its resources efficiently to be effective for all, then we can build on that vision through concrete actions. In the next chapter, we will share ideas about making that shared vision become a reality.

CHAPTER 3

The Steps of the RTI Journey: Creating Your Map

The best time to plant a tree was twenty-five years ago. The second best time is today.

—James Carville

Advance Organizer

✓ *Creating a clear plan for how your building will begin RTI implementation will make the start of the journey more effective.*

✓ *The five phases, or steps, of RTI implementation are commitment, leadership, assessment, instruction, and problem-solving organization and process.*

✓ *Feel stuck? Here are some lessons learned that might help.*

Implementing RTI can feel daunting. Continual problem admiring or waiting for the next new program or initiative to come along only prolongs the building of a complete system that works for all learners. Remember that RTI is an education framework for *all* students, with a concentrated emphasis on general education practices. The Secondary RTI Action Planning Guide (page 32) and RTI Implementation Status Checklist (page 39), included as reproducibles at the end of this chapter (as well as online at **go.solution-tree .com/rti**), will assist teams in walking through the elements and tasks within each step that secondary schools must take as they embark on RTI implementation.

Overall, we advise the following steps:

1. Establish a commitment to educate all students through ongoing consensus building.

2. Establish an RTI building-based leadership team.

3. Implement assessment.

4. Implement instruction based on the data.

5. Organize the school around problem solving and implement a problem-solving process.

Establish a Commitment to Educate All Students

The starting place for implementing RTI is a shared belief that we educate all children who come through our doors. While this sounds obvious, we need to be transparent with ourselves and others about our concerns, fears, and beliefs when it comes to this seemingly simple notion. Do the school custodians really believe it is their job to recognize positive behaviors they see in the hallways? Does the world language teacher expect a paraeducator to sit in back with the student who is visually impaired to teach him the lesson, or does he really believe it is *his* job to teach that student? Is the consumer science teacher annoyed by the high percentage of students who are unable to read the textbook, or does she see her role as teaching both content and strategies for accessing the content? *Do you really believe all kids can learn?* Commitment to this belief is the starting point, and a point to revisit regularly, during the RTI journey.

Commitment to Change at the System Level: School Culture

After addressing one's personal commitment to the fundamental assumptions that all kids can learn and it's our job to teach them, it's time to consider the next, more complex, and persistent context for change: a school's culture. Numerous definitions point to school culture as an established pattern of norms, values, attitudes, beliefs, rituals, symbols, and stories that exist in a school building (see, for example, Barth, 2002; Deal & Peterson, 1999). It is referred to as the *hidden curriculum* (Jerald, 2006), containing numerous unstated and assumed verbal and nonverbal behaviors, routines, attitudes, and practices. School cultures can be toxic environments, generally unsupportive of universal student achievement, or positive environments in which all students can and do learn because of what all staff members do (Deal & Peterson, 1999; Peterson, 2002).

Let's look at several aspects of school culture—the importance of "walking one's talk," the crucial roles of administrators, and the importance of consensus-building activities.

Walking the Talk

There is a tremendous amount of literature on educational change and reform, and the importance of establishing and sustaining buy-in (see, for example, Muhammad, 2009; OSEP Technical Assistance Center, 2006; Schmoker, 2006). The OSEP Technical Assistance Center on the SWPBIS website (www.pbis.org) suggests that before schools begin implementing any sort of system change, they achieve at least 80 percent buy-in from building staff (certified and noncertified) and building- and district-level administration (OSEP Technical Assistance Center, 2006). Achieving this level of commitment will surely ease RTI implementation from the start and ensure sustainability over time.

That said, our experience in secondary settings suggests that gaining this level of commitment is more difficult at the secondary than at the elementary level and takes longer. For example, many high schools started the RTI journey by implementing interventions at Tier 2 or by working on Tier 1 in a content area like science. Other schools start by spending a whole year building consensus and planning. Reeves (2008) states, "If, as a school leader, you wait to improve [insert whatever variable you want here] until you have total buy-in from the school community, then your school will be the last to change" (p. 91). So, while commitment building is a continual process, we must remember that *consensus* means *overwhelming agreement*, not *unanimity*. At some point you do have to start. In our professional experiences, the following are the top six ways to build consensus for RTI (counting downward):

6. **Start with a few motivated, charismatic staff**—These are the staff (certified and noncertified) who fully believe their job is teach all kids, are excited to think outside the box, and are critical, reflective, data-based decision makers. They are the ones Muhammad (2009) calls the *believers*. They are flexible in their practices; intrinsically motivated; well connected to students, parents, and community; and willing to challenge the status quo if it will lead to genuine and positive change. These early adopters are the go-to people for getting started on RTI.

5. **Make in-person connections**—It's not as convenient as firing off an email or leaving a phone message, and it does take more time; but in-person conversations are precious consensus-building times to discuss why a student needs a reading intervention or has to do progress monitoring during autos class or physical education. This is when staff have the opportunity to dialogue about that student's needs, to ask questions, and to express concerns. We also find that follow through on the part of classroom teachers and students increases considerably when teachers are personally involved in planning and implementing interventions through a face-to-face conversation.

4. **Give educators tools for remedial and basic skill instruction for academics and PBS**—Educators need high-quality professional development content in order to evolve and refine their instructional practices (Erickson, 2010). Asking secondary educators to implement RTI practices without quality time and training is like asking a pro basketball player to play in a major-league baseball game.

3. **Create time for staff to be involved**—There is no question that lack of time is one of the most common barriers to implementation. Administrators need to be creative and intentional about creating the time for staff to be involved in RTI. Some simple ideas to consider are omitting bus or hallway duty for a teacher who is willing to use some prep time for interventions, and scheduling meetings during prep time rather than before or after school. If a teacher is willing to go the extra mile to collect data or do an intervention, give him or her bus duty in May rather than in January. Pair up teachers who are willing to deliver interventions during supervision duties. You get the idea. Be creative.

2. **For every one new task added, eliminate two ineffective and inefficient ones**— RTI is about efficient and effective allocation of resources, not adding more tasks to the duties of already burdened school staff. Be willing to eliminate less important ones that aren't outcomes driven. Also, look for duplication of efforts: are there three committees in the building made up of basically the same people basically doing the

same things? The Team Audit reproducible (page 45 and online) is a tool for studying what your school's teams are trying to accomplish.

1. **Above all, show them the data**—The data will speak louder than words. Allocate two to five minutes at each staff meeting to share a student success story and current data. This will always help keep the process moving forward.

Roles for Administrators

The behaviors of school leaders trickle down to affect how policies, procedures, practices, and relationships among teachers and students are demonstrated, established, and maintained. School leaders are at the forefront of setting the agenda for a school's culture. The primary ways school leader behavior contributes to school culture are through the policies, procedures, and practices that they establish and the tone and quality of their relationships with school staff (Cotton, 1989; Leithwood, Louis, Anderson, & Wahlstrom, 2004; Muhammad, 2009). Administrators must lead open discussions about the current and desired school culture of their buildings if RTI practices are to be sustained over time.

Consensus-Building Activities

We recommend regular (monthly or bimonthly) consensus-building activities addressing the building's vision for RTI implementation, determining what progress has been made, and generating momentum around practices that are being established. One such consensus-building activity involves brainstorming and recording responses to broad questions about the topic under discussion. For this activity, staff need a meeting space that allows small-group discussion, a pad of poster-sized paper, and wide-tipped markers. Begin by posting four to six broad questions related to RTI for all participants to consider individually. Write each question on a separate poster-sized page. Questions can be written to suit your local situation but might include the following:

▶ What are your beliefs about what RTI is?

▶ What are your beliefs about what it means for a building to implement RTI?

▶ What are your beliefs about how children are affected when RTI is implemented?

▶ What are your beliefs about how we would know that RTI is implemented in a building?

After giving individuals time to reflect on these questions, divide the group into as many smaller groups as you have questions. (Count off, so that the smaller groups are diverse.) These groups work together to share their own reflections on their assigned question and write down their thoughts on the poster page. Groups then rotate through the posters, adding new ideas or piggybacking on what is already written.

A second consensus-building activity is a vision card exercise. To complete this activity, staff need a meeting space that allows small-group discussion, a large wall where material can be posted, belief posters from the first activity, lots of 4 × 6 cards, wide-tipped markers, and tape. Begin by reviewing the critical components from the belief posters. Then ask individuals to imagine a time three to five years in the future, and give them time to reflect on questions such as the following:

▶ What do you see that indicates comprehensive change activities have taken place?

▶ What do you see that is characteristic of teaching, learning outcomes, or our community that is consistent with our stated belief about response to intervention?

▶ What are some of our most significant accomplishments related to RTI?

Ask each group member to brainstorm a list of visions in response to these questions, placing a star next to those they believe are most vivid or significant. Have groups of three or four share their visions with each other, writing down each unique image from the group in concise form on a card. After the groups are done, collect one card from each group and post them on the wall. Allow each group to provide input into how the cards might be categorized. Continue to post new groups of cards, recategorizing as appropriate. Once all cards are posted, work as a large group to summarize the vision on the wall. After the meeting, have someone capture the information from the vision wall into a summary document that can be shared with the group and referred to on an ongoing basis.

Establish a Building-Based RTI Leadership Team

RTI implementation will not happen—or it will not happen with the degree of quality and fidelity needed—if the building administrator is not on board. We have, unfortunately, worked with numerous school teams where RTI practices were a grassroots effort among teachers. While these teachers are innovative and motivated practitioners, they sometimes become disgruntled when they reach the point where they cannot go further without leadership at the building or district level to address resource use and allocation. To start smart, leadership at each building must be actively involved and on board. More detailed discussions of leadership roles can be found throughout this text.

The action step here is to create an RTI leadership team at the building level. Members of the team must minimally include an administrator who can make decisions about resource allocation, general education teachers from diverse content areas, and a person who is an "RTI expert"—that is, who really gets what RTI is and how to implement it. He or she is the compass for RTI implementation. Some buildings designate an RTI coach. Most secondary buildings also include their dean, guidance counselor(s), the school psychologist, or school social worker (one of whom may be the local expert). A good guideline is to have no more than eight to ten members on your leadership team.

How to Choose Members for Your Leadership Team

Building administrators, choose team members thoughtfully! Emphasize including staff who are already committed to the philosophy of educating all students, function well within teams, are creative yet practical thinkers, and have high self-efficacy. Look to those who are the natural leaders among their peers. Also consider that this team affords golden opportunities to shape or mentor newer teachers who demonstrate initiative and innovation.

Some administrators include staff members who are not sure about or are even opposed to implementing RTI. Including these folks is an opportunity to positively influence staff who might otherwise hinder commitment and progress at the building level, as well as to dialogue openly about challenges and concerns that those who already buy in may not naturally sense or identify. Please note that if the team has too many members who are forced to participate or aren't really on board, however, RTI implementation will falter, and those who have bought in will become very frustrated.

The initial work of the leadership team is to take an inventory of practices currently in place in the building that support an RTI framework and those that require adjustment, as well as to develop a multiyear plan for training and implementation. The ongoing work of this team includes regular reference back to this plan to monitor progress and adjust plans as needed. The Secondary RTI Action Planning Guide and RTI Implementation Status Checklist (pages 32 and 39) are designed to assist secondary schools teams with walking through all the elements and tasks within each step that may form the basis of the building plan as they embark on RTI implementation.

Implement Assessment

Although RTI emphasizes that it is essential to use data for decision making if we are to close the gap for struggling learners, it is not a new idea, or one associated exclusively with RTI. In 1975, Dan Lortie wrote, "The monitoring of effective instruction is at the heart of effective instruction" (p. 141). Regular assessment tells us if our instruction is working or not. If it is not, that is not a time to take things personally, but rather a chance to respond by making a thoughtful instructional change. How can we know what to do instructionally if we do not have some kind of assessment information?

One of the first decisions the RTI leadership team needs to make is what types of data to gather for screening, formatively assessing, and eventually diagnosing more complex problems. The types of assessment data that are useful for secondary-level students for these different purposes are further discussed in chapters 3 (page 21), 7 (page 89), and 10 (page 137). We do not recommend that schools move forward with the next step—addressing instruction—until their assessment systems have been established and good data are being collected for the teams to use. Getting the assessment system established typically takes one year, with an additional year before staff start to feel some fluency.

Implement Instruction Based on the Data

After screening practices have been established, building teams should use this information to systematically focus on instruction. Research supports that students learn best when they are actively engaged, have high to moderate success rates and multiple opportunities to cover content, spend most of their time being directly taught by the teacher, and have instruction that is scaffolded, strategic, and explicit (Swanson, Hoskyn, & Lee, 1999). More information on best practices for instruction at each tier is included in chapters 4 (page 47), 5 (page 63), 8 (page 109), and 11 (page 149).

Implement a Problem-Solving Organization and Process

There are two parts to this step. The first is to determine how a system of problem solving will be organized and implemented across the three tiers of the building. That is, who will make decisions at Tier 1, Tier 2, and Tier 3 about which students need what level of instructional service, and when and how often they will meet? The next part of this step is to determine what specific process of problem solving or decision making will occur within the teams at each tier in response to student data.

Problem-Solving Organization

How decision-making systems are organized throughout a school building is central to the whole RTI operation. Being clear about the purpose for the teams in the building is a key place to start. One team can't really do it all in most secondary settings, so it makes sense to have multiple teams. Too often, however, there is duplication in team membership or purpose that causes confusion and lack of efficiency. We find, at the secondary level, that there are at least five key sets of tasks that a building needs in order for the RTI process to function efficiently and effectively. This may equate to five separate teams, as follows, or some number of teams less than five that divides these roles up in a manner that seems reasonable:

1. **Leadership team**—This building-level team is charged with leading the implementation of the RTI framework and develops the implementation plan. It regularly reviews buildingwide data, sets goals, and tracks progress for implementation of RTI. The role of this team is broader than just problem solving for individual students. This team extends its thinking and action steps toward continuous improvement of the entire building's RTI framework. Decisions made by this team will inevitably have an impact on individual students, but that is not the primary purpose or focus of discussion. For buildings implementing both academic RTI systems as well as behavioral RTI systems (SWPBS), another important function of this team is to develop systems of integration between these two areas.

2. **Tier 1 teams**—There are usually multiple teams at the Tier 1 level. What these teams are called can vary, but they may be referred to as professional learning teams, grade-level teams, departments, core teams, and so on. They collaborate on high-quality core instruction, a process sometimes called "growing the green." They meet on a regular basis to examine and develop deep understanding of grade-level or content-area standards, engage in ongoing mapping of the curriculum to these standards, work toward fidelity of implementation of a consistent core curriculum, and study and practice research-supported strategies for effective, differentiated instruction for all students. Collaboration on development and use of formative assessment and grading practices are two additional areas of important work at the Tier 1 team

level. We also advocate for the participation of special (art, gym, music, and so on) teachers and special education support staff on these teams. While this does add another meeting to the already full plates of these individuals, the opportunity it affords for them to understand what is happening in core instruction for the students they serve is invaluable. This is the most important work that a school can do. Team members should allot their time, attention, and resources accordingly. All intervention systems are built on top of this foundation, and it is critical to the success of an RTI system that it be solid.

3. **Tier 2 team**—This team meets to review progress of students involved in standard treatment protocol (STP) interventions. At the elementary and middle school level, grade-level teams can often manage the work of both core instruction and standard supplemental interventions (such that these two functions are supported by one team). However, we find that at the high school level—because these interventions so often occur in separate classes and because the size of the student body and organization of the staff often do not lend themselves to taking on both roles—a separate team is warranted. An important caveat: there must be quality communication among teams.

4. **Problem-solving team**—This general education problem-solving team guides and supports problem solving of academic and social and behavioral concerns for individuals or groups whose needs are not adequately addressed through differentiated core instruction *before* the student is referred for consideration of a special education evaluation. This team may be a clearinghouse for all referrals in a building. One outcome of the problem-solving process at this level is that a student may be assigned to a standard Tier 2 intervention, with ongoing follow-up by the Tier 2 team (described next). Other times, more complex individualized interventions (perhaps Tier 3) may be developed and monitored on an ongoing basis for students whose needs are not well addressed through a standard intervention. Alternately, the decision may be made by this team to refer to a student support team for evaluation of entitlement for special education services.

5. **Student support team**—The purpose of this team is to conduct evaluations to determine if a student is entitled to special education services and, importantly, to engage in ongoing problem solving for students receiving special education services. The problem-solving process should continue within the realm of special education in the same way as it is present in general education for students.

Note that in much smaller school buildings, each team may consist of all certified staff. In those cases, those staff will still need to schedule team meetings, but the purpose for meeting will change regularly depending on the tasks to be completed. For example, one week this small team will meet to look at fall screening data and make decisions about student grouping. The next week, these same staff will meet to discuss students with individualized education programs (IEPs). Two weeks later, the same staff will meet to review progress monitoring data for students identified through screening as being below target, and so on.

The point is that there is an important purpose for each team to meet and conduct problem solving with regard to specific kinds of student data (such as screening or progress monitoring) and tiers of instruction. Figure 3.1 provides a visual for how a typical secondary building would organize teams according to the three tiers.

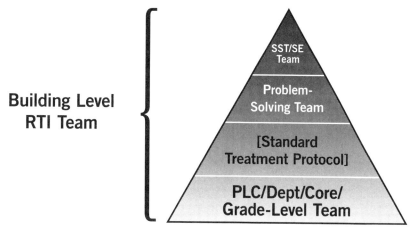

Figure 3.1: Organization of building teams.

Members of all teams must receive training on whatever problem-solving or decision-making process has been chosen (see the next section for more discussion of this point). In addition, there should be specific methods of documentation completed by each team in order to most clearly communicate across teams. Further, monitoring of effective team functioning is key to keeping meetings productive and maintaining the intensity of the problem-solving process. For Tier 2 teams, we have developed the Tier 2 Team Effective Behaviors Monitoring Form (page 46 and on online), which will be discussed in greater detail in chapter 10. For problem-solving teams, we have developed the Problem-Solving Team Effective Behaviors Monitoring Form (page 186 and on online), which will be discussed in greater detail in chapter 13. For all implementations, but particularly if districts are using an RTI process for identifying students with learning disabilities (discussed in chapter 14), the documentation arising from each of these teams will be paramount for this critical decision, making it necessary to have quality functioning teams.

Problem-Solving Process

As stated in chapter 1, this five-step process is what drives the decision making within the RTI framework. These five steps are repeated in table 3.1 (page 30).

We find that the RTI framework of many buildings lacks a structured, articulated process of decision making or problem solving. The critical questions your building needs to answer regarding problem solving are:

▶ What will your problem-solving process be for making decisions?

▶ Are the steps to the process grounded in research-based practices?

▶ What documentation will teams use for the varying levels of the problem-solving process? (For example, problem solving at Tier 3 is done much more intensively.)

Table 3.1: The Five-Step RTI Problem-Solving Process

Problem-Solving Step	Questions to Be Answered
1. **Problem Identification**	What is the discrepancy between what is expected and what is occurring?
2. **Problem Analysis**	Why is the problem occurring?
3. **Plan Development**	What is the goal?
	What is the intervention plan to meet this goal?
	How will progress be monitored?
4. **Plan Implementation**	How will intervention integrity be ensured?
5. **Plan Evaluation**	Was the intervention plan effective?

> ▶ Who will conduct the team training on the process?

> ▶ Who will be trained? When?

> ▶ How will fidelity of the problem-solving process occurring across teams be documented?

This process, as well as information related to implementation of this type of teaming, is described in full detail in chapters 6, 9, and 12.

Guiding Principles for Getting Started

Feeling overwhelmed? We sure did. That's why we created some reproducible checklists to guide teams through the steps we have summarized:

1. **Secondary RTI Action Planning Guide**—This form is designed to help a leadership team conceptualize the way RTI will look in its particular building. Use it to help define needs and next steps for RTI implementation (page 32 and online at **go.solution-tree .com/rti**.

2. **RTI Implementation Status Checklist**—This form is designed for teams to use in evaluating current RTI implementation and for goal setting for next steps (page 39 and online).

3. **Team Audit**—Use this form to help streamline the purpose of all building teams. Eliminate duplication, but ensure all needed work is addressed (page 45 and online).

4. **Tier 2 Team Effective Behaviors Monitoring Form**—This form is designed to provide feedback to teams that meet to review progress of students in supplemental interventions. Use it to provide feedback on effective behaviors (page 46 and online).

In addition, keep the following guiding principles in mind:

> ▶ **Start small**—As mentioned at the beginning of this chapter, many secondary schools find themselves immersed in doing RTI for a while, only to find that they feel

overwhelmed and cranky. While your data will give you good direction on where to start, don't try to fix everything all at once. Our emphatic advice is to start small—pick a grade, a content area, or even just a classroom or single student case to begin applying all the good practices of RTI implementation.

One place to start is with sixth grade if you are a middle school or ninth grade if you are a high school. Both are pivotal indicator years (Balfanz, 2009; Donegan, 2008; Quint, 2008). In addition, the largest research-based toolboxes out there for secondary learners are in the areas of positive behavior supports and literacy. Strong social skills and self-regulation create the conditions for students to learn; for acquiring academic content, knowing how to read is foundational. Consequently, our recommendation is to start with one of these areas.

▶ **Remember, it's a journey, not a destination**—Recall that RTI is not a program, an intervention, or a curriculum. It is a framework within which our daily instructional actions occur. This means that RTI will never be a task that gets checked off the checklist. It's what we do every day. This leads to the last guiding principle.

▶ **Persistence is the key**—There is no way around it: implementation of an RTI framework is hard work. We have learned that the difference between schools that have long-term success with RTI and those that don't is the persistence of the educators and their skill in responding to the inevitable frustration of temporary setbacks. Your team's ability to regroup and refocus when an intervention doesn't work or a team member doesn't follow through will be critical. Can you problem solve rather than problem *admire*? Can you stay focused on the vision ("we educate all our kids") despite the presence of kids who act as if they are unwilling to be educated?

Start cultivating persistence by adopting a live-and-learn attitude. Keep doing what is working. Stop doing what is not. Don't make the same error twice. Openly acknowledge and celebrate every step forward. See setbacks as opportunities to become more refined problem solvers. If it isn't working, do something different. And always remember—it's not about us, it's about kids. Keep your primary focus on whether or not it's good for them. If it is, you will not go wrong.

Conclusion

Getting any initiative started off on the right foot makes long-term implementation smoother for all. In this chapter, we have recommended steps to include broad staff study of RTI principles and visioning, along with small concrete first projects involving committed and energetic staff. Thinking in advance about what your assessment system, instructional options, and problem-solving organization will look like will help keep your system focused on creating a successful framework. In the following chapters, we will discuss assessment, instruction, and problem solving in detail at each tier.

Secondary RTI Action Planning Guide

This RTI planning guide is to be used to identify the action steps needed in your district or building in the short and long term. Year one is often used as a planning year, while you simultaneously pilot some steps. Year two is usually a kick-off year, when plans, policies, and procedures begin to be fully implemented districtwide or schoolwide. Be sure that the district-level and building-level action plans are aligned for sustainability.

Step 1: Commitment

Note that building and maintaining commitment and consensus is ongoing through the RTI journey.

   a.   Review the district and building (if applicable) mission statement.

   b.   Review the district and building (if applicable) vision statement.

   c.   Review the district and building goals for students.

Answer these questions. If you are unsure how to do so, determine what information you would need:

   a.   Is RTI still viable and applicable for you?

   b.   Are you currently reaching the goals set for students?

   c.   What do staff already do to demonstrate they are committed to the mission, vision, and goals for students?

   d.   What do you wish staff would do more of to demonstrate their commitment to the mission, vision, and goals for students?

   e.   What needs to be done next to move forward with generating commitment by the team completing this planning guide?

Action Step	For Whom? (Names and Grades)	When Will It Happen?	Who Is Responsible?	Measurable or Observable Outcome

   f.   How will the mission, vision, and goals be shared?

   g.   Who are the key stakeholders who need to hear them?

   h.   What is the plan for increasing their awareness and gaining commitment?

   i.   When will these tasks be completed?

j. Who is going to complete these tasks?

Who	Names or Grade Levels	Plan for Sharing (how and where will the information get distributed?)	When Will It Happen?	Who Is Responsible?
District Administration				
Building Administration				
Regular Education Teachers				
Noncertified Staff				
Special Education Teachers				
EL or Title I or II Teachers				
Related Services/Student Support Services Staff				
Parents and Community				

Step 2: Building-Based Leadership

A building leadership team can be an existing group, but this team must make the commitment to guide the building in implementing the RTI framework. *Note: We encourage districts and buildings to eliminate an existing team if they are considering creating a new RTI leadership team.*

Answer these questions:

    a. Do you have an existing team that would fill this role? Do some team members need to change to fill this role, or does a new team need to be created?

    b. What administrator will be attending the meetings each week and for the entire meeting time?

    c. Who on this team is skilled at managing and interpreting data?

    d. What professional development, resources, or support will it take to make this team work?

    e. Who are your teacher leaders in the building? What will their roles be either on this team or as key communicators from staff to this team?

List your RTI leadership team members. Although it is up to the discretion of each district or building, it is recommended that there be no more than eight members on this team.

Name	Role or Position
1.	
2.	
3.	
4.	
5.	
6.	
7.	
8.	

How RTI Works in Secondary Schools • © 2012 Solution Tree Press • solution-tree.com
Visit **go.solution-tree.com/rti** to download this page.

Step 3: School Audit—Tier Study

Note: You will need to review data from your district and building in order to fully complete the audit and action plan!

Review your answers to the Tier Study, and consider the following additional questions:

a. Do more people from your building or district need to participate in completing the Tier Study? If yes, who? When? How?

b. What are your areas of strength as a district?

c. What needs does your district have for further development?

d. How can you capitalize on your strengths while moving forward in areas of need?

e. What do you think is a reasonable timeline for implementing a full-scale RTI process?

Step 4: Action Plan

Use your school-needs assessment (data and needs checklist) to set goals and create an action plan for each strand.

Strand 1: Assessment

Short-Term Assessment Goals and Plan (for example, over the next academic year)

Goal(s)	Strategy (What is your game plan?)	Resources (Who or what people, time, funding, materials, professional development, and so on are needed?)	Due Date	Evaluation (Who and how often?)

Are there any barriers to carrying out your plan? If so, how will you address them?

Long-Term Assessment Goals and Plan (for example, phase-in process over years two to five)

Goal(s)	Strategy (What is your game plan?)	Resources (Who or what people, time, funding, materials, professional development, and so on are needed?)	Due Date	Evaluation (Who and how often?)

Are there any barriers to your long-term plans? If so, how will you address them?

Strand 2: Curriculum and Instruction

Key school data and audit questions will be needed to guide planning for this stand:

a. Is your building using a multitiered service delivery model? In each academic area? For each behavior?

b. Describe your existing data (percent in each category) and academic and behavior interventions at each tier. Are the interventions scientifically based? See the graphic Current School-wide System in the Area of Reading to guide the process (page 37).

c. Are there any instructional practices that should be abandoned because they aren't scientifically based? If so, list these practices or interventions.

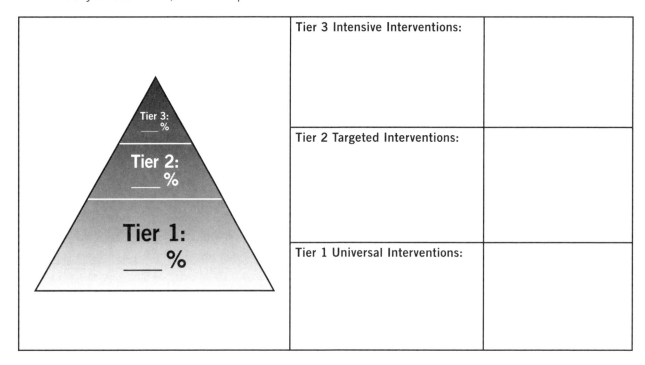

	Tier 3 Intensive Interventions:	
	Tier 2 Targeted Interventions:	
	Tier 1 Universal Interventions:	

Current Schoolwide System in the Area of Reading

Complete the percentages for the triangle across all three tiers. Indicate the intervention or curriculum used at each tier, and indicate the grade level(s) in parentheses.

Short-Term Curriculum and Instruction Goals and Plan (for example, over the next academic year)

Goal(s)	Strategy (What is your game plan?)	Resources (Who or what people, time, funding, materials, professional development, and so on are needed?)	Due Date	Evaluation (Who and how often?)

Are there any barriers to carrying out your plan? If so, how will you address them?

Long-Term Curriculum and Instruction Goals and Plan (for example, phase-in process over years two to five)

Goal(s)	Strategy (What is your game plan?)	Resources (Who or what people, time, funding, materials, professional development, and so on are needed?)	Due Date	Evaluation (Who and how often?)

Are there any barriers to carrying out your plan? If so, how will you address them?

How RTI Works in Secondary Schools • © 2012 Solution Tree Press • solution-tree.com
Visit **go.solution-tree.com/rti** to download this page.

Strand 3: Problem Solving and Schoolwide Organization

Short-Term Problem-Solving Systems/Organizational Goals and Plan (for example, over the next academic year)

Goal(s)	Strategy (What is your game plan?)	Resources (Who or what people, time, funding, materials, professional development, and so on are needed?)	Due Date	Evaluation (Who and how often?)

Are there any barriers to carrying out your plan? If so, how will you address them?

Long-Term Problem-Solving Systems/Organizational Goals and Plan (for example, phase-in process over years two to five)

Goal(s)	Strategy (What is your game plan?)	Resources (Who or what people, time, funding, materials, professional development, and so on are needed?)	Due Date	Evaluation (Who and how often?)

Are there any barriers to carrying out your plan? If so, how will you address them?

How RTI Works in Secondary Schools • © 2012 Solution Tree Press • solution-tree.com
Visit **go.solution-tree.com/rti** to download this page.

RTI Implementation Status Checklist

Parent Involvement	Not in Place	Limited Practice	Partially Implemented	Well Established	Don't Know
All parents are provided **information regarding the RTI framework** and what it means for them and their child.					
Communication with families exists in a **language** or mode that is meaningful to them.					
Parents are notified about their child's performance on schoolwide assessments.					
There is **meaningful communication** between families and staff about all students' strengths and needs—and additional collaboration when concerns are identified.					
Parents are notified when their **child begins a supplemental** (Tier 2 or 3) intervention.					
Parents are provided with a **description of assurances** of what general education problem solving will provide (for example, intervention plan, timelines, data to be collected, decision-making rules).					
Parent participation in the problem-solving process is solicited.					
Parents are provided with materials and training in the provision of curricular **supports in the home setting** when appropriate.					
Parents of children who receive interventions at any tier are provided reports on their child's interventions, goals, and **progress toward their goals**.					
Parents are informed of their **right to request** a special education evaluation.					

Comments:

How RTI Works in Secondary Schools • © 2012 Solution Tree Press • solution-tree.com
Visit **go.solution-tree.com/rti** to download this page.

School Climate and Culture	Not in Place	Limited Practice	Partially Implemented	Well Established	Don't Know
All educators have attended an **overview presentation** of the RTI framework that included information on implications for curriculum and instruction, assessment practices, and schoolwide organization and problem solving.					
All educators understand how the **RTI framework is represented** in their building (including implications for curriculum, assessment, and organization).					
All educators understand that RTI is a buildingwide framework designed to **benefit** *all* **students**, not solely or primarily related to special education.					
Building or district leadership **demonstrate active commitment** to and support of the RTI framework.					
Educators feel **shared responsibility** and play meaningful roles in ongoing activities to sustain the RTI framework.					
Research-based practices are understood and accepted by educators and are consistently incorporated within classroom instruction.					
Educators are committed to **ongoing professional development** regarding research-based practices and instruction of diverse learners.					
Consultation, feedback, and collegial exchange about curriculum, instruction, and behavioral expectations are supported by administration and valued by educators.					
Sufficient time and resources are allocated to **professional development** and related activities in support of the RTI framework components.					
All educators understand the **roles and responsibilities** of their colleagues to maximize capacity for student support.					
Shared responsibility for all children is evident among educators.					
Expectations for academic performance and positive behavior have been agreed on and shared with all stakeholders.					
Educators believe that **communication with families** and community is an integral part of their jobs.					
Growth and learning is celebrated with members of the school and community, and with families.					

Comments:

How RTI Works in Secondary Schools • © 2012 Solution Tree Press • solution-tree.com

Visit **go.solution-tree.com/rti** to download this page.

Curriculum and Instruction	Not in Place	Limited Practice	Partially Implemented	Well Established	Don't Know
There are clear, high-quality core curricula in academic and social behavior areas implemented with **well-defined scope and sequence** plans across grades.					
Teachers are **well trained** to implement core curricula.					
Ongoing work to **align** the core curricula with state standards is evident.					
Universal **screening results are linked** to ongoing discussions about high-quality core curriculum for academics *and* social behavior.					
The district has a plan for systematically evaluating the **fidelity** of core curriculum implementation on a regular basis and addressing deficiencies.					
Systematic **evaluation of the effectiveness** of core instruction is conducted on a regular basis.					
Teachers are knowledgeable about and implement principles of **effective instruction** (high rates of engagement, opportunities to respond, immediate error corrections, and so on).					
Teachers are knowledgeable about and implement research-based principles for effective instruction in **basic skill areas** (reading, writing, and math).					
Teachers understand how to embed basic skills instruction within **content area classes** and do this regularly.					
School **schedules** allow for maximum use of resources in the core classes (for example, through flexible grouping) and for daily, tiered supplemental intervention time.					
The school has **evidence-based curricula**, instruction, or strategies identified for tiered intervention supports of increasing intensity.					
Criteria and procedures for **moving between tiers** of intervention are set.					
Instructional staff members are **trained** in interventions to be used.					
Systematic **evaluation of the effectiveness** of supplemental, tiered instruction is conducted on a regular basis.					
By combining high-quality core instruction with intensive tiered supports, the school has a plan to **accelerate learning** for all at-risk students so they meet grade-level standards in one to two years.					

Comments:

How RTI Works in Secondary Schools • © 2012 Solution Tree Press • solution-tree.com
Visit **go.solution-tree.com/rti** to download this page.

Measurement and Assessment	Not in Place	Limited Practice	Partially Implemented	Well Established	Don't Know
The school or district has a clearly articulated local assessment plan that includes **screening procedures** for all students at least three times per year; **diagnostic assessment** as needed; a plan for **progress monitoring** those at risk; and **outcomes evaluation** at least annually.					
The measures identified in the local assessment plan are all **reliable and valid** for the purposes for which they are used.					
Professionals are trained to a high degree of reliability in the **standard administration and scoring** of all assessments used.					
Fidelity of assessment administration and scoring procedures are evaluated on a regular basis, and refresher trainings are provided as needed.					
Data are stored in a **database** that is easily accessible by all teachers and administrators in a timely manner.					
Educators understand and can communicate about the **purposes and value** of the assessments used, as well as their limitations.					
Educators are skilled at **interpreting assessment results** and making decisions based on these results.					
Schoolwide assessment data are used to evaluate the **effectiveness of core** academic and behavior programs.					
Schoolwide assessment data are used to **identify students** who may be at risk in academic or social-behavioral areas.					
Diagnostic assessments occur as needed to better understand specific needs of identified at-risk students.					
Schedules for **progress monitoring** are set based on the intensity of students' needs, and assessment occurs at least monthly for all identified students.					
Teachers regularly use data from progress monitoring to drive **instructional decisions** throughout the continuum of supports.					
Educators conduct an **outcomes evaluation** at least once per year to identify areas of strength and need for continuous program improvement.					

Comments:

Collaborative Teams	Not in Place	Limited Practice	Partially Implemented	Well Established	Don't Know
Grade-level, building-level, and district-level teams all consistently follow a **problem-solving process** to make data-based educational decisions that promote improvement in academic and social-behavioral outcomes for students.					
There is common understanding of the purpose and **unique roles** of each team within the building or district and of the ways in which these teams interrelate.					
All teams are viewed as having the primary mission and responsibility of supporting student success within **general education** and not as vehicles to promote special education identification.					
Team meetings at all levels are **regularly scheduled**, of sufficient duration, and frequent enough (monthly grade-level team meetings, weekly problem-solving team meetings) to complete necessary tasks. All members of teams regularly attend the meetings.					
Grade-level teams exist in grades 5–9 and include all general and special educators who serve students at each grade level.					
Building-based **problem-solving teams** exist and have balanced representation from all general and specialized teaching groups.					
Teachers who refer students to a problem-solving team **meet directly** with the team to discuss intervention options and plans.					
All team members are **trained** with regard to procedures, forms, and available resources for their team.					
Meeting **agendas** are clearly communicated and include goals and tasks.					
There is **effective facilitation**/leadership at each team meeting.					
The **building administrator** actively participates in team meetings.					
All team members attend regularly and **participate actively** during meetings.					
All teams **maintain records** on students they have served.					
Effective communication exists between teams.					
Data on team functioning are collected regularly (number of students served, fidelity to problem-solving process).					

Comments:

Page 5 of 6

Problem-Solving Process	Not in Place	Limited Practice	Partially Implemented	Well Established	Don't Know
Schoolwide **screening results** for academics and behavior are used to identify students for problem solving by grade-level or building-level teams.					
Team members effectively and efficiently **identify and prioritize problems** for every student or group of students served through intervention services.					
The prioritized problem for each student or group of students is observable, measurable, and described as a discrepancy between what is expected and what is occurring as measured on one assessment tool, with additional **converging evidence** from other sources.					
Teams generate multiple **hypotheses across domains** (ICEL) when considering the cause of the identified problem. These are relevant, alterable, and observable.					
Teams systematically analyze information from a **variety of sources** (RIOT) to support or refute each generated hypothesis.					
An individual, specific, and **measurable goal** is set for each student.					
Interventions selected by the problem-solving team are **supported by research**.					
Interventions selected by the problem-solving team **address the student need** identified in the discrepancy and hypothesis statements.					
Intervention plans are implemented in a **timely manner**.					
A plan to gather regular **progress-monitoring** data toward the student goal is a part of each intervention plan.					
Intervention fidelity is always assessed through direct observation, and any issues are quickly resolved.					
Intervention sessions are of sufficient intensity, duration, and frequency to **expect growth**.					
Student **responsiveness is evaluated** based on progress-monitoring data.					
Intervention plans are evaluated in a timely manner, and resulting **decisions are documented.**					
The team **cycles through** the problem-solving process again and again when students' performance is not sufficiently responsive to the current intervention.					

Comments:

Team Audit

	Team 1	Team 2	Team 3	Team 4	Team 5
Name of Team or Committee					
Meeting Frequency					
Meeting Purpose					
Members					
What Is the Research Base Behind Instruction Chosen by This Team?					
What Measureable Outcomes Are Evaluated?					
Comments					

What challenges do you identify?

What teams could be combined?

What teams could be eliminated?

Tier 2 Team Effective Behaviors Monitoring Form

To complete this form, determine what section(s) of the problem-solving process will be addressed for each student on the agenda. Award one point for each behavior listed that is observed by the team for each student. (Partial = Key people teaching students are absent. No = The majority of teachers who teach the students are missing.) At the end of the meeting, add up the points for a final score.

Item	Yes	Partial	No
1. Meeting includes staff who teach the skills of focus to the group of students being discussed.			
2. Purpose of the meeting is stated ("Today we are looking at progress-monitoring data and making decisions about our groups."), or an agenda is handed out.			
3. Data to be reviewed are provided (on paper, via LCD projector, on the computer, or by other means).			
4. Data being reviewed include general outcome measures. Other data may also be reviewed.			
5. Progress graphs for individual students or small groups of students are shared.			
6. There is discussion of progress, lack of progress, or maintained progress for each student or small group of students, or a subset of all students was preselected for discussion, and all those preselected were discussed. (Partial = Some but not all are discussed.)			
7. Based on Item 6, team members discuss possible reasons (hypotheses) for progress or lack of progress, and these hypotheses are based on alterable variables.			
8. Instructional changes proposed are linked to the hypotheses generated.			
9. Teams struggling with why one or more student is not making progress with Tier 2 interventions consult with the RTI team or a representative of the team for additional considerations. (If teams don't struggle with intervention ideas for any students, mark Yes.)			
10. Changes in instructional groups are made explicit: who is teaching, what strategies or programs are being taught, when the instruction is to be delivered, and when it will start. (Partial = Some but not all details discussed.)			
11. Graphs have evidence of prior instructional changes if data indicate need for change. Phase changes are indicated on some graphs.			
12. Discussion of topics other than student data, progress, and instructional planning is kept to a minimum.			
13. An opportunity to discuss the progress of other students not currently receiving intervention or not currently monitored is available (new students or students newly identified during the screening period).			
14. The next meeting date is announced and is within six weeks of this date. (Partial = Date is announced, but it is not within six weeks.)			

CHAPTER 4

Tier 1 Assessment: Screening for Secondary Students

The monitoring of effective instruction is at the heart of effective instruction.

—Dan Lortie

Advance Organizer

✓ While secondary schools have many types of existing screening data, building teams should attend to some specific quality indicators for those data.

✓ When using screening data for making decisions about Tier 1 instruction, building teams should attend to how data collection procedures are articulated and how cut scores are selected. Screening measures within a secondary RTI system include existing data sources and general outcomes measures.

✓ Screening assessments will differ between middle and high school.

Now that you have some initial information on the rationale for developing an RTI framework, ideas on getting started, and an example of one site with rich implementation, it is time to focus on the details of building an RTI framework. We begin here—where we suggest that you and your leadership team begin—by establishing a measurement system that allows you to effectively screen all students and identify any who may be at risk for academic or social behavior difficulty.

This critical component of an RTI framework is every bit as important at the secondary level as it is at the elementary level. Proactive screening at all grade levels is necessary so buildings do not wait for parent or teacher referral of students of concern, which has greater potential for bias and constitutes a "wait until the student is failing" model. You need to decide early in the process what screening instruments (screeners) to use. Screeners should have quality characteristics for this purpose, meaning that they do a good job picking out the students who need help and not picking out students who don't. Technically speaking, teams will want to consider the reliability and validity of screening measures.

Quality Psychometric Indicators for Screening Instruments

In this section, we will describe attributes of quality screeners, describe some reasons why class grades often do not meet these standards, and offer an alternative: curriculum-based measures, also known as general outcome measures.

Reliability and Validity

In general, the *reliability* of a test refers to its consistency. Teams consider the degree to which a student would earn the same score on the same test across multiple administrations (test-retest) and the level of consistency seen across alternate forms of the assessment (alternate forms), as well as across items within the same test (internal consistency). If a student's scores vary widely, teams cannot have confidence that they have defined that student's performance. That is why reliability of assessments is very important. Reliability is measured on a scale from 0 to 1.0. While no test is perfectly reliable, those with reliability coefficients above 0.80 are considered highly reliable, and those with reliability coefficients below 0.50 are not considered reliable.

Validity refers to the extent to which a test measures what it is intended to measure. A test can be very reliable but not valid. However, most often, tests that are valid are also reliable. Often, validity is established by determining that student scores on one test are highly correlated with student scores on another well-regarded test of the same content. This is called *criterion validity*. Validity coefficients also range from 0 to 1.0, with validity of 0.70 and above being considered good. Two other types of validity are also important, though more qualitative. *Content validity* refers to the extent to which the content of the test matches all the instructional objectives, or said another way, the extent to which the content of the assessment is representative of the total content being tested. *Construct validity* refers to the extent to which the test outcomes correspond to a given theory.

Using Formative Assessments and Grades for Screening

Although locally developed formative assessments and grading are critical to teaching and learning, both of these feedback systems typically lack established reliability and validity. Formative assessments allow teachers to understand the quality of concept mastery on important instructional outcomes and to adjust instruction meaningfully to address the needs of students on an ongoing basis. Likewise, grading systems provide an opportunity for teachers to communicate about student content mastery. However, *for the purpose of screening* they are not the strongest choice from a measurement standpoint. It would be possible to develop formative assessments with adequate technical features, but in the vast majority of cases, this test development work has not been done.

Another point about most teacher-created formative assessments is that they are designed to measure mastery of particular content (photosynthesis or spread of democracy, for example) rather than basic component skills (like general reading or math skill). It is the latter we assess in the broad screening systems we are advocating. Course grades, which would be considered to have high content validity for the courses in which they are earned, most often are not awarded with absolute consistency across teachers or classes. Even if they are low, course grades do not necessarily indicate difficulty with academic skills. Students may demonstrate low course grades due to not turning work in, social or emotional difficulty, drug dependency, boredom, and any number of other reasons. For these reasons, we encourage schools to select screening instruments of basic skills that have established reliability and validity coefficients in acceptable ranges and to use these *in addition to* other formative assessments that inform content mastery. Use this and other data, like grades, as converging evidence. Armed with the results, teams will be able to have more confidence in their identification of students who need extra support and those who do not, as well as what kind of support may be needed.

Using Curriculum-Based Measures as Screeners

Curriculum-based measures (CBMs) are a set of assessments commonly used for screening within an RTI framework. These deceptively simple assessments measure the fluency with which students perform basic academic skills such as reading aloud or silently, completing math problems, writing, or spelling. Though they each take only a few minutes to administer and score, research has shown them to have impressive psychometric characteristics (both reliability and validity) for screening in academic areas (Ardoin & Christ, 2008; Christ & Ardoin, 2009). We characterize curriculum-based measures as tools that can be used as formative assessments of basic skills. The National Reading Panel specifically supports the use of CBMs to evaluate the skills and progress of students in reading (National Institute of Child Health and Human Development, 2000).

General Outcomes Measures

Early research in CBMs utilized assessments derived directly from curriculum content. Over time, the practice was adopted of creating the assessments from content outside the specific curriculum but still representative of the content. These measures are still curriculum-based, but they are sometimes referred to as *general outcomes measures* (GOMs) to make it clear that they are representative of grade-level content but are not direct excerpts from local textbooks.

GOMs have key features that provide many practical advantages:

▸ They are standardized, norm-referenced assessments that are reliable and valid indicators of student achievement.

▸ They are simple, efficient, and of short duration in order to facilitate frequent administration by teachers.

▸ They provide curriculum-linked assessment information that helps teachers plan better instruction.

▶ They are comprised of tasks of about equal difficulty that are given throughout the year, so that growth toward a final goal may be measured.

▶ They are sensitive to the improvement of students' achievement over time.

▶ They are easily understood by teachers and parents.

GOMs are useful in answering questions about *intra*individual improvement (for example, is intervention A more effective than intervention B?) and *inter*individual differences (how severe is this student's reading problem?). Using GOMs provides a way to use measurement for planning, evaluating instructional programs for students, and making peer-referenced comparisons—for example, assessing severity (Fuchs & Deno, 1991). These measures may be used to establish school and districtwide norms, identify students who are experiencing difficulty, evaluate instructional programs, aid teacher decision making, and facilitate communication between parents, students, and professionals (Shinn, 1989).

Why We Prefer GOMs to Traditional Within-Curriculum CBMs

Moving to a system of GOMs rather than traditional CBMs addresses two potential problems with CBMs. First, because textbooks, by design, grow more difficult from start to end as new content is covered, creation of alternate forms at consistent difficulty levels is more challenging. If probes given over time are not consistent in difficulty, then it is hard to know whether changes in student scores are a result of student growth or test difficulty level. Creating GOMs of equivalent difficulty allows the measures to be used in alternate forms across time to monitor growth.

Second, when measures are developed from the local curriculum materials, the whole measurement system must be recreated with every new curriculum adoption, and comparison of student performance across the two curricula is not possible. GOMs are administered and scored the same way as CBMs, but are designed to have alternate forms of consistent difficulty so that growth over time may be measured. When using assessment materials from outside the curriculum, the effects of curriculum changes may be measured through the use of GOMs.

Where to Find GOM Materials

Materials for use in general outcomes measurement are currently available from a variety of sources. The AIMSweb® product (now sold through Pearson) offers both the probes for assessment and a web-based system for storing and graphing the data. Yearly Progress Pro (McGraw Hill) offers a similar product, as does Edcheckup (Edcheckup LLC). DIBELS (University of Oregon CTL) is another well-known product providing GOMs and a data management system; however, the probes are created only through grade 6, so they are less useful in a secondary setting. Pro-Ed publishes a program called Monitoring Basic Skills Progress (MBSP), and includes GOM assessments for math computation and applications (word problems). These are sold as blackline masters, and the program does not include a data storage system. As with all assessments, we strongly encourage you to read the technical manuals available with each of these products to identify the reliability and validity coefficients for the screening instruments.

Academic Screeners

In the following section, we will describe specific screeners for reading, math, writing, and vocabulary from the family of curriculum-based measures. We will also describe two other assessments commonly used as screeners: the NWEA MAP test and state high-stakes tests.

Reading

Two curriculum based measures that assess reading skills are curriculum-based measurement of reading (CBM-R) and the maze assessment.

Curriculum-Based Measurement of Reading

Curriculum-based measurement of reading, also sometimes referred to as oral reading fluency (ORF), assesses the number of words a student reads aloud correctly in one minute on grade-level passages. Standard passages are typically provided through eighth grade.

Maze

The maze assessment is a silent reading test. In the text, every seventh word is removed. In its place, three options are provided. Often the choices are constructed so that one option is the correct word, one option is a near distractor with correct syntax but incorrect semantics, and the third option is a far distractor with incorrect syntax and semantics. Students are given three minutes to read and circle the word from each group of three that best fits in the sentences they read. The total number of words correctly identified in three minutes is the score.

Math

In the area of math, two common CBM screening assessments used are Math Applications, which focuses on math problem solving, and Math Computation, which focuses on computation.

Math Applications

The math applications assessment is an eight-to-ten minute test of mixed math problems (for example, story problems, ratios, fractions, geometry, measurement, money, charts and graphs, numeration, number concepts, and other such problems). Students complete as many problems as possible in the allotted time and are awarded points for each problem completed correctly in the given time. This assessment may be administered to groups of students.

Math Computation

In the math computation curriculum-based measurement, students receive a set of mixed math computation problems (typically adding, subtracting, multiplying, and dividing of whole numbers, fractions, and decimals, depending on grade). The number of correct answers they generate in two minutes is their score. This assessment may be administered to groups of students.

Written Expression

In the written expression curriculum-based measurement, students receive a story starter and have thirty seconds to think and three minutes to write. Students' written products may be scored by counting total words read, total words spelled correctly, total correct word sequences, or total correct word sequences minus total incorrect word sequences. A correct word sequence is two adjacent words, correctly spelled and syntactically and semantically appropriate to the sentence. This assessment may be administered to groups of students.

Vocabulary

In curriculum-based measurement of vocabulary, students receive lists of vocabulary words and their definitions and must match words with definitions in a specified amount of time, often five minutes. This measure has been studied most often as a measure of content knowledge for academic courses with upper elementary and middle school students. The number of correct matches a student makes is the score. This assessment may be administered to groups of students.

NWEA MAP

The Northwest Evaluation Association Measures of Academic Progress (NWEA MAP) assessment is a computer-adaptive, nationally normed assessment of reading, math, and language. Each test is approximately one-hour long and uses item-response theory to offer different levels of questions until students' proficiency levels are found. Scores are reported in Rauch Units (RIT scores), which is an equal interval scale like feet and inches. This means the difference between any two consecutive scores represents the same amount of change. RIT scores range from 145 to 250 in the area of reading and 150 to 280 in math. Students typically start at an RIT score of between 170 and 190 in the second grade and progress to the 230 and 260 range by high school. Student scores may be compared across grade level. The goal of the MAP testing is to record individual student growth over time. Reliability estimates of the MAP test are consistently above 0.80. In addition to a total score, tests also provide strand scores that offer some diagnostic information regarding areas of relative strength and weakness for students.

State Assessments

State assessments have become very salient in the era of NCLB. These assessments are used in outcomes evaluation to determine the level of success of a particular school or group of students. They may also be used as a screening instrument, identifying the students who score at or below a particular score level. Because state accountability tests are typically designed to measure students' proficiency levels on the state instructional standards, they provide an important measure of success. However, as with all assessments, care should be taken to understand the psychometric properties and limitations of state tests, so that reasonable interpretation of the results can be made.

Selecting Cut Scores for Screening Instruments

Deciding the cut score, that is, the score or range of scores that will indicate increased risk for each screening instrument, is a critical decision for teams to make. There are a number of ways to do this. Three are described here, along with the benefits of each option.

Local Norms

Local norms may be used for screening. To do this, first administer the screening instrument either to all students or a large sample (at least one hundred students per grade level). Then determine the mean and standard deviation by running descriptive statistics on the list of scores in a spreadsheet program such as Microsoft Excel. Often, students who score one standard deviation below the grade-level mean are considered at risk. For example, if a building administered a reading assessment to all grade 8 students, and the mean score was 161 with a standard deviation of 34 points, then the cut score for indication of risk would be 127. All students scoring at or below 127 on the reading test would be considered to be at risk based on this assessment. Use of local norms may be desirable particularly for schools whose students, as a group, are very high or very low performing.

National Normative Data

A second method for determining the cut score for screening instruments is the use of national normative data. Often, students who score below the 25th percentile relative to national norms on a particular assessment may be considered at risk. For example, if the 25th percentile score on a grade 8 reading assessment was 106, then all students scoring at or below that number could be considered at risk. Use of national norms is helpful for understanding how students in a local system are performing compared to a larger sample. One commonly referenced national normative sample is published every few years by Jan Hasbrouck and Gerald Tindal (2006).

Criterion-Referenced Benchmarks

A third method for determining the cut score for screening instruments is the use of criterion-referenced benchmarks that are predictive of high-stakes outcomes. In most instances, the high-stakes test used is the state accountability test for NCLB. Inferential statistics may be used to calculate scores on a screening instrument that predicts a student's ability to pass the state accountability test. For example, in east central Minnesota, students in grade 8 who score 170 on a reading screening test have a 75 percent chance of passing the Minnesota Comprehensive Assessments Series-II (MCAII) test that spring, while those scoring 109 have only a 25 percent chance of passing the same test. The connection to salient expectations for academic outcomes provides a strong rationale for using this method of determining cut scores. More details related to criterion-referenced benchmarks are included in chapter 8.

Screening Procedures

Once a secondary team has determined what assessment tools to use for the purpose of screening and what cut scores will indicate at-risk status, it is ready to develop a buildingwide plan. Four components of a comprehensive screening system are discussed in this chapter:

1. Regular ongoing academic screening for all students through grade 8

2. Regular ongoing screening for all students in grades 9–12

3. Screening for all students in preparation for a building-transition year (often grades 6, 7, 9, or 10)

4. Screening individual students in grades 9–12 as they join the system

Screening All Students Through Grade 8

The practice in our local districts, which we endorse, is to screen all students through grade 8 three times per year on academic skills. Once schools have selected the assessments to use in screening and the cut scores that will indicate instructional risk, it is time to consider the logistics of collecting the data. For assessments such as curriculum-based measures of reading (CBM-R), which are administered individually, it's advantageous to employ an assessment team for data collection. This is a team of staff members who have been trained on standardized administration and scoring procedures and who put their regular school duties on hold for one to three days (depending on the size of the school) to assess each student. Assessment teams can be made up of special or general education teachers, paraprofessionals, administrators, counselors or psychologists, retired or substitute teachers, or community volunteers. In all cases, training in standardized administration and scoring procedures in addition to observations to confirm fidelity to assessment procedures is critical.

If all English or reading classes are scheduled for testing at the time of their regular class period, testing can be completed in the same number of days as there are concurrent sections of English or reading for a given period. In some cases, schools reserve a large commons area, and classroom teachers bring their classes down to that area according to a predetermined schedule for assessment. In other cases, the assessment team sets up desks in the hallway outside of class groupings and moves from hall to hall through the school to complete assessments.

Collecting CBM-R data takes about five minutes per child, so a team of six could assess a class of thirty in twenty-five minutes; a team of eight could complete the assessment in twenty minutes. Materials for CBM-R can be organized into assessment binders that include student copies of each of the passages to be read and teacher copies that have been laminated or placed in page protectors. Teachers who use dry-erase markers for scoring on these protected copies can erase and reuse the assessment over and over, saving paper. Expo® makes a dry-erase marker with an eraser on the top, which is nice, but any rag will get the job done. Teachers also need timers. We have found digital kitchen countdown timers to be preferable to standard stopwatches because they are silent while timing and beep audibly at the end of the timed period, so the teacher does not need to keep one eye on the clock while testing.

For assessments such as curriculum-based measures of math application, which may be administered to groups, the assessment team can often place sets of the assessment, along with a written script for administration, in teachers' mailboxes with a request to have students complete the assessment within a specified window of time. Following this model, some schools have their math teachers collect the math assessment and score their own class assessments, following standardized scoring procedures. Other sites have used para-educators or other support staff, hired substitute teachers, or trained community volunteers for scoring the assessments. One tip for scoring the math assessments (which works for any of the group-administered written assessments) is to create an answer key on a copy of the assessment and print it on a transparency so it can be placed on top of the students' pages and scored with a dry-erase marker.

A few factors are important when considering the timing of screening data collection. First, we have found that the best way to get class lists for recording scores is from the student information system in the building. In order for these to be most accurate, we recommend waiting until late registrants and course substitutions have been entered, usually the second or third day of school, to export the lists. On the other end, schools typically like to have their assessment data scored and compiled prior to fall conferences, so teachers can share results, together with school plans for addressing those results, in meetings with parents.

Some schools have used pencil-and-paper methods to report scores, which are later entered into a database. Others have created electronic data-recording forms (using Microsoft Excel, for example) and housed them on a shared drive that teachers can access. Some screening database programs, such as AIMSweb, offer additional electronic means for data entry. Our experience has been that it is most helpful to enter scores into a local database (created in Microsoft Excel or Microsoft Access) first, and then to import this database into other programs as needed. We have a few reasons for this suggestion.

First, assuming district databases, such as AIMSweb or other web portals, are actually web based, those completing the data entry are dependent on the speed of their Internet connection for efficiency. Depending on the capacity of the district server, some connections may be very slow at times—and therefore very inefficient. Second, if student data are to be sent to multiple databases, each one will likely have a unique set of parameters for imports. By creating one file that has all field names required by any database, subsets of that file may be sent to any other database with relative ease.

For example, our districts want to be able to view student CBM data in the AIMSweb database because of the graphs that are automatically generated within the system. However, they also want the CBM data to be loaded in our district web portal so they can access a report for students that has CBM, MAP, and high-stakes testing data together. The AIMSweb uses the student AIMSweb ID number to match scores with student names; however, the state ID number is used for state testing. So, to be able to view both data points, we need to link the students' AIMSweb IDs and state IDs. In any case, districts need one or more persons who are adept with data and manipulation transfer to ensure that data are readily available to staff for decision making in whatever databases are being used.

Some buildings have adopted the practice of reporting screening scores on student report cards as an alternative or in addition to sharing feedback with parents at conferences. Teachers and parents have found this practice tremendously useful. To ensure that data are available at key times, however, it is important to plan data collection in relation to the timing of these conferences or reporting periods.

Screening Students in Grades 9–12

In our buildings, the use of CBM to screen all students three times per year ends after eighth grade for all students who have met grade 8 targets. We do continue to screen students in grades 9–12 on grade 8 measures if they have not yet met our performance expectations on those measures. In addition, we believe NWEA MAPs can be used for screening ninth or tenth graders buildingwide. We suggest that the NWEA math assessment is useful through grade 10, but the reading assessment seems to cease being useful after grade 9. Other data for screening at this level include office discipline referrals (ODRs), attendance, and credits earned toward graduation. While there tends to be less reliability and validity associated with these variables, they are already being collected and are key indicators for secondary student engagement. If you have a large student population with already-existing risk indicators (for example, high ODRs, high mobility, or predominantly low socioeconomic status [SES]), it would be advantageous to do a schoolwide screening with the NWEA MAP to get a good look at how students are performing in response to core instruction across all grades. You may not consider this each year, but it is a good check to do occasionally.

The notion of regular screening for academic difficulty for students who did show proficiency on grade 8 screening measures does continue, but in revised form. Measures of basic skills understandably become less relevant when the large majority of students are already proficient, so having other means of identifying students who may be at risk becomes important. We suggest four common measures for identifying at-risk students in grades 9–12. First, we flag any student with three or more office discipline referrals in one semester for additional consideration. Second, any student who fails two or more classes per semester is identified as at risk. Third, any student who earns less than one-quarter of the total number of credits needed to graduate each year is identified as at risk. Fourth, any student who does not earn a passing grade on the high-stakes state assessment offered in the given year is identified as at risk. It is largely the building guidance counselors who review these data on a semester basis, meeting with identified students to interview them in an attempt to understand the cause of the problem. The counselor brings the names of identified students to the building RTI team in order to plan supports. It is wise for buildings to develop a concrete list of indicators that will be checked for all students on a regular basis for the purpose of catching any instance of student risk.

Another tool for screening high school students is important to mention at this point. The National High School Center's Early Warning System (EWS) Tool, now in its second edition, is available free of charge at the www.betterhighschools.org website. This tool was developed to manage data that identify students who are at risk of dropping out, based on research-supported indicators for this problem. It runs in Microsoft Excel and is customizable.

Screening in Preparation for a Building-Transition Year

Even within districts that operate in a tight top-down management style, individual buildings tend to operate as independent unique environments. This may be due, among many reasons, to different demographics among students being served, different building cultures and sizes, or different age groups served. The differences between elementary and middle or secondary schools, and even between middle and high schools, are particularly significant due to changes in scheduling, which result in the upper grades in many more teachers interacting with a particular student within a given day. In general, teachers in middle and secondary schools tend to interact with many more students than their elementary school counterparts.

A philosophical underpinning of an RTI system is that the level of success a student experiences in school is attributed primarily to the quality of interaction between the child and the instructional environment. With a change of buildings, there is most often a significant change in that environment, and as a result, changes in student performance. The rationale for having a strong screening system for incoming classes is twofold: to help ensure a smooth transition between environments for as many students as possible and to proactively plug students into the supports they need to reduce needless struggle for both students and teachers.

The school-year transition process begins in the early spring of the preceeding school year with a look at the high school master schedule. Administrators work to set the schedule at this time as much as possible, in order to identify areas of flexibility or to allow for the possibility for altered programming. With this background knowledge, transition planning continues with a meeting of staff from both the sending and receiving schools. For example, the transition-planning group might include the following: from a middle school, the school counselor, dean, school psychologist, assistant principal, reading teacher, and intervention teacher; from the high school, the assistant principal, counselors, school psychologist, and intervention teachers. The purpose of this meeting is to identify students who may be at risk for failure in grade 9 based on their performance in grade 8 and to design a proactive plan to support them through the transition year. A specific predetermined set of data is collected and compiled prior to this meeting to assist with decision making.

Building staff members often wonder what data is best to use for these types of screening decisions. In his policy and practice brief, "Putting Middle Grades Students on the

Graduation Path," Robert Balfanz (2009) shares results of over a decade of research, development work, and direct field experience in identifying risk factors related to high school dropout. In short, researchers found there were specific indicators for students in grade 6 that accurately predicted dropout instances:

> We found that sixth graders who failed math or English/reading, or attended school less than 80 percent of the time, or received an unsatisfactory behavior grade in a core course had only a 10 percent–20 percent chance of graduating on time. Less than 1 of every 4 students with at least one off-track indicator graduated within one extra year of on-time graduation. (p. 4)

It stands to reason that these indicators would be among those data points schools would consider when planning for at-risk students. In addition to screening for dropout prevention, schools might consider results of the federally mandated high-stakes tests of state standards given in every public school at least through grade 8, in addition to other academic screeners. Our local districts use the NWEA MAP test as well as general outcomes measures of academic skills through grade 8 for screening students entering middle or high school.

Carefully consider what assessment scores will be available in preparation for this transition-planning meeting. For example, in Minnesota, students take the state test in May, with results first available in August. So, in thinking about the transition from grade 8 to grade 9, the most recent MCAII score that can be utilized is the one taken in the spring of the grade 7 year. Likewise, the local achievement test and general outcomes measures are offered three times per year, with the winter testing season being the last one prior to transition meetings. Results of spring testing may ultimately change a team's decision about student placement for some students; however, we have found that decisions based on broad converging evidence have typically been solid for planning, despite having test data that is a few months to one-year-old. Table 4.1 shows a typical Excel file set up for transition meetings with a column for each screening indicator.

Table 4.1: Example of Excel Template for Summarizing Eighth-Grade Student Transition Data

Student Name	Grade 8 GPA	Number of Fs	Attendance Rate	Grade 8 ODRs	Winter Grade 8 MAP Reading	Winter Grade 8 MAP Math	Winter Grade 8 ORF GOM	Winter Grade 8 Math Applications GOM	Spring Grade 7 MCAII Reading	Spring Grade 7 MCAII Math

In addition to assessment scores, middle school staff also bring specific knowledge about the students under consideration and the instructional programs in which these students have participated. High school staff bring knowledge of the current intervention options available in the building and open minds about what possibilities could be developed to meet the unique needs of members of the incoming student class. For example, the high school staff might know that they have one section of supplemental and remedial English available; students would participate in regular English in addition to this period of reinforcement of essential skills. They may have a vision for the number of participants for that class and an understanding of how participation in it would affect other details of a student's schedule. The middle school staff may be able to identify more possible students for this class than would fit into one section. In that case, staff from both buildings would work together to consider how to meet the needs of the remaining students at risk.

At this point it is important to note that the purpose of these transition meetings is not to build more and more supplemental programs to support large numbers of students. Coming back to the triangle model (fig. 2.1, page 17), we are still striving for a core instructional program that fully meets the needs of at least 80 percent of students served. So, if in our example transition meeting, the middle school identifies numbers of at-risk students that are too high, this will be a clear indication that two sets of core planning meetings need to take place. First, the eighth-grade team will need to identify ways in which it can use its resources to get more students meeting grade-level expectations. Second, teachers serving ninth grade will need to identify ways that the core instructional offerings can be intensified to meet the needs of a broader population of students.

An outcome of the transition meetings is a list of every identified at-risk student, with a plan for what standard program or programs that student will participate in starting the following fall. Table 4.2 shows the results of one such meeting.

Table 4.2: Outcome of a Transition Meeting

Student Name	SPED	RTI 9	Pre-Alg	Science Topics	Alg1/Sci Skinny	Math Lab	Not Prof Read MCA	Not Prof Math MCA
Adams, John								
Aikins, Jill					X		X	
Beck, Beth		X			X	X	X	
Bostern, Boyd					X			
Cray, Michael				X				
Cummings, Maura	X	X	X	X		X	X	
Dahl, Edward							X	

In table 4.2, the standard academic services offered in ninth grade include special education (SPED), a double period of English that includes remedial reading instruction (RTI 9), a pre-algebra class (pre-Alg), a remedial science class, the option to take shorter class periods of algebra and science all year long (Alg1/Sci Skinny, known as the "skinny" option) versus longer class periods for one semester each in a block schedule and a supplemental math lab for work on missing prerequisite math skills.

Once students are identified for the specific supplemental intervention programs available in ninth grade, teachers of those courses spend time in the spring planning for how these courses need to be altered to meet the unique needs of the incoming group. One group might be particularly weak in writing or might have many students with multisyllabic word decoding difficulties. Teachers might plan to spend a greater portion of the intervention time on these weak areas, or even select specific supplemental curricular materials. Any additional training needed for staff should be put in place as soon as possible.

The timeline followed by one high school (table 4.3) provides an overview of annual events designed to provide a smooth transition and effective student support for all incoming ninth graders.

Table 4.3: Overview of Annual Events Providing Effective Support for Incoming Ninth Graders

February	Master schedule is adjusted for the upcoming year.
March	High school assistant principal (AP) and middle school administration and staff put together initial list of at-risk students and their data.
April	High school principal, AP, and school psychologist review student needs to develop the Tier 2 course concept: what is needed instructionally, and what are the building-level needs?
May	Middle and high school staff meet to plug students into the grade 9 schedule of supports.
June	Hire new staff (if needed).
August	Meet with new teachers to discuss the class/intervention concept, data, and progress monitoring.
Fall/Spring	Teachers receive ongoing professional development.

Screening Individual Students in Grades 9–12

If families never moved, then the one-time comprehensive screening procedure for incoming students would catch all students who need support throughout high school. However, families and kids do move, so a system needs to be in place to connect students with needed supports as soon as they join a new school system. It is important that educators take the time to understand academic needs quite early on, so that supports for success can be put in place. Some would advocate for not knowing a student's history when they begin teaching that student, to avoid bringing any preconceptions to the instruction. We feel that the potentially detrimental consequences of this thinking outweigh any benefits. If we allow students to become overwhelmed or fail, then we have two problems to deal with—the need for the intervention that we could have originally implemented and the challenge of reconnecting the student to instruction.

An additional screening policy for newly enrolled students in grades 9–12 has been helpful to our districts. These students meet with a staff member (often school counselor) within their first few days of school to complete the screening instruments. This practice ensures that if this new student might be at risk for academic difficulty, the team knows about it right away and can plan effective supports. It also helps with initial class placement, which can be challenging for newly enrolled students.

For them, screening begins with a review of the student file, including the transcript from the previous school. Typically, the guidance counselor conducts this review, looking at high-stakes-test outcomes, grades, attendance, and courses taken, and makes a judgment about whether the data from the file indicate solid performance in each area or whether follow-up is needed. Table 4.4 illustrates a template for such a review.

Table 4.4: Sample Screening Data Template for Students New to the Building

Student Name: _____ **Grade:** _____ **Date:** _____

Directions: For each row, check satisfactory performance or follow-up indicated, based on review of student files.

Review Area	Satisfactory Performance	Follow-Up Indicated
Most Recent NCLB High-Stakes Test		
Course Grades: English Language Arts		
Course Grades: Mathematics		
School Attendance		
Course Credits on Track for Graduation		

For reviewing high-stakes-test outcomes, counselors look at the most recent assessment of math and reading, in particular, and determine whether the student earned a passing or *meets standards* score. Often, students who move into a building are moving from elsewhere in the same state, so building staff are accustomed to interpreting scores on the NCLB test. If the student is from out of state, staff might need to do some sleuthing to learn how to interpret the score.

Counselors also look to see if there is any history of failed classes. Seeing grades in the A to C range is expected, whereas Ds raise some concern, and Fs are definitely a cause for follow-up. Recall that even a single failed course in middle school, particularly in language arts or mathematics, puts students at increased risk (Balfanz, 2009).

School attendance is important to review as an indicator of connectedness to the previous instructional setting. Counselors expect to see attendance rates above 90 percent. Note that a 90 percent attendance rate, which equates to one missed day every two weeks, is cause for concern. Here, a local norm can be helpful by determining what the average and standard deviation are for the building attendance rate and can help clarify what is discrepant.

The last check is for whether students are on track in terms of courses. The counselor makes two parallel considerations. First, he or she sees whether the student is on track in terms of credits earned and required courses. In Minnesota, for example, students must pass the assessment in math taken in grade 11 in order to earn a diploma. This assessment includes typical algebra II concepts. Therefore, to be on track for courses, students are expected to take algebra in grade 9 and geometry in grade 10. Students whose transcripts indicate courses on a slower track are identified for follow-up. In New York, to earn a state diploma, students must complete math courses I–III. An eleventh grader in course I raises a red flag. Second, counselors are looking to see whether there is any indication that the student has been enrolled in remedial or intervention-level courses. This is a slightly different issue from taking on-level courses at a slower pace.

Once this initial screening via file review is completed, students might participate in a second round of screening if there is an indication of concern. For example, if a student has failed high-stakes tests and has failing grades, low credits earned, or evidence of remedial courses, that student receives academic screening. Commonly, this will mean that the student will complete CBM reading, math, and writing probes using grade 8 level assessment materials. If the district utilizes other achievement tests with students, the student may take those tests as well. The NWEA MAP test, for example, is one that students can take at any point in the school year.

Conclusion

Setting up a comprehensive screening system for secondary students is critical to an RTI framework. The indicators used for screening change as students grow older, but the conceptual framework remains the same. Once the measures and cut scores are selected and an efficient system for gathering data is designed, schools will be able to use these data for two important purposes. The first is to identify students who need supplemental supports. The logistics of data reviews and planning and the implementation of Tier 2 instruction are discussed further in chapter 8. The second outcome of strong screening is the ability to use these data for evaluation of the quality of the core curriculum discussed in chapter 5 (page 63).

Tier 1 Core Instruction: Academics

Tier 1 must meet the needs of 80 percent of the learners, because Tiers 2 and 3 cannot handle more than 20 percent. Building a strong Tier 1 with highly defined and measureable curriculum gets broader gains for an organization.

—Charles Johns, former principal,
Rolling Meadows High School, Rolling Meadows, Illinois

Advance Organizer

✓ *An organized and well-articulated plan for effective Tier 1 instruction is non-negotiable within an RTI framework.*

✓ *There are some distinct features to attend to and implement to ensure quality Tier 1 instruction at the secondary level.*

✓ *How do we know Tier 1 core instruction is working? A plan for evaluation is an essential feature to include in the implementation plan.*

✓ *Steps and ideas for problem solving when Tier 1 academics are ineffective.*

The question asked throughout this book is, Do we believe we can educate *all* kids? Tier 1, or core, instruction is what we are teaching—or are attempting to teach—all students in the building. As educators, we dream of the day that our students are all truly engaged in authentic learning—learning that demands rigorous thinking and substantive knowledge, learning that is relevant to students. What educator wouldn't want to have all students in a class focused, interested in the content, engaged in learning, and demonstrating high-level outcomes?

While this sounds good, achieving it is a daunting task. Extensive research, lengthy debates, and lots of money have gone into telling educators to improve the quality of secondary educational systems, but the best method for achieving that goal is unclear. Making core instruction work for at least 80 percent of secondary learners is a challenge. No one-size-fits-all approach is likely to succeed. We have found, however, that implementing a response to intervention framework offers a robust and efficient *opportunity* to create effective instruction for all. And for RTI to be effectively managed, there *must* be an effective Tier 1 base of services. Given this close relationship, let's look more closely at Tier 1, effective core instruction.

Why Are Effective Tier 1 Services Important?

In the current educational climate, there seems to be an ever-increasing focus on accountability based on a defined set of criteria for learner outcomes, most commonly through NCLB (state tests). In addition, schools are responsible to the community they serve to be the best stewards of the limited resources given to them. It would be a rare school site in which staff would say they have all the resources they could possibly need to achieve the NCLB goal of proficiency for all, let alone other local expectations.

Fact: Basic educational formula allowances in, for example, Minnesota have increased by a total of $50 per student from the 2007–2008 to the 2010–2011 school year (Strom, 2010). Many states face similar or worse funding scenarios. Without an endless supply of people, time, or materials to individualize instruction for every pupil perfectly, secondary schools need to be extremely efficient with what they have; these services need to be effective for large numbers of students. The goal is for Tier 1 services to meet the needs of 80 percent of our students, as shown in figure 5.1.

Imagine if Tier 1 instruction met the needs of only 50 percent of your students. That would mean that half your students would need something in addition to core instruction to meet grade-level expectations. Trying to address the needs of such a large percentage of students through supplemental supports would be a tremendous strain on resources. How could anyone defend a Tier 1 system that met the needs of only half the students? The answer is that no one *should* accept that as effective schoolwide programming. As budgets are reduced and funding continues to decline, schools must work smarter with their money. The national government, state educational system, local community, and most importantly, our students expect that of us.

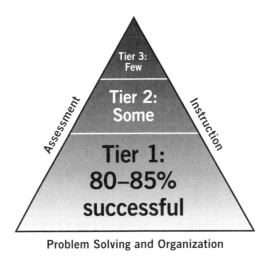

Figure 5.1: Tier 1 services successfully reaching 80–85 percent of students.

If We Know What's Needed, Why Isn't It Happening?

There are many reasons effective Tier 1 services aren't happening in schools around the United States. Let's explore a few of the ones we've identified.

Time Constraints

Time is one of the most precious commodities in education. We know from research that academic engaged time is one of the most significant variables for student success (Gettinger & Ball, 2008). To just "make time" or reallocate time to focus on instructional priorities is such a simple idea that we can lose site of the complexities involved in making that happen. As discussed in chapter 9 (page 121), the master schedule drives everything in a secondary setting. But just building time into the master schedule will not be the one-shot fix for low student achievement. We also need to think about time for professional development, time for teacher collaboration, time for planning, and time for preparation related to what the additional student time will consist of. A lack of time devoted to these things is a barrier to developing effective Tier 1 instruction.

Content Specialization

Compared to their counterparts in elementary buildings, educators in secondary settings increasingly become content-area specialists. While the idea of focusing on a content area has many advantages (for example, extensive knowledge or focused study), a primary disadvantage is the potential lack of cohesiveness and continuity in the overall curriculum. This emphasis on content can contribute to a culture of resistance to teaching or instructing outside one's area of study, which in the end will limit effectiveness of the instructional system as a whole. Secondary school administrators trying to implement increased reading instruction in their buildings are commonly met with such statements as "I teach social studies, not reading," or "I teach computer classes, not math." Resistance of this type is most commonly a symptom of fear and anxiety. Let's face it, change is difficult. It's difficult for any of us to stretch ourselves outside our comfort areas, let alone do so in front of thirty teenagers! To implement effective Tier 1 services, staff must be willing to be exposed to new ideas, participate in staff development activities, and reflect on the implementation of a new idea. This change in roles and responsibilities is part of changing a school's culture (see chapter 6).

Characteristics of Secondary Students

Anyone who has spent any amount of time in a secondary school can quickly identify differences between secondary and elementary students. From an adolescent development viewpoint, one typical characteristic is the desire of secondary students for greater independence. Although adolescent psychologists espouse how critical it is to provide appropriate opportunities for independence, it can be tricky for teachers to integrate them into a classroom. In their quest for independence, secondary students demonstrate a need for choice, power, and control, for having a voice in a situation. It is the job of the adults in their lives to acknowledge this need and provide support and boundaries. This is a characteristic, among many other developmental traits, that secondary educators must recognize as part of many considerations for implementing RTI.

Lack of Administrative Leadership

Administrators must be active in all aspects of implementing an RTI framework. While the implementation process in the classroom is hard work, often administrators and other building leaders face a different set of challenges. The resistance of their staff to changing the status quo of a building can be an uphill battle. Once administrators or leadership teams have worked to build consensus and have their staff believing in changing their system, they can be met with a new challenge—the fact that few research-based math interventions exist for high school students. How then can they provide adequate professional development in this area? School leadership must continue to be supportive and persistent to problem solve these challenges.

In summary, we see that lack of time, content specialization at the expense of cohesive instructional planning, the characteristics of adolescent learners, and lack of administrative leadership can all be significant barriers to effective Tier 1 instruction. Given the importance of achieving this outcome, however, we are compelled to work toward this goal.

Striving for Effective Tier 1 Services

The good news is that there are a number of practical strategies schools can employ to increase the effectiveness of instruction. While none of these is a silver bullet that will work on its own or in every situation, we offer these suggestions to schools who are striving to make their core instruction more effective for greater percentages of students served.

Knowing Your Standards

Teachers need to know the standards to which they are teaching. It is reasonable to expect that every staff person would be able to provide a cogent overview of the standards in his or her area of instruction and the salient specifics related to rigor and unique details provided within those standards. This level of understanding does not come from a single-day workshop or a myopic study of a single grade level or subject area. Rather, ongoing collaborative work around standards that elicits an understanding of changing expectations across grade levels and connections across subjects is needed. A study of how standards are evaluated on federally mandated tests is also helpful in understanding desired learner outcomes.

A multiple-read strategy may be helpful to staff teams when working with standards. First, staff read over their standards to get the overall gist and note the general layout of the full document. To reflect on this, ask staff members to work with a partner from the same content area to share a topic from the standards they have addressed in the past month that neither of them fully understands, along with one thing that was a surprise. Next, have them reread the standard, highlighting the verbs in one color to focus attention on the level of understanding required and highlighting the nouns in another color to focus attention on the content to use. To help staff reflect on this activity, create vertical teams within a content area to look at the way skills build across years. Finally, have staff reread the standard with an eye toward identifying the essential competencies called for in their grade level and subject area, and this time, through discussions with colleagues across content areas, discuss connections across the curriculum. See table 5.1 for an illustration of benchmark progression through Standard 1 in Reading Literature and Informational Text.

Table 5.1: Benchmark Progression Through Standard 1 in Reading Literature and Informational Text

Grade 6	Grade 7	Grade 8	Grades 9–10	Grades 11–12
1. Cite textual evidence to support analysis of what the text says explicitly as well as inferences drawn from the text.	1. Cite several pieces of textual evidence to support analysis of what the text says explicitly as well as inferences drawn from the text.	1. Cite the textual evidence that most strongly supports an analysis of what the text says explicitly as well as inferences drawn from the text.	1. Cite strong and *thorough* textual evidence to support analysis of what the text says explicitly as well as inferences drawn from the text.	1. Cite strong and thorough textual evidence to support analysis of what the text says explicitly as well as inferences drawn from the text, *including determining where the text leaves matters uncertain.*
CCR Standard: READING LITERATURE AND INFORMATIONAL TEXT 1				
Read closely to determine what the text says explicitly and to make logical inferences from it; cite specific textual evidence when writing or speaking to support conclusions drawn from the text.				

Source: National Governors Association Center for Best Practices and Council of Chief State School Officers.
© Copyright 2010. All rights reserved.

   A second strategy that has been helpful to some schools is working together on an extended study of a small number of standards over the course of a year. The Common Core Standards for English Language Arts (National Governors Association Center for Best Practices and Council of Chief State School Officers, 2010), which have been adopted by many states, have been an ideal set for this work because of the standards for ELA in science and social studies that are included for grades 6–12. For this study, teams of teachers, grouped either by grade level or department, take one standard for study per month. In a meeting, this group of teachers reviews the College/Career Anchor standard and grade-level benchmark, noting the verbs and nouns as described previously. Next, the group reads the benchmarks for the grade level above and below their own, taking specific note of the rigor demanded at their level in contrast to the two others. Finally, the group discusses ways in which they are, or could be, more effectively addressing this benchmark in their instruction. This discussion can reasonably occur in twenty minutes, but the power of the exercise is in having these discussions on a regular, ongoing basis, which results in deep understanding of the standards.

Aligning Curriculum

Curriculum mapping is the next strategy we suggest for building a strong Tier 1 program. This ongoing process of aligning instruction to the standards and ensuring that all course pathways result in adequate mastery of content in the standards is critical to ensuring positive outcomes. We find that deep understanding of standards documents makes a huge difference in the quality of mapping activities. We also find that using the standards documents to anchor classes (as opposed to particular textbooks) results in more continuity across courses and grade levels.

Supporting Active Reading Throughout the Day

Kids who read succeed, right? Much has been written about the amount of text students read in a given day and the related positive outcomes (Cunningham & Stanovich, 1988; Stanovich, 1986; U.S. Department of Education, 1999). Given this knowledge, it makes sense that, as secondary educators, we would strive to build educational systems that include significant time for students to be reading each day. And yet we find that for many sites, improvement in this area is needed. A common instructional practice used in many classrooms is *round-robin reading*, a practice by which each student is called on to read a paragraph, while the rest of the class listens. This offers every child a small amount of practice, and everyone who is listening hears the content being read. Overall, however, it is a weak strategy. Actual reading practice for each student is fairly small compared to the total text covered in a session. Further, students who are poor readers are typically asked to read less often or are assigned shorter paragraphs, in order to save them potential embarrassment and the class potential frustration. The result is less practice for the students who need it most. Further, if there is any discernible order in which students are asked to read, many will spend time prereading theirs in order to perform well. Not only are they receiving an unfair advantage, but they are not listening to the content offered by other readers. A good consensus-building activity for a staff is to break into small groups and develop lists of reasons why round-robin reading is not a good use of class time—your small groups will come up with more reasons than those listed here! Not all suggestions will work in all classes or at all times. The idea is to have options like the following from which to choose when working to create an instructional environment that includes rich practice in reading for students:

▶ **Prepractice**—If you are going to do a round-robin read anyway, consider preassigning the paragraphs and giving all students three minutes or so to silently practice their assigned paragraph before reading the text as a class. This will provide targeted practice time that students appreciate—so they are ready! Following this procedure, students will be more likely to listen to the content when the class does start to read, because they have already had the chance to work on their own paragraph. Struggling readers are more likely to read their assigned section with better speed, accuracy, and expression.

▶ **Choral reading**—"Keep your voice with mine as we read the next paragraph." This strategy gives everyone in the class practice reading, with the teacher's voice as a model for correct pronunciation and pacing.

▶ **Close reading**—"I am going to read the next paragraph to you as you follow along with your eyes and finger. When I pause, your job is to read the next word aloud." This strategy is a good way to get through content quickly and increase the likelihood that students are tracking as you read. One caveat to this strategy: students should read aloud words that are central to the main idea of the section you are reading. Having them read nonessential words actually reduces their comprehension of the passage.

▶ **Silent reading including check-ins**—If students are silently reading in class, teachers can monitor this activity by checking in with students. One way to do this is to set up a system in which students expect that when the teacher taps them on the shoulder, they will begin *whisper reading* so the teacher can hear the quality of their reading. As they do, teachers can check off their names on a class list they are carrying with them. Teachers can also make notes about which students are struggling to read the text with fluency and need follow-up support.

▶ **Partner reading**—Pair students up to practice reading text together. Students can alternate paragraphs, reading aloud to each other and gaining much more practice than if they were listening to the whole class take turns. As an alternative, you can assign partners to A and B roles, with partner A, the stronger reader, reading a paragraph first, and partner B reading that same paragraph back again after hearing it once. If you have one or two very discrepant readers, we suggest you put these students with two partners. A strong member of the triad reads first, then the second member and the struggling member read chorally.

Building Effective Instructional Strategies

If staff have deep understanding of the standards to which they are teaching, and have developed (and are always continuing to refine) thorough maps by which alignment of curriculum with these standards is demonstrated, the next body of work we suggest is to consider quality instructional strategies that can be employed across teachers to yield positive outcomes for students. Many readers are, no doubt, familiar with the nine high-probability instructional strategies that were identified from an impressive meta-analysis of research related to effective instruction and published by Robert Marzano, Debra Pickering, and Jane Pollock (2001). We list them here as a start to the conversation about strategies that are likely to improve Tier 1 effectiveness:

1. Use activities in which students *identify similarities and differences* through comparison or classifying tasks, for example, resulting in deeper understanding of content.

2. Encourage *summarizing and note taking* as ways to synthesize information.

3. *Reinforce effort* over smarts and *provide recognition* for achievements.

4. Provide *homework and practice* to build competency.

5. Use *cooperative learning* to enhance learning through interaction.

6. Employ *nonlinguistic representations*, such as mental images, physical models, and kinesthetic activities.

7. *Set objectives* for explicit learning targets and *provide feedback.*

8. *Generate and test hypotheses* through "what if . . ." questions, for example.

9. Use *cues, questions, and advance organizers* to help students predict what they will learn

Marzano (2009) wisely warns that these are not the only effective instructional strategies and that teachers should not expect that all these strategies will always be effective in every setting. Taking these warnings to heart, one powerful outcome of this list is to focus our attention on the idea that staff can work collaboratively to engage in strategies that promote explicit instruction, effective practice, and deep content mastery among students. Even the best-aligned curriculum will be enhanced with this type of ongoing work.

Building Effective Engagement Strategies

The fifth broad suggestion for building core instructional effectiveness that we share relates to increasing student engagement in instruction. Many teachers have entered the classroom quite knowledgeable about their content area and how to effectively deliver the subject information, but with little training and few tools for effective classroom management. The term *classroom management* refers broadly to what teachers do to foster the social and academic behaviors we expect of students in our classrooms. When it comes to the science of teaching, classroom management needs to be intentionally planned, implemented, refined, and changed based on what our learners tell us through their data and behavior. Thoughtful and positive classroom management will play a large role in the degree to which secondary students are engaged in learning.

While the kids who come to our doorstep share some common, predictable characteristics, they most assuredly have differences as individuals and groups around a multitude of factors, some of which include the following:

▶   Prior learning of content

▶   Academic self-efficacy (the "I believe I can" attitude)

▶   Cultural/linguistic background

▶   Self-regulation skills

▶   Range of problem-solving or coping skills

▶ Outside-of-school support for learning and social or emotional needs

▶ Stage of physical development and maturity

Because of this diversity, what works for one group of ninth-grade learners may not be effective for another. So, we need a toolbox of effective classroom planning and management strategies. We also need to be persistent problem solvers for kids who don't fit with how we typically plan our classrooms to function. Even in secondary settings, so much of student engagement depends on the daily routines, rules, practices, and expectations in our classrooms. We have a tremendous amount of control over these variables, because much of it has to do with our own behavior. It follows that, as educators, we must regularly revisit our practices and think about designing classrooms and instruction that are academically engaging.

The next few sections summarize research and translate it into practical strategies for content delivery in academically engaging secondary classrooms (Gettinger & Ball, 2008; Morrone & Schutz, 2000; Perlman & Redding, 2009; Vaughn, Bos, & Schumm, 1997). Chapter 6 provides further strategies for creating positive classroom environments and student relationships.

Planning Instruction

What are the expected learning outcomes for the course, the unit, and the lesson? What is the expected routine for accessing the identified learning outcomes? Secondary staff need scheduled time to plan within teams. This planning time must have clear, expected outcomes if there is to be a sufficient impact on learning (Perlman & Redding, 2009). After spending this time planning, teachers need to tell students what to expect in terms of content, social behavior, and classroom routines. Tell them as often as they need to hear it. Remember: drift happens. You may have to practice and discuss expectations again after the first month or two months.

A great resource to assist with content planning is the strategic instruction model (SIM™). SIM contains research-established routines designed to bring order and priority to content. Of the fourteen routines, six are for content enhancement (what teachers do to plan and deliver content), and eight are strategies to teach students how to access and comprehend the content. Go to www.kucrl.org/sim for more information.

A practical suggestion for how to begin incorporating the SIM strategies is to start with training modules in the winter and spring. Have follow-up or debriefing meetings with the staff using these strategies. Let the time between winter and spring be an opportunity for teachers to try out their learning and get feedback from peers. Plan for full implementation the following fall, and plan also how you will establish fidelity of implementation. In addition, consider support for fidelity through peer observation or coaching from those who are more experienced with SIM strategies.

Differentiating Instruction

In order to respond to diverse learners, educators need to adjust their instructional approaches based on the group of students they have. This can be done through differentiating instruction, which is simply designing instruction so students with diverse academic needs can master the same academic content.

There are a wide range of strategies for differentiation for secondary learners. We think of differentiating content of instruction, process of instruction, and student product. A short list includes consideration of the instructional group size, allowing alternative products or means by which students can demonstrate the attainment of learning outcomes, being flexible with time allocations for activities, and modifying learner outcomes. As an example, a teacher may use a preassessment to determine the level of knowledge students already have on an upcoming topic, and then differentiate the activities students work on depending on their current level of mastery (Wormeli, 2006; Wormeli, 2007). The keys are to be knowledgeable about the learners in your classrooms through their assessment data, and then to thoughtfully plan content, process, and product according to the instructional needs of diverse learners (Tomlinson, 2010).

Manage the Instructional Environment

How instruction is planned—from the minute a student enters the classroom to the second the end of class is signaled—has a marked influence on overall student engagement. Here are strategies for structuring three critical times of a class period (Shinn, Phillips, & March, 2008; Sprick, 2006):

The First Seven Minutes

1. Greet students as they enter.

2. Connect lesson focus to previously taught skills.

3. Display enthusiasm. (Fake it if you have to.)

4. Present clear directions, and share the objective for the day's lesson.

5. Respond to students who follow directions.

6. Ensure opportunities for *all* students to respond.

7. Provide differential feedback for cooperation.

8. Know whether all students responded correctly.

9. Establish a routine for students who complete the initial instructional task.

The Last Five Minutes

1. Give a signal about five minutes before the end of class.

2. Post homework assignments and materials that students need to take home today or bring to school tomorrow.

3. Acknowledge students who are following classroom rules for end of class.

4. Have a filler activity for students who are ready to leave class. Examples include writing in a journal or starting on a homework assignment.

5. Have students turn in exit slips explaining what they learned that day as they leave.

Independent Seatwork

Over the course of over one thousand classroom observations completed, we have learned that regardless of age or grade level, content area, or years of teaching experience, secondary students typically remain legitimately academically engaged in independent work for a maximum of ten minutes, with most classrooms beginning to show signs of one or more students being off-task within the first three to five minutes.

Just giving kids the time to learn isn't instructionally meaningful (Perlman & Redding, 2009), especially for less-engaged learners. Quality and use of that time are paramount. However, when most secondary educators schedule independent seatwork time, students are expected to be on task and self-monitor while the teacher catches up on some work, takes attendance, or circulates to help individual students. Even five minutes of independent seatwork time for a chronically off-task student during a fifty-minute class period is a loss of 10 percent of instructional minutes. During a nine-week quarter, that amounts to 225 lost minutes of learning. Imagine if that happens in each of five, six, or seven daily classes for a student who is already behind in his or her learning. The gap just continues to grow.

Learning time that yields high engagement will be structured, have clear learning outcomes and products, contain tasks that are inherently relevant and interesting to students, and—if considered independent seatwork time—last no more than ten minutes before there is some kind of direct teacher involvement to bring attention to or assess the current learning objective (Perlman & Redding, 2009; Rock & Thead, 2009; Sprick, 2006).

Table 5.2 (page 74) summarizes teacher characteristics and behaviors that create classrooms that range from not engaging to highly engaging. Note that there is a progression of skill acquisition and performance as teachers gain more experience and knowledge with tools for fostering engagement. Teachers of highly engaging classrooms are objectively metacognitive about their current learners and motivated to be flexible in content delivery without sacrificing quality. In doing so, they foster student ownership of learning and the educational process.

Table 5.2: Examples of Teacher Behaviors in Nonengaging, Emerging Engaging, and Engaging Classrooms

	Believe	**Say**	**Do**
Nonengaging	Some kids are smart, and some kids just won't get it. All the content is important, or teachers wouldn't teach it. My classroom, my rules. Teachers shouldn't have to reteach or reinforce appropriate behavior for secondary learners. Kids should just know what the expected rules and routines are. Teachers are not responsible for whether kids care about school. Parents just don't care about school.	"If Billy paid attention in class, maybe he'd be passing." "You'll never get into a decent college if you don't get serious and study." "Why did you put off starting the horticulture project until the night before it's due?" "You got the outline written, which is good, but you didn't finish the paper." "How come your parents didn't show up for conferences last night?" "Hey! Knock it off, or you'll find yourself in the front office."	Blame students for class failure. Assume students will ask for help. Give large amounts of independent seatwork time. Focus on acquisition of facts and information. Allow students to sleep or be off task. Publically reward students who earn As. Emphasize repetitive tasks and worksheets. Use sarcasm or cool talk to relate to kids. Grade on a curve.
Emerging Engaging	If only parents would do more at home, then kids would care more about school. Teachers should teach routines and rules at the beginning of the term. Some kids will be disengaged no matter what, right? Have high expectations for most learners, but expect that some will not achieve as much.	"Don't say you'll never understand geometry. You'll get it." "You're not dumb, and I don't want to hear you saying you are." "Good job!" "I'll give the whole class a pizza party at the end of the term if we have perfect attendance." "There is no more computer time for the rest of the semester if you don't quiet down right now."	Give praise. Ask questions that are factual or knowledge based. Allow some off-task behavior to occur. Intermittently enforce rules and routines. Give some worksheets and repetitive tasks, but not exclusively. Solve problems for students rather than giving them ownership to solve them.

	Believe	**Say**	**Do**
Engaging	All kids are capable of learning, and it's our job to figure out how to help them. Teacher actions will increase or decrease student engagement and motivation. Not all the content is of equal importance. Teachers should use student data to make important decisions. It's OK to make mistakes. Parents are important influences, but they are not the only reason kids fail. Teachers need to teach routines and rules as frequently as kids tell us they need to learn them.	"I can tell you're really thinking about this." "Mistakes are OK." "It sounds like you're really struggling with geometry concepts right now." "You got two points higher on this week's quiz. Next week, try to beat your personal best." "You have some creative ideas for your science project. What things will you consider to decide which one to choose?" "Do you have any idea why other kids passed the test?" "It seems as if you are confused about what to write for your English essay. I bet you can come up with ideas to get started. Let me know if you'd like to talk about your ideas, and I'd be happy to listen and help if I can."	Emphasize learning because learning is a good thing. Give tasks that are moderately challenging. Use questioning to provoke interest and critical thinking. Build in elements that students can control. Tell students learning outcomes daily. Grade based on effort. State high expectations for all learners. Teach steps for identifying and solving barriers to student goals. Give authentic, specific praise. Give ownership of problem solving back to the student.

How Do We Know if Our Tier 1 Instruction Is Effective?

As discussed in chapter 4, each school must define what types of data are important and why. Since the passage in 2001 of No Child Left Behind, a large measure of school success has been based on the adequate yearly progress exam and status. While this is not optimal, it is our reality. Thankfully, however there is much more than an exam to determining if your school has effective Tier 1 services.

All secondary schools have a variety of data available to determine the effectiveness of their Tier 1 services. In fact, we find there is an overabundance of it: attendance, office discipline referrals, suspensions, class grades, credits earned, state tests, ACT, SAT, PLAN, PSAT, and so on. In addition, many districts use the NWEA MAPs (measures of academic progress) or ACT EPAS (educational planning and assessment system). As discussed in chapter 4, the NWEA MAP has a learning continuum that assists with more practical instructional application of the test scores. This type of test can help the leadership team answer the question, Is our Tier 1 instruction effective? It can also help the team determine a course of action. For example, if a school's NWEA MAP reading test results show 85 percent of its students meeting the grade-level benchmark, Tier 1 reading instruction is likely effective.

Many teams struggle with how to view and summarize data. The key is to find a succinct format of reporting that can quickly and reliably identify areas of progress and needed growth. Being able to create charts and graphs is a huge plus. Chapter 4 outlined a few database options. Take the time to review a variety of databases and their reports to find what works best for your school.

Finally, it's important to set and schedule when and how the data will be reviewed. The timing of these reviews is important. Why did you give the test? How will you use these data to impact instruction and student learning? Data reviews are covered in detail in chapter 8 (page 109). The take-home message here is: get them on the calendar and do them.

Conclusion

At the heart of RTI implementation is robust, research-supported core instruction that is aligned to standards, articulated, and relevant to today's secondary students. This chapter covered specifics for supporting reading content areas, planning, organizing, and differentiating content, and strategies for effective classroom management that build relationships and foster high levels of student engagement in learning. Following the same concepts we have discussed for academics, next we turn our attention to Tier 1 services for social-emotional, and behavior support.

CHAPTER 6

Tier 1 Core Instruction: Schoolwide Positive Behavior Supports

The continued logic of focusing solely on curriculum will ultimately fail without considering the social context in which learning occurs

—Timothy J. Lewis

We just started doing RTI, and now we have to do PBS?

—Conversation in the staff lounge

Advance Organizer

✓ *Positive behavior supports are the "behavior" side of the RTI triangle.*

✓ *Just as with academics, there are unique and critical features for implementing PBS in secondary settings.*

✓ *Classroom PBS is focused on positive and proactive classroom management to engage diverse secondary learners.*

Recall that core instruction in an RTI framework is everything we do instructionally for kids. An essential element of all instruction has to do with how positive behavior supports (PBS) are implemented. PBS is "a systems approach for establishing the social culture and behavioral supports needed for a school to be an effective learning environment for all students" (Horner, 2010). This chapter focuses on the secondary applications of PBS at Tier 1.

Schoolwide PBS emphasizes proactive creation of positive school environments for all students. It also replaces the need to develop numerous individual interventions for students who engage in similar inappropriate behaviors. Just as with academics, the adults in the building are making a commitment to using a framework for assessing, instructing, and problem solving for social and behavioral issues across multiple tiers that is research-based and data-driven, and to maximize the efficient use of building resources.

To implement PBS, school teams participate in the following ongoing activities:

- ▶ Select and define expectations and routines

- ▶ Teach behavior and routines directly (in all settings)

- ▶ Actively monitor behavior (*Move, Interact, Scan*—don't MIS anything!)

- ▶ Acknowledge appropriate behavior

- ▶ Review data regularly to make decisions

- ▶ Correct behavioral errors

The OSEP Technical Assistance Center on Positive Behavior Interventions and Supports (www.pbis.org) has a wealth of information as well as specifics for middle and high schools.

Is PBIS Different From RTI?

As we have mentioned, there may be confusion over PBIS (positive behavior interventions and supports) and RTI, because they appear to be mutually exclusive initiatives. In reality, both share a common framework for implementation. The name *PBS* is clearly associated with social and behavioral issues, even though there is a well-established correlation between cognitive and affective aspects of learning (Bowen, Jensen, & Clark, 2004). While RTI and PBS have developed on two relatively separate roads in research and academic literature, they both naturally converge in practice. This convergence (table 6.1) is also acknowledged by the OSEP Technical Assistance Center on PBIS (Sandomierski, Kincaid, & Algozzine, 2007). Table 6.1 provides examples.

Table 6.1: Convergence of PBS and RTI

	Literacy	Social and Behavioral
Team	General educator, special educator, reading specialist, school psychologist, and so on	General educator, special educator, behavior specialist, school psychologist, and so on
Universal Screening	Curriculum-based measurement	Systematic Screening for Behavior Disorders (SSBD), record review, gating
Progress Monitoring	Curriculum-based measurement	ODR, suspensions, behavior incidents, precision teaching
Effective Interventions	Five-specific reading skills: phonemic awareness, phonics, fluency, vocabulary, comprehension	Direct social skills instruction, positive reinforcement, token economy, active supervision, behavioral contracting, group contingency management, function-based support, self-management
Decision-Making Rules	Core, strategic, intensive	Primary, secondary, tertiary tiers

Source: School-wide positive behavior support and responsiveness-to-intervention. *Keynote presentation of paper by G. Sugai at the Southern Maryland PBIS Summer Regional Conference, Waldorf, MD, August 1, 2007.*

Why Implement PBS at the Secondary Level?

Consider the following summary of a 2008 court case:

> [The] student's special education teacher is not entitled to qualified immunity where it is alleged that she sharply rebuked the student for talking to a classmate, taped his mouth shut with masking tape and ripped it off when he tried to speak to her through the tape. A reasonable educator would have known that forcefully taping the mouth of a child [with asthma] amounted to a constitutional violation. (W.E.T. v. Mitchell, 49 IDELR 130 [M.D. N.C. 2008])

While this is an extreme example, consider that (a) it actually happened, and (b) the circumstances under which the teacher found herself may have made such a response, however misguided and abusive, seem instructionally appropriate to her at the time. While there are many factors that influence any decision a teacher makes to control classroom behavior or institute discipline, the implementation of a PBS program may assist. Consider the following. Were schoolwide policies and procedures clear and agreed on? Did she have the resources and time to plan for preteaching and corrective teaching for challenging student behavior? Did she have supportive administrators if she needed to refer a student out of class? Did she have a team with whom she could problem solve tough cases? Were there policies in place to identify a teacher with personal issues or stress levels that were so high she might be driven to behavior like this? Valuable hindsight would suggest that if the answers to these questions had been *yes*, this unfortunate event may not have happened.

Behavior challenges often arise because students struggle academically (Bowen et al., 2004). By the time secondary learners at risk for school failure come to our doorstep, they have had many years of practicing maladaptive (yet effective) strategies for escaping instruction and obtaining lots of negative attention from adults. Common challenging behaviors observed in classrooms include distracting adults' attention from teaching through disruptive behaviors, such as talking to peers during instruction, making off-task noises with objects, having off-task conversations with peers during group work, or not following the instructions of the teacher. Passive avoidance behaviors include looking quietly around the room, doodling or sleeping in class, working only when the teacher is looking, looking busy, texting peers, completing other preferred schoolwork, and simply not doing work at all.

The cost to these students and educators is that greater amounts of time are spent on interpreting problem behavior to figure out whether the underlying issue is a lack of basic academic skills or not. By the time these students reach middle school, they are well down a path of being disconnected from learning altogether. Given that these students have a greater likelihood of dropping out of school (Alliance for Excellence in Education, 2008; Balfanz, 2009; Christenson, Sinclair, Lehr, & Hurley, 2000), and our time is limited, we want to intervene quickly. A focus on PBS within a comprehensive RTI framework provides the tools to do this.

What Does PBS Look Like in Secondary Settings?

PBS implementation consists of addressing both a school culture (sometimes referred to as school climate or atmosphere) and school practices. Recall that in chapter 2 (page 13), a shift in school culture was identified as a defining feature of whether RTI implementation was successful. In establishing or healing a school culture, the emphasis is on modeling and teaching proactive positive verbal and nonverbal communication; conveying genuine caring, respect, and trust among staff and students; and communicating high expectations for student achievement.

We find that it takes longer for a school culture than it does for academics to change. Why? Think about choosing and implementing a new math curriculum or instructional technique for writing. There is a clear start and end point, direction for how to do it, and immediate feedback to the teacher on whether students learned or not. Changes in beliefs and values that underlie social and cultural expectations and shifts in norms that have been in place for years or decades are more personal and have a deep context and history that is less explicit and defined. These changes happen in iterations over time, cumulatively, with considerably variable responses to them based on the unique characteristics of the members within the educational community. A school culture is made tangible by what school staff and students do and say every day. Mahatma Gandhi once said:

> Your beliefs become your thoughts. Your thoughts become your words.
>
> Your words become your actions. Your actions become your habits.
>
> Your habits become your values. Your values become your destiny. (English Forums.com, n.d.)

In this example, of all these variables—beliefs, thoughts, words, actions, habits, values— add up to become the school culture. You could visualize this as the cycle shown in figure 6.1.

The more that adults demonstrate positive behaviors, the more students will do so. Those behaviors influence values, which become part of a belief structure. It follows, then, that the schoolwide expectations for positive behavior will become a natural part of the school's milieu, thereby establishing the culture.

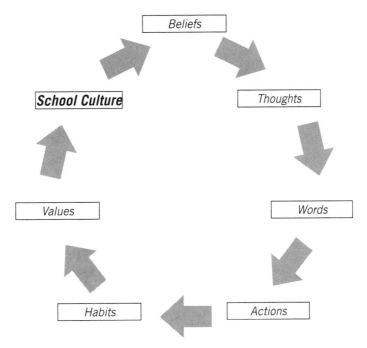

Figure 6.1: The cycle of school culture.

PBS practices within an RTI framework center on positive, consistent, proactive practices for teaching and managing student behavior among all adults in the building. This is particularly challenging when student schedules change frequently, kids are striving for increased independence, and there is less overall time for relationship building. While the following PBS practices should be expected to exist to some degree in all schools for all ages, secondary settings emphasize:

▶ Efforts to develop positive relationships with all students, even students who don't seem to need anyone

▶ Active supervision by adults during unstructured time, such as passing time, before and after school, and so on

▶ Student input for classwide and schoolwide expectations

▶ Explicit communication of behavior expectations, even if it seems as if students should just know what they are

▶ Regular acknowledgment of appropriate behaviors

▶ Time management: arriving to school and classes and completing work on time

▶ Appropriate greetings and dialogue with all school staff including custodians, cafeteria staff, office assistants, and others

▶ Appropriate language that shows respect for the time and the place, as well as individual self-worth

- ▶ Appropriate clothing that shows respect for the time, place, and self-worth

- ▶ Connections made to how present behavior influences future postsecondary training, career, and increased diversity of relationships

- ▶ Safe driving on and around school property

- ▶ Increased options for mental and chemical health support

Designing Positive, Safe, and Respectful Classroom Cultures

In chapter 5, strategies for planning and disseminating content to maximize academic engagement were discussed. This section discusses strategies for designing a positive, safe, and respectful classroom environment to complement and augment content delivery and learning.

In *Discipline in the Secondary Classroom*, Randall Sprick (2006) summarizes a framework for positive classroom management around the following concepts and tasks, about which educators need to be knowledgeable:

- ▶ Understand the basics of behavior: it's learned, it serves a purpose, it's predictable, and it's changeable.

- ▶ Understand motivation and what instructional and environmental factors can be manipulated to increase it.

- ▶ Understand the importance of high expectations for student academics and behavior and how to maintain them.

- ▶ Understand the importance of personal, positive relationships with students and how to build them.

- ▶ Develop, implement, teach, and reinforce specific behaviors for success.

- ▶ Make adjustments to the classroom management plan based on the needs of your students.

Have you ever experienced frustration when your common classroom rules, routines, and practices work for four of the seven sections you teach but not for the others? How about when each of your six sections needs its own individualized classroom management plan? Do you ever have a classroom of learners who are so unique and diverse that you feel you can only teach to the middle and hope the rest will get it? Have you ever said to a colleague, "We can't make kids care"? We may think of students who cause us to have these thoughts as unmotivated or disengaged learners. Let's briefly explore what it means for a secondary learner to be engaged or disengaged from learning.

Engagement: What Does It Mean?

Stop and think for a moment. Identify one student who you would describe as disengaged from school. What is that student like? How does he act (or not act)? What does she say (and not say)? If we videotaped that student for one day, what would we see on the tape? (You may want to write down your response.)

Now, identify one student who you would describe as an engaged learner. Complete the same activity. What is that student like? How does she act (or not act)? What does he say (and not say)? If we videotaped this student for a day, what would we see on the tape? Hold on to the descriptions of these two students while you continue to read.

In practice, most secondary educators would define *motivation* as whether or not students care about school, learning, and education. But really, when we say a student doesn't care, we are really describing a student who behaves in ways that suggest he or she is not excited about or reinforced for or engaged in the academic and social behaviors that will lead to successful educational outcomes.. The degree to which students are motivated or engaged is also highly influenced by what they think about themselves as learners, and what they think about learning itself. So, for instructional purposes it is highly advisable to think of whether or not students are motivated to achieve in terms of engagement. This makes the concept of motivation more observable, measureable, and able to be directly influenced as opposed to another student characteristic we do not have control over. In order to directly influence student engagement we need to think about it in terms of both the cognitive beliefs a student has toward learning, and how they actually behave toward learning

Table 6.2 (page 84) gives a brief overview of what constitutes the beliefs, talk, and behavior of students who are disengaged versus those who are engaged (Brophy, 2004; Morrone & Schutz, 2000; Rathvon, 1996).

Do these descriptors reflect characteristics of disengaged and engaged learners you identified earlier? Chances are, they do. You probably have many others. We all know who these kids are. Now, no one can *make* a student (or anyone else for that matter) care about anything. We can, however, decide what *our* responses to maladaptive comments and behaviors will be and what we will choose to reinforce. We can tactfully, patiently, and tenaciously prompt and reinforce changes in the belief and behaviors of students who are disengaged from school. It is through our prompting and reinforcing of their efforts that struggling students will see concrete evidence of small incremental gains in achievement. When they see even these small gains tied to their own effort, this increases their self-efficacy and affects their thoughts about themselves as learners and learning itself. Learning will naturally start to become more self-directed the more learners experience increasing success (Jinks & Morgan, 1999, as cited in Doll, Zucker, & Brehm, 2004).

This is going to require a shift in *our* thinking about learners who are disengaged. There are a lot of factors we cannot control in kids' lives. We *can* determine whether the reasons that students are disengaged are because of skill deficits (unable to do), performance deficits (will not do), or some combination of both. This will also require persistence and patience on our part, as the adaptive behavior change takes almost as long as the maladaptive behaviors did to develop.

Table 6.2: Some Differences Between Disengaged and Engaged Learners

	Believe	Say	Do
Disengaged Learners	They are not responsible for their own behavior. They cannot control what happens to them. Lack of success is due to their own innate (lack of) ability or luck. Persistence will not pay off. They cannot solve their own problems. They engage in all-or-nothing thinking (absolutes). Learning is a means to an end.	"My teachers don't care if I fail their class." "They want me to fail." "I had my homework done. I just don't know what I did with it." "If the teacher would have asked questions on what I studied, I would have passed the test." "I'll never go to college, so why should I care about passing my classes?" "If I don't get help in the resource room, then I will fail math again!" "I can't write." "I will never be good at writing." "I'm just dumb in writing."	Assign blame to others. Fail to organize materials for efficient use. Fail to have needed materials for the task. Pretend or look busy but do not do schoolwork or the assigned task. Avoid talking to teachers and parents. Complain about teachers or situations being unfair. Perform well in one or two classes but fail others. Start strong but fail to follow through. Fail to anticipate how actions today affect future outcomes. Sleep in class.
Engaged Learners	Learning is important for the sake of learning. Their effort is the primary influence on their outcomes. They have control over what happens to them or their responses. Effort will lead to achieving goals and success. They are the first source of finding a solution to a problem. There are many solutions or possibilities that can produce acceptable outcomes.	"Next time I'll put my homework in my textbook so I remember it." "The test had questions I wasn't sure of, but I gave the best answers I could." "If I practice enough, I know I can pass the class." "I had to work really hard to get a B in biology this term." "Because I have play practice, I'll have to set up a time to meet with Mr. Smith either before school or during study hall to get help on this." "I'm not sure if this is what Mrs. Jones wants for this paper. I'll show her what I started. She gives good feedback on my writing." "Well, this presentation isn't going to finish itself."	Have positive, prosocial relationships with peers and adults. Have strategies for remembering. Pay attention in class. Ask for help. Actively participate in class. Use coping and problem-solving strategies when setbacks or challenges arise. Set realistic goals. Identify and solve problems that block success toward their goals. Systematically select and implement actions to make progress.

Engagement as a Skill Deficit

Let's explore this concept through an example. Assume that you are given a sheet of music containing a song and asked to play it on the piano. From a skill perspective (cannot do), what are all the possible reasons that would present challenges to you in completing this task? One might be your ability to read music. What do the black notes mean? How about the open ones? What about the notes with lines and the ones with lines and little flags? Also, you need to know what the symbols and abbreviations mean. Further, where do you put your hands on the keys? Do they go on the white keys or the black ones? Do you place them in the middle of the keyboard or at the ends? Without having these skills, chances are you are not going to feel very positive about the task. Consequently, you probably are not going to feel very engaged in this task.

Now think about student engagement in school. We can anticipate a number of skills that students would need to know in order to actively engage in their learning. For one, they need to know *how* to organize their materials, class work, and time. Do they use a planner? Is it electronic or paper? What information should be recorded? Where? Students also need to know how to obtain information when they don't understand something. Do they know how to get the teacher's attention? Do they understand when it is time to ask questions? Do they know the first step in completing an assigned task? If they don't, do they have an idea or two about how they could find out?

Students also need to know who the adults are in the school building who are resources for them, what questions those adults can help answer, and what the routines are for accessing those adults. Hopefully, you are getting the idea. A student who doesn't have specific skills to demonstrate the academic and social behaviors needed for school success is less likely to be engaged in doing them in the first place.

Many educators assume that by the time students are in high school (and even middle school), they should already know how to do these things. This assumption makes it much easier for us to believe that being disengaged or unmotivated is a performance (will not do) rather than a skill (cannot do) problem. When we have individuals or groups of students who are disengaged, we should approach problem solving from a skills deficit approach before assuming it is a performance deficit.

Engagement as a Performance Deficit

The "won't do" behaviors are also common features in students who are disengaged. These are kids who clearly have the ability to perform the skill, but for some reason perform it intermittently or not at all. These students are the ones who make us the most frustrated, and consequently, we fall back on the "it's their choice" response to their lack of achievement. To a certain degree, it is their choice.

Think of it as a cost/benefit analysis. If kids learn that with enough nonperformance we will eventually just leave them alone, they see the short-term benefit of avoiding work (and making adults unhappy) as more beneficial than doing the work they don't want to do. Struggling students do this kind of calculation all the time. The student who is willing to get into arguments with adults and peers feels that the benefit of the negative attention outweighs the cost of being disliked, getting suspended, or failing classes. As educators, our job is to create the conditions that will enable these students to see more benefit from demonstrating appropriate academic and social behaviors than from not doing so. We need to give students relevant and meaningful reasons to use their powers for school success rather than school failure.

We can begin by relationship building and positively reinforcing small increments of the desired behavior. As Ron Renchler (1992) writes, "If [educators] are equipped with the wisdom that comes from humility, sensitivity, and a constant reflection on the way that motivation functions in their own lives, it will probably be much easier for them to find ways to motivate their students" (p. 2).

Strategies to Create Engaging Classrooms

There is much literature on how to create classrooms that are engaging for diverse learners (see Gettinger & Ball, 2008; Morrone & Schutz, 2000; Perlman & Redding, 2009; Vaughn et al., 1997). Table 4.1 (page 58) summarized the *behaviors* of teachers who create engaging, emerging engaging, and disengaging classrooms. This section summarizes three key *strategies* to foster positive behavior supports in classrooms.

Building Relationships!

We cannot overstate the importance of respectful, healthy, positive student-teacher relationships. Like instruction, relationships are variables that have a powerful effect on whether students are engaged in learning. As Donald Deshler has remarked, learning—far being only a cognitive undertaking—is also an emotional, affective, and visceral one (as cited in Cooper, 2005). Greetings, smiles, and questions that show genuine interest in students personally set the stage for being able to invite students on the journey of learning.

Having a relationship is not equivalent to being good friends with a student or being concerned with whether students like you personally. Nor are classrooms the place for pure democracy. Adults must maintain their role as authority figures—with that authority grounded in knowledge and expertise, and not simply in position (Danielson, 2007). Adults are also instructional authorities who cultivate safety, support, challenge, and creativity in their classrooms. Find the balance between rules and relationship, but be sure the relationship is there. Disengaged students will simply not respond without it.

A note about sarcasm: while informal dialogue and humor are important features of connecting with adolescents, there needs to be a clear distinction between humor and sarcasm. In general, students with emotional, social, or behavioral skill deficits will not understand that you meant the sarcasm to be funny or that it was an attempt to relate. Instead, they will interpret it as a put-down, which will result in damaged trust and diminished adult credibility. It will forfeit—or at best, significantly hinder—the chance of establishing a positive relationship with students. Further, sarcasm will set the stage for a classroom or school culture that is negative, demeaning, and divisive. Just *don't* do it! Keeping humor positive and neutral is a more effective and safer relationship-building strategy.

Establish a Classroom Culture of Respect

Positive relationships in engaging classrooms are accomplished through teacher behaviors that not only establish appropriate roles and boundaries but also create a culture of respect. Thankfully, secondary students will tell us how they define respect and what behaviors adults can demonstrate to cultivate it in the classroom.

In 2008, Rob March presented research on 2,580 middle and high school students in four states who were asked, "What are some ways that teachers show you respect?" (Shinn et al., 2008). Out of 3,800 responses, the following were listed 200 or more times (items in parentheses are very similar responses that were included in the totals). Teachers:

- Talk privately to students when a problem occurs. (They do not embarrass them in front of their friends.)

- Use a calm tone of voice, even when they are upset. (No yelling.)

- Respect personal space. (They don't touch, grab, eyeball, or crowd.)

- Listen without interrupting.

- Have a sense of humor.

- Display student work around the classroom and school.

- Make learning fun and prepare exciting lessons.

- Let parents or guardian know the student did a good job sometimes.

- Use students' names when talking to them. They address students as ma'am or sir.

- Are available during nonclassroom times.

- Return work promptly. Let students know how they're doing.

- Smile or say hello to students as they enter class.

Acknowledging student birthdays was also frequently mentioned.

Use Daily Grading

Grading is a daily practice that can be intentionally designed to influence student engagement. According to traditional grading policies for secondary students, all content is equally important, classes are graded on a curve, and grades are a result of a summative outcome (Marzano, 2010; Sprick, 2006). These practices communicate two maladaptive messages. First, learners have to learn all the material or figure out the learning objectives to earn a good grade. Second, and more importantly, individual student grades are influenced by how other students in the class perform rather than on a student's own performance and mastery. Both of these are frustrating for all learners, but they are defeating for disengaged learners.

A practical solution is to develop a grading system that acknowledges student effort in small increments (for example, biweekly) and is related to discrete learning objectives or content standards on a formative rather than summative basis. In describing a grading system that gives feedback on behavior and effort, Sprick (2006) states, "An effective grading system at the secondary level must teach less sophisticated learners the skills that more sophisticated students learn on their own" (p. 35). By grading on effort and using a formative process, the grading system itself will teach students that small increments of behavior have important and immediate effects on their academic outcomes.

Conclusion

Within an RTI framework, core instruction consists of a focus on basic academic skills as well as schoolwide positive behavior supports. To best understand the behavior of student engagement, we must consider engagement as both a skill deficit and a performance deficit. And we must believe it is a critical variable that we can influence and change. A targeted focus on developing a positive school culture coupled with practices that promote positive relationships with students will yield an increase in overall student engagement in learning and prosocial behaviors schoolwide.

Tier 1 Problem Solving: The Systems Level

Problem solving refers to the systematic approach used to conceptualize a problem situation and identify needs, analyze factors contributing to the problem situation, design strategies to meet those needs, and implement and evaluate the strategies.

—Sarah J. Allen & Janet L. Graden

Advance Organizer

✓ *When collecting systemwide screening data, target a few important outcomes.*

✓ *Tier 1 teams can stay in the driver's seat by considering reasons for problems over which you have control.*

✓ *Designing a systems level plan will advantageously position your building to meet its goal.*

✓ *Drift happens to the best of us: teams must continually work at implementation integrity.*

✓ *Celebrate all growth, and always keep working at it.*

The problem-solving process introduced in chapter 2 is used as the basis of our work at all tiers within a schoolwide RTI framework, with increasing intensity and specificity for each tier. There are many varieties of problem-solving models, each having anywhere from four to twelve steps. Basically, they all accomplish the same thing, with different ways of dividing the tasks or thought processes.

The model we advocate is derived largely from the work of John Bergan and Thomas Kratochwill (Bergan, 1977; Bergan & Kratochwill, 1990; Kratochwill & Bergan, 1990). We advocate for our model (fig. 6.1, page 90), in part because a relatively small number of steps is easier to remember. A four-step model that is also used (Ikeda et al., 2007; Marston, Lau, & Muyskens, 2007) is very similar, except that we separate problem analysis from problem identification, giving us a fifth step. In our minds, understanding what the problem is and why it is occurring are separate, critical designations. In any case, the exact problem-solving model your system adopts is not nearly as important as ensuring that you implement it consistently and that stakeholders are fluent with the vocabulary and the steps. The communication tool shown in figure 7.1 will help your system operate effectively.

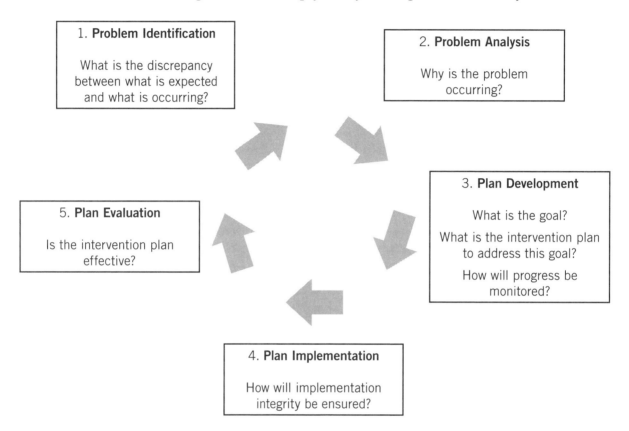

Figure 7.1: Five-step problem-solving model.
Source: St. Croix River Education District, 2011. Used with permission.

In this chapter, we describe how this five-step model operates within a Tier 1 or core instructional system. In Tier 1, we pay careful, ongoing attention to developing and maintaining high-quality core instruction, instruction that results in the strong majority of students within the local system meeting grade-level standards, as well as instruction that results in all students making acceptable growth over the course of the year. We make mention of this second standard in order to ensure that growth for all students continues to be a central expectation of the instructional environment—even those who start the year above target. To help us think about problem solving in Tier 1, we restate in table 7.1 the questions for each of our steps as they relate to core instruction.

Table 7.1: The Five-Step RTI Problem-Solving Process

Problem Identification	Is there a problem with our core instruction? Are more than 20 percent of our students in need of something in addition to core instruction to meet grade-level standards? Do we have students who are starting the year at or above grade-level expectations who are not making acceptable growth?
Problem Analysis	If there is a problem with our core instruction, why is this happening?
Plan Development	What is our goal for improving core instruction? What is our plan to meet this goal?
Plan Implementation	How will we be sure our core instruction is delivered with fidelity?
Plan Evaluation	Did our plan work? Are we closer to our goal?

Problem Identification

In a problem-solving model, we begin by identifying the problem as a discrepancy statement. This is a much more specific standard than a general statement of concern. To develop a discrepancy statement, we say both what we expect and what is occurring in specific terms. This is one of the primary intersections among schoolwide screening, setting of cut scores (as discussed in chapter 4), and problem solving. We use our screening data to help define what is expected. For those whose performance is not as expected, the same data tells us what is occurring.

To make this efficient at the systems level, our best advice is to identify a small number of critical outcomes that are most significant to the success of enrolled students on a buildingwide basis. Most often, this will be a subset of desired skills in reading, math, or writing; social behavior; and task or homework completion. The areas a building identifies as being most critical to the success of students are those for which the building should collect systemwide data on all students. This screening system allows buildings to identify the expected level of performance, keep their fingers on the pulse of critical outcomes, and identify whether and where student performance is not meeting expectation.

We offer the following five-step process for developing a discrepancy statement:

1. Identify the broad area of concern that your team wants to address (for example, reading).

2. Identify a measurement tool you will use to quantify this area of concern (for example, NWEA MAP, SAT10 Reading, maze).

3. Determine the expected or desired score on the measurement tool (for example, 100 percent of sixth graders should score at or above 214 RIT on the Reading MAP assessment in the fall of the school year).

4. Determine the score that is occurring on the measurement tool by screening all students on the selected measure (for example, 84 percent of sixth graders scored at or above 214 RIT on the Reading MAP).

5.   Gather and describe convergent evidence that supports the stated discrepancy (for example, outcomes on other assessments such as state tests).

For example, a school might identify a broad concern for reading comprehension skills among high school students. Perhaps the measurement tool they use is the tenth-grade high-stakes NCLB test. They expect that at least 97 percent of students should pass this test, but over the previous three years, an average of only 74 percent have passed. Convergent evidence can be found by reviewing results of other district assessments, interviewing teachers, or reviewing student work.

Schools can answer the problem identification question by reviewing results from school-wide screening and deciding if an acceptable percentage of students have met the criteria set by the building leadership team. In middle school settings, updated screening data can be collected on a variety of academic and social and behavioral topics. For example, oral reading fluency or maze assessments may provide a screening indicator for students in need of additional support in reading; the NWEA MAP assessment might provide a screening indicator for reading, math, or language skills; and office discipline referrals can provide a screening indicator for students in need of social and behavioral instruction and support. In high school settings, ongoing screening for social and behavioral skills might be in place through behavior incident reports, but very often, new schoolwide screening for academic skills is not completed. Instead, high schools often look at grade 8 data for incoming freshmen and identify those students who did not meet spring grade 8 targets as at risk. Continued screening can be conducted on this subset of students as they progress through the 9–12 system. Other assessments, such as state NCLB tests, PLAN, ACT, PSAT, and SAT tests, can provide additional opportunities for building teams to identify secondary students at risk. Students do not typically take these assessments every year, nor do all students take the assessments, with exception of NCLB testing; these parameters limit the opportunity of teams to use these data in a screening capacity. Often grades or credits students have earned can also be a useful metric for identifying students at risk in secondary settings. Spending time ensuring consistency of grading among teachers will improve the usefulness of this information.

Another important notion about screening assessments is that, by using them, we hope to have data that identify students as at risk *before* a high-stakes outcome has passed. This provides teachers with the opportunity to intervene in time to promote a desirable outcome. The lack of time to make valuable interventions is why an eleventh-grade graduation requirement test is not an ideal screener. Instead, we are looking for ways to predict which students may need more support than the general core curriculum offers to build the skills needed to pass that high-stakes graduation requirement test.

At this point, while we are considering expectations for our buildings within an RTI model, it is important to revisit our famous triangle and think deeply about what the 80-15-5 percentages mean (and do not mean) for our expectations. Let's begin with the section at the base of the triangle. Some see the 80 percent designation as a quota system to mean that 80 percent of students should be served through core instructional programming only (essentially no more than 20 percent of students can receive any supplemental support). Many consider the 80 percent designation as a goal-attainment system, meaning that if a system is meeting the needs of its students effectively, then 80 percent of all children served by the system will meet the target scores set for them. We suggest a hybrid meaning that has a higher standard than either of the first two alone: the 80 percent designation means that 80 percent of students should be meeting grade-level targets *with no additional assistance* beyond what is already included in the core program. Therefore, while we easily recognize that a school sitting at 70–20–10 is not operating at the desired level, a school that manages to get 80 percent or more of students to target by providing 35 percent of its students supplemental interventions is not yet performing at the 80–15–5 level either—even if their summary scores look that way.

The real question here, as it relates to Tier 1 problem solving, is whether the core instruction is robust enough to result in at least 80 percent of students served meeting the grade-level standards *without* additional support. We expect that many of the students whose scores fall outside the green range will also meet grade-level standard as a result of the additional support they are provided. The 80–15–5 triangle provides a goal for both in terms of skills attainment and the resource allocation it will take to get there. This is why we are asking whether no more than 20 percent of our students need supplemental support to meet grade-level standards, and whether students who start the year on target stay on target for the whole year. These questions are much more specific than the broad question of what percentage of the total student population is at or above the current expectation. Whereas this latter question provides insight to the system in total, our first two questions narrow our focus down to core instruction.

Problem Analysis

If your school is not yet at the 80–15–5 point (and most aren't), the second question of the problem-solving process is to determine why. At this point, a very important detail must be well understood: challenges over which a building has little or no control represent a dead end for problem solving. Without denying that many factors in students' lives lie outside the control of the school, teams must avoid problem admiration and focus instead on those things they can control. A good question to ask is, What will it take for this group of students to meet our expectations of success? This shift in attitude and attention puts teachers in the place of power they deserve to be—with a clear vision about what they intend students to accomplish, as well as a sense of efficacy about their role in making that happen.

In a review of various problem-solving models, you may notice that other models appear to skip right over the problem-analysis step. Given the challenge of good problem analysis, this might, at first, seem desirable! We argue that the published four-step models actually roll problem analysis into the problem identification step. We maintain, however, that it is important to call out problem analysis as its own unique and important phase of the problem-solving cycle. Problem analysis is the work that teams do to be sure they are engaging in intervention or systems change work that is actually needed and well matched to problems identified. It is the critical evaluative step that focuses intervention planning on the right problem.

At the systems level, buildings are interested in identifying overarching considerations that are contributing to lower-than-expected proficiency. Reasons for low effectiveness in core instruction may be quite varied. The acronym ICEL (instruction, curriculum, environment, learner) provides buildings a framework for thinking broadly about the possible reasons for lack of sufficiency in the core curriculum. There could be a lack of clarity regarding the scope and sequence of courses in a particular topic (instruction). Materials used in courses may not be well matched to standards (curriculum). There could be widespread problems with regular attendance at school (environment) or behavior in the classroom (environment). One 7–12 high school in east central Minnesota surveyed its students and learned that most read less than ten minutes per day, including reading during class time, and that they visited the library only to use the computer (learner). It is important to note that teams should collect data to support or refute hypotheses they are considering, rather than relying on hunches.

An example from the medical field illustrates this point well. If a patient visits a doctor with a high temperature, the doctor works to determine whether the cause of the fever is a virus or bacterial infection, or some other cause. Treatment plans for high temperature vary widely based on the identified cause of the problem—an antibiotic won't cure a virus, and taking antibiotics needlessly may lead to other problems for the patient in the long term.

Regular Review of Standards

Circling back to chapter 5, an important question for building staff to consider is the extent to which the content in the courses offered matches the relevant national, state, or local standards. Ensuring a high overlap between course content and expected learning standards is a vital first step for strengthening core instruction. Two lessons we have learned on this topic are that review of standards needs to be a regular part of ongoing staff development and discussions, and concrete practices, such as curriculum mapping and identification of course pathways, can help keep standards relevant and central in teachers' minds. A common, helpful practice is spending time rewriting benchmarks in student-friendly language. A beneficial outcome of this practice is that teachers share these benchmarks with students, who then have a better sense of course outcomes. The more near-term benefit, however, is that through the process of rewording and summarizing benchmarks, teachers develop a much deeper ownership of the content in these statements.

Review of Instructional Quality

A second step related to core instruction strength is identifying research-supported instructional practices in place within courses. It is possible for the content of a course or a particular curriculum to closely match the standards but to be organized in an instructionally ineffective manner. Reviewing course instruction for outcomes related to total student active engagement time, quality of class discussion, rates of accurate participation, use of teacher modeling, and other markers of quality teaching can assist schools in identifying whether ongoing professional development in this area would help students reach standards in greater numbers. The match between content and standards and the quality of instructional delivery are two of the most common areas identified for improvement in core instruction by school teams when analyzing the cause of lower-than-expected student performance.

Plan Development

What is our goal for improving core instruction? What is our plan to meet this goal? How will we monitor our progress toward this goal?

Setting Goals

The plan development stage provides the opportunity to create an action plan for remediating the identified problem. To keep this process data based, teams should first select a goal. This goal must be quantifiable. It is best that the measurement tool used to identify the original problem be the same one used to measure progress toward the goal. For example, if the original problem related to an unsatisfactory percentage of students scoring as proficient on a high-stakes assessment, then the goal should state the desired percentage of students who score as proficient on that assessment by a certain point in time. If the original problem is related to a higher-than-expected rate of office discipline referrals, the goal should state the desired rate of office discipline referrals by a given time. As discussed in chapter 4, goals can be derived from local normative data, broader published normative data, criterion-referenced targets, or professional expectations (Fuchs & Shinn, 1989). At this point, teams can engage in meaningful discourse around the goals that they set for their systems.

Sometimes groups external to the school or district set standards that affect a school system's choice of goal. For example, with the NCLB legislation, state agencies identify the number of students who must be proficient on state assessments of reading and math for the building to be considered as making adequate yearly progress. This determination might drive the goal a building would set for percent of students scoring proficient. For example, if a building needs to have 78 percent of its eleventh graders score proficient on the high-stakes math assessment for a given year, that may become the goal. Other times, philosophical or ideological characteristics of a system might drive the goal. Schools at which the notion of proficiency for all resonates would likely not set a goal for only 90 percent of students to meet proficiency standards. Which of our students are in the 10 percent for whom our goal is lack of proficiency?

Building teams may also think in terms of amount of growth from one year to the next, or amount of growth within one year for a single cohort. In addition, those teams should be thinking in terms of how a goal for the current year fits into a longer-term system of goals for the building. Whichever method is employed, it's important to consider the relative aggressiveness of the goal. A more aggressive goal requires a more intensive plan to attain it. Our guidance is to make the package of goal plus intervention plan feasible and plausible. That is, the educators involved in the process must believe that the plan that has been designed can and will really be implemented—and, if this happens, that it is likely the goal will be met. So, it is fine to have an aggressive goal as long as there is an intensive, believable plan in place to achieve it.

Finally, when writing goals, take care that they are written in a way that helps avoid unwanted practice. This occurs with simple goals written to reflect an increase in the percent of students reaching a set proficiency target. While the transparency of this type of goal is appealing, a potential problem might be created if the implementation plan overemphasizes supporting students who are just below target at the expense of those who are more discrepant. The result may well be that the goal is met, but actual improvements may not be as systemic as desired. An alternative is to write goals for percentages of students to reach certain targets and for all students to demonstrate a set amount of growth.

At the secondary level, it is reasonable and advisable to communicate with students about building-level goals. Public posting and discussion of their importance for students specifically encourages students to focus their efforts. In addition, drawing explicit connections between students' individual goals and larger systemwide goals helps students see the impact of their participation in goal attainment work. Be sure to build in positive reinforcement that recognizes student contributions to the goal.

One last point is the connection between goal setting for systemwide problem solving and goal setting commonly done in professional learning communities. A gift that the PLC structure brings to problem solving is the notion of teams in shared study of a topic area for the purpose of building skills and expertise that will benefit students. A community of grade-level teachers might review data for their students, identify a broad concern, then develop a specific problem-identification statement, conduct problem analysis, and set a goal for improvement teachers wish to support. Imagine a team developing a problem identification statement in math. Perhaps in its analysis it determined that teachers had too many students who struggled with fractional thinking. What if this team spent a year working together studying this topic in order to develop stronger instructional strategies and a more explicit plan for teaching this?

Determining the Intervention Plan

Given a quantified statement of the problem, a hypothesis about its cause, and an agreed-on goal to remediate it, building teams move to develop the actual plan that achieves the goal they have set. At the systems level, they are thinking of initiatives that will be implemented broadly—for all students in a building or grade level, for example. If curriculum mapping completed in the problem-analysis phase revealed that students across grades were getting less instruction than expected across years on a certain standard, a plan might be built to add more instruction on that standard across course pathways. If a building team identified that a spike of office discipline referrals were coming from the cafeteria each day, a review of cafeteria traffic flow might be conducted and a plan to clarify and teach lunchroom behavior expectations and award compliance might be instituted.

In the case of the Minnesota school where students reported low levels of independent reading, the building team developed a plan to ensure that every student read text for at least ten minutes each class period of the day. Further, at the secondary level, we believe staff should know about the Content Literacy Curriculum through the strategic instruction model from the University of Kansas. This model supports high-quality instruction across content areas and has been demonstrated to be an effective model of secondary systems change (for example, Fritschmann, Deshler, & Schumaker, 2007; Scanlon, Deshler, & Schumaker, 1996). As Stephen Covey (1998) writes:

> Remember the flight of the airplane. When an airplane takes off it has a flight plan. However, during the course or the flight, wind, rain, turbulence, air traffic, human error, and other factors keep knocking the plan off course. In fact, a plan is off course about 90 percent of the time. The key is that the pilots keep making small course corrections by reading their instruments and talking to the control tower. As a result a plane reaches its destination. (pp. 9–11)

To complete plan development, building teams determine how they will monitor progress toward their goal. In other words, they identify what indicators to rely on in order to know whether they are on track. Like an airline pilot, school teams would rather not be surprised at the end of the year (or flight) by finding out they missed the goal. It is much better to have a handle on progress so you can make midterm course corrections. So, we set up our instrument panel and talk with our control tower to keep us on track.

If the testing measure that was used to identify the original problem and set the goal happens to be one that can be administered frequently over time, it makes sense to use it, because it is the most direct measure of progress. Office discipline referral rates might be summarized biweekly or monthly, for example, and give teams a good sense of the trend of their data over time. However, it is not always possible to collect formative data on the measure used to set the goal. If, for example, the building goal is set based on proficiency rates on a test given annually, there are no opportunities to measure midterm progress toward proficiency on that test. Instead, select measures that are suitable for more frequent progress monitoring based on their ability to predict the outcome on the assessment stated in the goal.

Achievement tests such as the NWEA Measures of Academic Progress have been shown to have reasonable predictive validity to state assessments in many states. The MAP test may be given a few times per year. Often building teams choose to collect data once in the fall and again midyear to help understand progress toward the year-end goal. General outcome measures may also be used in this manner. Though monitoring is often completed on a very frequent basis for individuals or small groups of students receiving intervention, it is typically considered overly cumbersome and unnecessary to collect weekly data at a systems level. This is not to say that it could not be done. In fact, for some applications this may be quite feasible (weekly rates of schoolwide on-time homework turn-in as monitored through electronic gradebooks, for example). However, if the purpose of collecting the data is to be able to make course corrections to the intervention as necessary, it makes sense to collect data at a frequency rate that is roughly equivalent to the frequency with which it is possible to make changes. Because it is unlikely that an entire buildingwide initiative is going to be altered on a weekly basis, collecting data that often may not be the most effective use of resources. So, in addition to determining what data the team will collect to monitor progress, the team needs to determine the frequency of data collection so that it has enough data available to reasonably keep its fingers on the pulse of the intervention—but not more than the team will be able to use. At the secondary level, data reviews at the end of each term or trimester are most common.

Plan Implementation

How will we be sure our core instruction is delivered with fidelity? As Francis Bacon wrote:

> It's not what we eat but what we digest that makes us strong; not what we gain but what we save that makes us rich; not what we read but what we remember that makes us learned; and not what we profess but what we practice that gives us integrity. (Thinkexist.com, n.d.)

Plan implementation is the fourth step of our problem-solving process, and it is important to take it very seriously (Lane, Bocian, MacMillan, & Gresham et al., 2004). C. A. Peterson and S. R. McConnell (1996) note that intervention integrity is correlated to desirable student outcomes. So it makes good sense to invest in efforts to ensure that we implement our plans well. The best intervention in the world on paper has no chance to be effective if it is not implemented with integrity, yet logistical and other challenges quite often result in interventions that fall by the wayside. Intervention integrity or fidelity is an outgrowth of teacher knowledge of and competency in implementing effective instructional techniques and of teacher beliefs that specific interventions, when implemented with consistency, will solve well-defined problems.

At Tier 1, fidelity of implementation takes into consideration the degree to which all processes at the school level are being conducted for all students. Processes include schoolwide formative and summative assessments, the degree to which the core curriculum has an empirical base and is implemented as intended, and how schoolwide data are used to drive decision making. Ensuring fidelity at this level is critical for ensuring that students are not referred for strategic (Tier 2) services when curricular, instructional, classwide, or schoolwide issues are interfering with their ability to be successful. Treatment fidelity at Tier 1 ensures that 75–80 percent of the students are making adequate progress given the instructional, assessment, and problem-solving practices being implemented. In addition, treatment fidelity at Tier 1 ensures that 95 percent of students meeting benchmark targets in the fall are also meeting them in the spring.

A memorable exchange on this topic happened once at an interdistrict meeting of teachers and psychologists involved in intervention systems. Clearly agitated, one teacher spoke up to say, "I have been a certified reading specialist for twenty-five years, and I am offended to hear you are suggesting that someone would need to come check up on me to be sure I know how to do my job." Without missing a beat, a psychologist in the group said, "Well, I've been a licensed school psychologist for thirty-two years, and I still read every test item verbatim out of the manual each time I give an IQ test, even though I could probably recite them in my sleep, because I know that drift happens to the best of us."

Discussing implementation integrity as a system can be difficult, because it may cause some to feel they are being checked up on. On the contrary, these systems stem from a healthy acknowledgment of the potential of drift in practice and a commitment to delivering the very highest quality instruction possible. In fact, we see that outside monitoring to check on implementation fidelity, while important, may be an uphill battle if the team has not paid attention to building consensus around the ideals of fidelity within intervention implementation. Given this orientation, the following factors have been most helpful in working toward good integrity of intervention implementation.

One important lesson we have learned is to make a clear and explicit distinction between the personal integrity of the human being conducting the intervention and the integrity of implementation of the plan. Some schools have carefully chosen terms such as *fidelity* rather than *integrity* to help clarify this difference. High-quality completion of the plan development stage in the problem-solving process is also paramount. Specifically, having a very clear written description of the intended intervention helps communicate the plan to all involved. This intervention description is most helpful when details are spelled out, so that anyone could pick up the description, read it over, and implement the plan with confidence and accuracy. We look more closely at intervention scripts (one way to do this) in the chapters related to Tier 2, but scripts are just as beneficial here in Tier 1.

A second factor affecting implementation integrity is the professional development offered to those providing the intervention to students. In the case of a systems-level intervention, consistency across staff members is key. For example, if an updated schoolwide policy regarding student dress code is implemented, integrity of implementation may be enhanced to the extent that all staff members have a clear understanding of their role in implementing it and the confidence that they are not the only ones who are following the policy. Imagine a staff development meeting in which staff members hold up cards displaying sketches of students in various outfits to decide whether an outfit is within the bounds of the new dress code. Building agreement on these norms among staff benefits students by allowing teachers to provide consistent messages about expectations.

Third, direct observation of the intervention in action, along with explicit feedback to interventionists about this observation, significantly affects intervention integrity (Noell et al., 2000; Noell et al., 2005). At a systems level, this practice may include teachers of the same course observing each other teaching a lesson and providing feedback about adherence to the curriculum map, consistency of strategy instruction, or language usage across classes. Some districts employ curriculum chairpersons who have time to observe in classrooms and give feedback on integrity of implementation for any systems-level initiative. One midwestern high school made the decision to increase use of explicit reading comprehension strategy modeling and instruction across classes. The building administrator added the following two items to her regular walkthrough observation feedback chart for the year:

▸ Were there permanent products displayed in the classroom showing a reading comprehension strategy?

▸ During the observation, did the teacher provide a model of, or instruction in the use of, a reading comprehension strategy?

In addition to the considerable work done to be sure that building staff are well trained and that they consistently and correctly implement the interventions, student participation in the intervention is also an important factor to measure. If we design an intervention that is to be implemented daily for a month so that students would participate in twenty sessions, but students actually participate in only twelve sessions, on average, due to vacation days, special assemblies, fire drills, and student absences, then there is an integrity problem that we need to address.

Plan Evaluation

Finally, plan evaluation allows a building or district to decide if the plan it implemented had the desired effect. At the systems level, interventions are implemented in core instruction—that is, in instruction (for both academics and social behavior) that is provided to all students. We know the core instruction is working when students are showing proficiency rates at the levels we expect and when most students are not getting extra support in order to demonstrate this proficiency. We know that the core instruction is *not* working when we have too many students missing our goals or needing something extra to meet the goal.

Because the goal was set prior to implementation of the intervention, the simple answer to this question is quite straightforward: either the goal was met or not. If the goal was met, celebrate, and then discuss the next steps for continuous improvement. In particular, determining the most effective aspects of the successful intervention is important so that those same aspects can be used again in future. If the goal was not met, celebrate any growth toward the goal. Then, engage in an in-depth discussion about why the goal was not met to help the building or district understand what to try next. Perhaps the hypothesis about the cause of the problem was incorrect. Perhaps the hypothesis was right on, but the plan was not robust enough or was not implemented consistently. This self-evaluation allows buildings to make another course correction before beginning work again to improve important outcomes for students.

Table 7.2 and figure 7.2 (page 102) display systems data for reading from a middle school seventh-grade team. In table 7.1, results of the fall and spring NWEA assessment are recorded. The team reviews the number and percent of students scoring in each of the three tier ranges as defined by criterion scores predicting success on the state high-stakes test. Because this is a measure designed to capture growth, the team can also compare growth rates to national averages and can calculate the percentage of students meeting their individual growth goals. Breaking down screening outcomes by tier is helpful to teams, because they can consider whether their instructional programs are meeting the needs of students across the continuum of need levels. In this example, students who began the year at or above the Tier 1 target, on average, grew 122 percent of their individual growth goals, and 62 percent of those students attained their individual growth goals (which are set based on typical growth for students nationally with the same fall score).

Table 7.2: Results of the Fall and Spring NWEA Assessment From a Middle School Seventh-Grade Team

Percent in Tiers	Goal	Fall MAP		Spring MAP		Fall to Spring Averages			
		Number	Percent	Number	Percent	Actual Growth	National Growth Goal	% of Expected Goal	% of Students Meeting Goal
Tier 1	80%	37	**59%**	40	**62%**	3.7	3.0	122%	62%
Tier 2	15%	18	**29%**	18	**28%**	5.1	4.7	108%	56%
Tier 3	5%	8	**13%**	7	**11%**	10.3	8.8	117%	75%

Another way our teams have looked at their NWEA MAP data to identify needs at the systems level is through comparison of strand performance. Figure 7.2 (page 102) displays student performance across the four strands of the assessment. In this fairly traditional box plot, the average range performance is shown in the boxed area. Superimposed on the boxes are horizontal lines that denote the cutoff point between Tiers 1 and 2 and between Tiers 2 and 3. Remember that students who meet or exceed the Tier 1 target score have at least a 75 percent chance of passing the upcoming high-stakes state assessment. At the systems level, a grade-level team can use these data to consider needs for core instruction. Which strand has the largest percentage of students scoring the lowest or highest relative to the targets? Which strand has the broadest range of needs? By looking at these charts over time, staff can note growth and change. Are there strands with more or less growth across test administrations? Each of these questions allows a team to think about systems-level issues and needs. Because the unit of consideration is the grade level for these data points, the unit of intervention is designed to be the same.

For oral reading fluency, the team can not only look at straight percentages of students in tiers, as in table 7.3 (page 103), but it can also look at movement between tiers. A hallmark of a strong core curriculum is that students who begin the year on grade level also end the year on grade level. Table 7.4 (page 103) illustrates how to evaluate the core curriculum based on this idea. In this example, 98 percent of the students who met their Tier 1 criterion score in the fall also met the Tier 1 criterion in the spring. Because the criteria grow from fall to spring, these students demonstrated growth rates steep enough to keep them at or ahead of expectation. This is a very desirable outcome and suggests effectiveness for the core instruction.

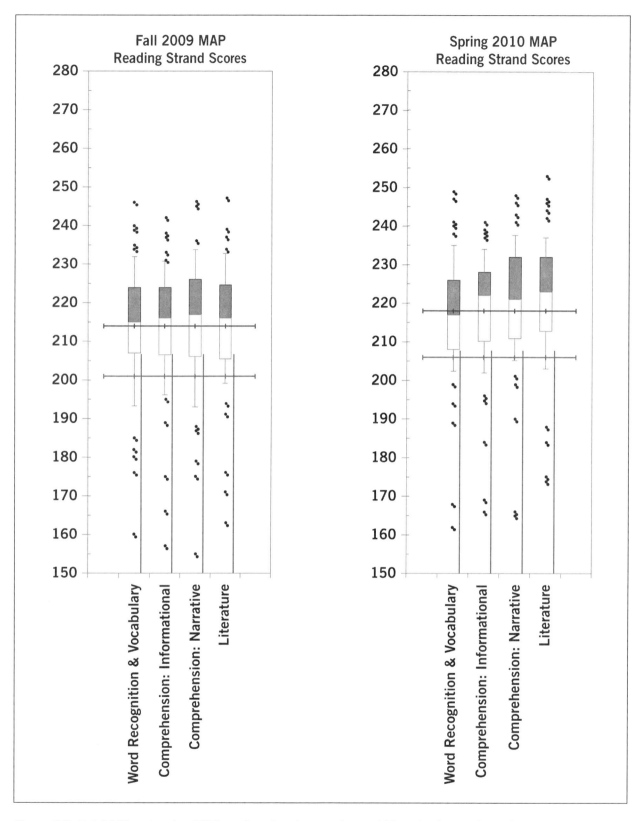

Figure 7.2: Fall 2009 and spring 2010 reading strand scores for a middle school seventh-grade team.

Table 7.3: Oral Reading Fluency in Percentages of Students According to Tier

Percent in Tiers	Goal	Fall ORF		Winter ORF		Spring ORF	
		Number	Percent	Number	Percent	Number	Percent
Tier 1	80%	45	73%	46	72%	48	75%
Tier 2	15%	11	18%	13	20%	11	17%
Tier 3	5%	6	10%	5	8%	5	8%

Table 7.4: Effectiveness of the Core Curriculum by Tier

Summary of Effectiveness	Goal	Fall to Winter		Winter to Spring		Fall to Spring	
		Number	Percent	Number	Percent	Number	Percent
Tier 1 to Tier 1	95%	42	93%	45	100%	43	98%
Tier 1 to Tier 2		3		0		1	
Tier 1 to Tier 3		0		0		0	
Tier 2 to Tier 1	50%	2	18%	2	15%	2	18%
Tier 2 to Tier 2		8		11		8	
Tier 2 to Tier 3		1		0		1	
Tier 3 to Tier 1		0	0%	0	0%	0	0%
Tier 3 to Tier 2		2	33%	0	0%	2	33%
Tier 3 to Tier 3		4		5		4	

In this way, staff members can look at the problem-solving process at the building level as a continuous improvement model. In upcoming chapters, this same process is described as it relates to subsets of students or individual students. The steps remain the same, but specificity and intensity increase as identified problems become more focused or narrow.

A Tale of Two Tier 1 Outcomes

Let's walk through a couple of real-life examples. Take the following two scenarios, and see how a five-step problem-solving process is applied to Tier 1 instruction.

Scenario A: Tier 1 Instruction Is Working

In reviewing the school's statewide results on the reading test, this school found that 88 percent of their seventh graders were proficient.

Step 1: Problem identification
Answers the question: What is the discrepancy between what is expected and what is occurring?

You may question, How is it a problem if your data indicate you have effective Tier 1 services? This is a common dilemma that good schools face. *Good schools* are the ones that seem to be functioning well and have effective instruction for students, as evidenced by their performance on state and national exams. This phenomenon of being a good school can be the greatest barrier to becoming a school of excellence. Problem identification centers around answering questions like: How is the message that RTI is for all students—or that high performers must also continue to grow—reinforced? How do administrators convince staff not to become complacent with success? Further, how does this school continue to focus on allocating resources to support students who aren't yet proficient? The problem identification of this scenario focuses on how a school can continue to improve.

Step 2: Problem analysis
Answers the question: Why is the problem occurring?

A better question in this scenario may be, what barriers do you have to continually improving? To answer this question, you need to refocus your team on the purpose and framework of RTI. Within an RTI framework, improvement and refinement is continual, because the current needs of learners change regularly. One semester or one year your learners may need more vocabulary strategies in content areas. Next, a new group of learners—or even this same group—may tell you they need an increase in active supervision in the hallways and lunchroom due to inappropriate behavior. We do not abruptly stop all areas of growth once we've met a certain target or score. We continually celebrate success, sustain improvement, and let the data tell us where to refocus our problem-solving energy.

Step 3: Plan development
Answers the questions: What is the goal? What is the intervention plan to address this goal? How will progress be monitored?

How would you create a goal for something that appears to be working? Let's say the Tier 1 ACT performance suggests that 88 percent of your students are meeting the target benchmark for reading. When the building leadership team reviews these data, they identify that one substrand, for example the math substrand, is not at or above the national average. Further disaggregation reveals that a certain subgroup, for example students who are identified as receiving free or reduced lunch, is also well below the target. This information points your team in a direction for further problem solving and a possible new goal.

Next, your team would need to determine the intervention to address the goal. This is an articulated series of action steps to make a meaningful change in instruction, the learning environment, or the curriculum. The team also needs to specify who is going to do what to move this plan forward. The intervention could start with a review of the test specs or content as they relate to what is being assessed. Next, you might explore how the current math curriculum aligns with the state standards and the ACT math test items. The team would then need to explore specific staff development on math skills in which students are relatively weak. It is important to note that whatever the goal is, the plan must be related to the goal.

Once these issues have been addressed, the next step is progress monitoring, which is essential to ensuring the plan is working. A school that is working on a substrand of the ACT could use the tenth-grade PLAN test to help predict student achievement on the ACT or the maze assessment to monitor if reading comprehension is being addressed (see chapter 4, page 51, for a review of maze assessment). Finally, set a date on the calendar to review data to determine if your plan has worked. Communicate clearly who should be in attendance and how long the meeting is expected to last.

Step 4: Plan implementation
Answers the question: How will we be sure our core instruction is delivered with fidelity?

This step in problem solving can be one of the most intimidating to implement. All too often, educators rely on professional judgment to ensure that training or skill development is being implemented. Ignoring or not being proactive in implementing this step ensures failure in any plan! At this step, administration involvement is especially critical. Administrators must be willing to not only establish the process for fidelity checks but also to follow up with staff that are not meeting established criteria. One suggestion for establishing fidelity checks in Tier 1 services is creating a yearly staff development plan detailing who will review which examples of work and when.

Step 5: Plan evaluation
Answers the question: Did our plan work?

If the problem-solving steps have been applied effectively, the team will be clear on what data will be reviewed on what date (step 3). During this step, the team meets to review the effectiveness of its plan. In the example of reading comprehension, the team would review the maze results and decide whether or not it has met its goal. The beauty of a problem-solving process is that, in either case, you have a framework to move forward. Let's say the team reviews the data and discovers it has not met the goal. The team would resume the problem-solving steps to determine if it should continue with the plan and collect more data or change the plan. While this may seem like failure, we encourage teams to focus on even small amounts of progress gained in addition to taking a hard look at what they learned that did not work.

Now, consider what would happen if the team *determined* the goal had been met. It's wonderful! It's time to celebrate the success! Again, the beauty of the problem-solving process is that you're never really done. Because your school and team are regularly reviewing data, you should be in a constant state of problem solving and moving on to the next identified area of growth. In either outcome, report your results to your entire staff. Whether you are successful or have more work to do, it's important for consensus that all staff know about the process, the work involved, the outcomes, and the next steps. Keeping all staff in the school informed communicates that RTI is a priority for everyone and not just certain teams or staff members.

Scenario B: Tier 1 Instruction Is Not Effective

Let's now consider a school that discovered after reviewing its statewide testing data that only 41 percent of its ninth-grade students were proficient on their reading exam. This school has acknowledged student reading scores are not where staff wish them to be. They are, however, unsure of how to proceed. Thankfully, the problem-solving process provides the necessary steps and framework to help address this problem.

Step 1: Problem identification

Answers the questions: What is the discrepancy between what is expected and what is occurring? Or, in this specific example, is the core program sufficient?

Defining this problem can seem overwhelming and demoralizing. The public pressure to meet state averages in proficiency rates can be immense. The leadership team knows that only 41 percent of students being proficient is not acceptable. Statewide, 82 percent of ninth-grade students scored at the proficient level on the state reading exam. An example problem identification statement would be: "When given the state reading exam, 41 percent of ninth-grade students performed at a proficient level compared to 82 percent of ninth-grade students who performed at a proficient level statewide."

Step 2: Problem analysis

Answers the questions: Why is the problem occurring? Or, in this specific example, why isn't the core program sufficient?

At this step, the leadership team generates multiple hypotheses for why the problem might be occurring. During this process, the team might determine that more data need to be collected in order to answer this question. This is often a necessary step, because good problem analysis generally does not happen without multiple sources of data and information.

Once all data are collected, the team generates hypotheses that are focused on reasons the problem is occurring due to instruction, curriculum, or the learning environment. For example, one hypothesis might be that staff do not having an adequate understanding of the state content standards being assessed. Another might be that the core curriculum does not align with the state content standards. Another might be that the core curriculum has not been adequately mapped. Still another explanation might be that there is no vertical or horizontal dialogue about curriculum maps occurring among staff within and across buildings. Further, there may be high rates of students arriving late to class or receiving office discipline referrals. You get the idea.

After the team has generated a comprehensive list with an emphasis on alterable variables, the next step in problem analysis is to align the data and information with the various hypotheses in order to support or refute their viability. The team then narrows the list down and agrees to one hypothesis using the following criteria as guidance:

▶ The hypothesis must be a variable that can be altered through intervention.

▶ The hypothesis must be supported by at least two pieces of data, one of which must be quantitative.

Step 3: Plan development

Answers the questions: What is the goal? What is the intervention plan to address this goal? How will progress be monitored? Or, in this specific example, how will the needs identified in the core program be addressed?

In following this example, a goal the team might choose is, when given the annual state reading exam, 80 percent of ninth-grade students will perform at a proficient level.

The plan may consist of each professional learning team researching various strategies or activities that support the statewide language arts standards and agreeing on one or two of those strategies that will be systematically implemented in their classrooms. If the team decided that a systematic review of the standards was a part of the plan, this would facilitate an examination of exactly what needs to be addressed in the core curriculum. Through a systematic process of reviewing the standards, staff will have a deeper understanding of what skills, strategies, and concepts are expected. An essential aspect of this process must be an analysis of what strands the staff are adequately covering and what needs to be adjusted to incorporate the standards expectations. This phase may uncover a need for staff development to support staff understanding and implementation of learning standards identified in the state standards.

Because the team has selected a goal with only one data point to indicate whether or not the goal has been met, careful consideration must be given to what will be done for progress monitoring. Teams need to know well before the summative state exam whether they are making progress. For this goal, teams might consider setting an additional goal using CBM maze, because that assessment can be reasonably collected schoolwide and is a technically adequate general outcome measure for reading.

Step 4: Plan implementation

Answers the questions: How will we be sure our core instruction is delivered with fidelity? Or, in this specific example, how will the effectiveness and efficiency of the core program be monitored?

At this level, fidelity of implementation takes into consideration the degree to which all processes at the school level are being conducted for all students. Processes would include schoolwide formative and summative assessments, the degree to which the core curriculum is empirically based and is implemented as intended, and how schoolwide data are used to drive decision making. Ensuring fidelity at this level is critical for ensuring that students aren't referred for Tier 2 services when curricular and instructional, classwide, or schoolwide issues are interfering with their ability to be successful. Fidelity checks on this intervention plan could be done by walkthroughs by building administration or other team leadership staff. Team members also have opportunities to observe in each other's classrooms to enhance the feedback given to staff and to broaden the professional growth of all involved.

> *Step 5: Plan evaluation*
> *Answers the questions: Did our plan work? Or, in this specific example, have improvements to the core program been effective?*

At this stage, teams need to do a check on progress toward the goal and determine whether the intervention plan has had a positive impact on the core reading curriculum. Rather than focus on whether the answer is yes or no, it is important to consider where growth has occurred—on both the small and large scales—and what accounts for the growth or lack thereof. Teams can learn just as much from what didn't work as they can from what did. The truth is that even if it didn't meet its established goal, the team can have faith that it has a problem-solving process and organizational framework it can rely on to continually work on the identified issues.

Our hope is that, through this tale of two schools, you have a template for how to apply a problem-solving process to determine whether the core instruction is working and—whether your answer is yes or no—that you continue to refine and improve practices to achieve the goal of meeting the instructional needs of all our kids.

Conclusion

This chapter presented a five-step problem-solving process as it relates to Tier 1, or systems level, considerations. We also demonstrated many intersections between problem solving and screening assessments and problem solving and instructional planning. The three sides of our RTI triangle are significantly interdependent! As we move on to a consideration of Tier 2, you will see that the essential tenets of assessment, instruction, and problem solving remain the same, only with an increase in intensity and specificity.

CHAPTER 8

Tier 2 Assessment: Progress-Monitoring Options

All assessment is a perpetual work in progress.

—Linda Suske

The difference between perception and fact is that fact changes.

—Ron Krouch

Advance Organizer

✓ *Revisiting quality screening practices will assist with developing quality progress-monitoring practices.*

✓ *The critical considerations for progress monitoring are choosing who to monitor more frequently, choosing the right measures to use, and developing a logistics plan that is efficient and effective.*

✓ *It is wise for teams to take the extra time to do a good analysis of progress-monitoring data and apply that to instructional decisions.*

We need to use data not only to better identify and understand our learners and our profession but also to assist and improve the lives of the students we serve.

In chapter 4, we discussed setting up a screening system designed to help ensure that all students at risk for academic difficulty were identified in a proactive manner. Screening helps catch potential problems early, in order to maximize intervention opportunity, and helps reduce possible bias that occurs from a referral system that relies solely on individual staff members to refer as they see fit.

Note that no series of screening assessments will perfectly identify all at-risk students every time. We hope that most students are categorized correctly in each set of screening data. That is, we hope that students who appear proficient on the screener are, indeed, proficient, and those who appear at risk on the screener really do need intervention support. We must anticipate that a small number of students will be incorrectly classified. Some who appear at risk based on the screening assessment might go on to become proficient without additional support. And some who appear proficient on the screener will need intervention support (although if we have a quality screening instrument, this discrepancy will be rare).

The outcomes are shown in figure 8.1. Students who we correctly predict will be successful based on screening comprise our Happy No Surprises group. Those who we correctly predict will need intervention are our Unhappy No Surprises group. For these two groups, our screening system works accurately, in that it tells us who needs additional support and who does not. Students who look to be at risk but are, in fact, successful are our Happy Surprises. They do well even though we predicted they would not. This group of students may end up receiving unnecessary intervention support, which does create added expense for the building and requires an unnecessary expenditure of time for the student. Although a large number of Happy Surprises could waste district resources or dilute services for others, we argue that providing interventions that are not needed is a better mistake to make than failing to provide interventions for students who do need them. The final group, the Unhappy Surprises, are students who looked like they were on track based on screening results but were actually not.

Figure 8.1: Four types of screening outcomes.

When systems are setting criterion-referenced targets for decision making, it is this exact balance that they are trying to set. The goal is to set cut scores for screening instruments at points that minimize unhappy surprises and happy surprises while maximizing the no surprise groups. The technical analysis procedure for this work is *logistic regression*, in which the dependent variable (categorical) is whether or not the student met the criterion (passed the high-stakes test, for example), and the independent variable is the score the student earned on the screening tool (CBM, for example). This analysis yields a percentage likelihood of meeting the desired outcome on the criterion measure at each given CBM score. See the work of Benjamin Silberglitt and John Hintze (2005) for detailed information on this topic.

In addition to setting our targets for screening carefully, other considerations may be especially helpful for those students close to the cutoff. First, considering other data available for these students may help teams determine whether there is converging evidence of a problem. For example, if a student who is new to the school performs poorly on the screening assessment but her transcript shows good grades in on- or above- grade-level classes and passing scores on achievement tests, the level of concern may well be lower than for a student whose transcript reveals no completed math or science classes or nonproficient scores on state tests. Second, teacher report of student behavior in class and review of permanent student products from classes can provide qualitative support or lack of support for a screening outcome. Some systems develop a purposely gated screening system. For example, all students may participate in the maze assessment in the fall. Those students performing below a specific criterion score or normative level are then assessed using CBM-R. These additional data points are helpful to teams in making accurate decisions about student placement in intervention programs. Data do not belong in a vacuum. They must be considered within the context of all other information available to promote accurate decision making.

One method for ensuring better decision making after screening is collecting additional data on a regular basis. While not necessary for most students, for the subgroup of those in each grade for whom there is some concern, more frequent data collection is helpful. A technical way to think about the use of more frequent data collection to supplement screening is consideration of sensitivity and specificity. A good screener will be *sensitive*, meaning that it will accurately identify students who are at risk, and it will be *specific*, meaning that it will accurately identify students for whom the core instruction is working. We become more certain we have identified the right kids when we see students identified as at risk via screening measures who do not demonstrate adequate growth on the more frequent measures as a result of targeted instructional support.

At first glance, the idea of collecting even more data about students may not seem palatable. Don't we test enough already? There are many rationales we could offer for why more data collection is a good idea. As S. S. Yeh (2007) states:

> Comparisons of student achievement effect sizes suggest that a system in which student performance in math and reading is rapidly assessed between 2 and 5 times per week are 4 times as effective as a 10 percent increase in per pupil expenditures, 6 times as effective as voucher programs, 64 times as effective as charter schools and 6 times as effective as increased accountability. Achievement

gains per dollar from rapid assessment are even greater—193 times the gains that accrue from increasing preexisting patterns of educational expenditures, 2,424 times the gains from vouchers, 23,166 times the gains from charter schools and 57 times the gains from increased accountability. (p. 416)

Fiscally speaking, use of data to frequently monitor student progress in this study, a core feature of an RTI framework, was the most cost-effective policy for schools. This is not to overlook alternative efforts toward student achievement, such as charter schools, that may also be successful in some circumstances. However, the study draws attention to a specific practice that has yielded significant gains in student achievement for a fairly low cost. What better way to know whether or not interventions are effective than using data, and how validating to know that this is not only an effective means to answer the question but also a fiscally conservative one.

Whom Should We Progress Monitor?

If you agree that more frequent data collection is a good idea for a subset of your students, the next decision is which students would benefit. Often, schools that begin implementing more frequent data collection, even outside of an RTI framework, do so for students receiving special education. A next step within RTI is to choose to collect more frequent data on all students receiving some sort of Tier 3 intensive intervention (regardless of their special education status) or to collect more frequent data on all students receiving any Tier 2 or Tier 3 support. Some buildings teams choose to collect more frequent data on all students not meeting grade-level expectations, regardless of participation in supplemental support programs. This choice represents the largest proportion of students in a building, as most buildings do not enroll 100 percent of all students not meeting grade-level standards into an intervention course. Rather, in most buildings there is a group of students who may be performing just below expectations who need greater consideration and differentiated instruction within core classes, but whose skill deficits are not significant enough to warrant an additional course of study. In some cases, the percentage of students performing below grade-level expectation is so large that it would be impossible to schedule and deliver supplemental courses for them all. In this case, the school is best served by working diligently to strengthen the core instructional programs to meet the more intense needs of the student population. In such situations, the school team might choose to collect more frequent data to monitor effects of improvement efforts. Figure 8.2 provides a visual portrayal of the various subsets of the entire school population that might be identified for more frequent monitoring.

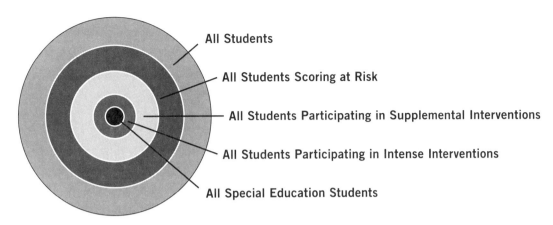

Figure 8.2: Deciding whom to progress monitor.

In summary, the decision to collect more frequent data regarding student progress and the decision to provide additional intervention support to students are separate. A team may opt to collect regular progress-monitoring data for students while they are participating in the typical core instructional program just as a way to check in, to be sure that the students are making needed progress. We do not advise engaging in supplemental intervention work without adding a layer of frequent monitoring into the program.

What Assessment Should We Use?

A question of tools often emerges at this point: what assessments are appropriate for more frequent data collection, such as we have suggested? Fortunately, there have been a number of projects undertaken for the purpose of identifying quality progress-monitoring tools. The National Center on Student Progress Monitoring created a list of progress-monitoring tools with appropriate psychometric characteristics for the purpose. Go to www.studentprogress .org to view their recommendations. Another organization that has continued the work of disseminating information on progress-monitoring tools is the National Center on Response to Intervention (www.rti4success.org).

Most of these suggested progress-monitoring measures fall into the category of curriculum-based measures (CBMs). Curriculum-based measures are used predominantly for progress monitoring because, in addition to being reliable and valid tools, they are also practical, brief, repeatable, and sensitive to growth. These measures are created with a large number of alternate forms, so that a different assessment can be given each time. All alternate forms are developed to be at the same level of difficulty. Because the difficulty level of the assessments does not change throughout the school year, changes in student score can be attributed to changes in student proficiency. This attribute of the assessments makes them different from other within-program assessments, such as unit tests. The multiple forms of these very sensitive measures allow for repeated measurement that captures growth over time. As described in chapter 4 (page 47), these measures also carry the weight of research support as technically adequate standardized measures. This makes them different from most formative assessments that are individually or collaboratively created by teams of teachers to measure performance on course content.

How Often Should We Collect Data?

Data collection frequency can vary widely depending on the need for the information. If screening happens three times per school year, more frequent progress monitoring may mean collecting data one time during each of the months not already assigned to screening. At the other end of the frequency continuum, it may mean collecting data twice each week for a particular student. The more often data are collected for a student, the more quickly a team can collect a sufficient number of data points to be able to evaluate growth over time (measured as slope). Research related to reliability of slope estimates suggests that 12 to 15 data points on CBM measures are needed in order to reduce the standard error of slope to an acceptable level (Christ, 2006). If you can collect data two times per week, the slope of growth for a student can then be reliably determined after six to eight weeks of intervention.

However, not all measures (even CBMs) are sensitive enough to make twice weekly (or even weekly) data collection a reasonable practice. Consider curriculum-based measurement of writing, for example. Normative research indicates that typical growth on this measure is one-half of a correct word sequence per week (Fuchs, Fuchs, Hamlett, Walz, & Germann, 1993). Because the scoring system does not allow for partial scores, you would typically need to wait two weeks to see a one-point difference. More frequent data collection doesn't make much sense, because you would reasonably expect to be measuring a fair amount of error on a more frequent basis. In general, we collect reading CBMs and tests of math facts weekly, writing and maze tasks two times per month, and math application CBMs on a monthly basis.

Progress-Monitoring Logistics

A variety of organizational structures may be put in place to achieve frequent progress monitoring for students. You can see that, depending on the extent to which a school plans to implement progress monitoring, potentially 20 percent or more of the student population would be involved. To implement the system in an efficient and sustainable manner, it is therefore critical to focus on the logistics of data collection. In some buildings, staff who are leading study halls or teaching intervention classes are able to collect data from students assigned to their sections. In other buildings, special education paraprofessionals are given a list of students from whom to collect data on a rotating schedule. Hall passes may be given to students to pull them from class for a short time to go to a central location for data collection.

An important project for some groups of leaders of this initiative within the building will be to design and communicate a very explicit plan regarding frequent data collection for students. This team must first decide which students are to be monitored (given the considerations raised previously), and for each student name on that list, the team must decide which measure or measures will be used and how often data will be collected. Once the team has that three-column list (who, what, and how often), they can begin to design a master plan for the when, where, and by whom. CBMs such as math applications, maze, or written expression can be administered to groups of students together. It makes sense to administer these only during periods of the day when students who need to be monitored are gathered for classes, or when at least small groups of them can reasonably be gathered together. An example would be choosing to administer a maze assessment every other week to all students participating in a supplemental reading class, or having the teacher covering the fifth-hour study hall collect a written expression probe every other week from the four students assigned to that room who need it. The read-aloud CBMs of reading must be administered individually, so a different set of plans must be put in place for collecting data on that measure for students. One option is to use paraprofessionals as described previously. Other times, an assessment that might have been group administered is planned, but a student's schedule does not align easily with times when other groups of students are being assessed on the same measure. In this instance as well, an individual testing session must be planned.

As teams are considering what progress-monitoring tools to use for secondary students, data from research studies will be informative. Based on some empirical research, maze has been suggested as the preferred progress-monitoring tool for secondary students in reading relative to CBM-R. Although the reliability and validity on maze at the secondary level is not quite as robust as CBM-R (reliability $r = 0.79 - 0.96$ versus $r = 0.93 - 0.97$; validity $r = 0.75 - 0.88$ versus $r = 0.76 - 0$ k.89), the maze measure is seen as more sensitive to growth over time for this age group (Espin, Wallace, Lembke, Campbell, & Long 2010; Ticha, Espin, & Wayman, 2009). In the realm of math, some scholarly work has been completed on measuring growth in algebra skills that may further extend the reach of math problem-solving measures (Foegen, 2007; Foegen, Olson, & Impecoven-Lind, 2008).

A contingency that this leadership group would be wise to plan for is how staff should respond when students don't show up for data collection. Students miss their assessments more often when they test individually (as opposed to with a class). There is little that is more frustrating to an intervention team gathered to review student progress than finding out that, because the student has been skipping assessments, they have nothing to evaluate. Staff conducting the assessments need to know whether or not they are expected to track students down for testing if they fail to show up. Staff also need to know with whom they should follow up regarding the missed testing. For example, should they inform the school counselor, dean of students, RTI leadership team facilitator, problem-solving team facilitator, or anyone else? Also, recognizing that anyone might miss one testing opportunity (or even a few more), it is helpful to decide how many missed testing times can be accrued before the behavior is considered a problem.

Scoring Assessments

As the list of decisions to be made continues, you must plan scoring assessments and collection of the related data. CBM-R is the only one of the measurements for which scoring happens simultaneously (or briefly after) assessment. For the group-administered assessments, it is possible to collect the data and pass the probes to someone else for scoring. For such assessments, teams need to figure out who will do the scoring. The benefit of spreading out the scoring is that it reduces the work that any one person has to do. The benefit to limiting scoring to a smaller group is greater ease of training on scoring procedures, as well as the likely increase in inter-rater reliability. Many schools will assign one or more paraprofessionals to complete the bulk of the scoring.

Graphing and Storing Data

Once the data are collected, leadership teams must make a decision about how to store and display the data. Some buildings use Microsoft Excel, or a freeware equivalent, to keep spreadsheets of student data that can be displayed in graph form. A few online graphing tools exist as well, such as ChartDog or easyCBM. There are also products for purchase available for this purpose. AIMSweb and Yearly Progress Pro both offer CBM assessment tools through the eighth-grade level with web-based data management, including progress-monitoring graphs. It is wise to develop some way of displaying the progress-monitoring data in a graphical format (rather than just a table) to assist with decision making.

Setting Goals

In order to set up a progress-monitoring graph, noting the baseline score and the date the score was collected are obvious starting points. But you need to make a few decisions. Deciding how frequently to collect data is a fairly obvious decision. Less obvious, however, are the decisions about the length of time for which data will be collected and the goal score for that end point in time. In general, we advocate for progress-monitoring graphs to be set up for the length of the academic year, with baseline data collected in the fall and the goal set for just before school lets out. For grade levels involved in gradewide screening (through grade 8), the fall benchmark data can be used as the baseline point. The goal can be set for a student to achieve a certain score on the spring benchmark assessment. Although it is certainly possible to set up graphs for shorter durations (a quarter or semester, for example), that often results in putting multiple graphs together over the course of one year, which is just extra work. Particularly when progress monitoring with a general outcome measure (such as CBM), we know we are measuring growth in general achievement in the subject area, so we can work on a variety of subskills during the year and still expect to see growth on our general measure.

For goal setting for students within the general education setting, we strongly advocate, in our buildings, that the criterion-referenced Tier 1 targets we have set for spring on our GOMs are used as goals. This is the equivalent of saying that our goal is for students to reach grade-level expectations by the end of the year. For which general education students would we not have that goal? Given the starting point of some of our students, expecting grade-level achievement within one year does represent a very aggressive goal. This means that a very intensive intervention is needed for those students. Research tells us that given the same instructional program, students who are aware that their teachers have more aggressive goals for them experience more growth than students who are aware that their teachers have moderate goals for them (Fuchs, 1989). Students may not meet these aggressive goals, but if we can accelerate their slope of growth by doing something as simple as setting and communicating lofty goals, why wouldn't we?

Reviewing Data

Some helpful guidelines exist to help teams review progress-monitoring graphs to determine whether progress has been sufficient. One such method involves looking at the most recent three or four data points that have been plotted on the graph and comparing them to the aimline (a straight line drawn from the baseline, or first data point on the graph, to the goal point). Following this guideline, if the most recent three or four data points are all above the aimline, the data suggest that the student may be ready to have his or her goal revised to be more aggressive, or that he or she may be ready to have a less intensive intervention. If the most recent three or four data points all fall below the aimline, the data suggest that the student may be in need of an alteration to the current intervention in order to encourage an increased pace of growth. If the most recent three or four data points are neither all above nor all below (that is, if they are on both sides of the aimline), then the intervention, as currently implemented, is understood to be resulting in the desired rate of growth and may be continued.

A second guideline for reviewing data is to consider the trend line, or line of best fit, from the data. The slope, or steepness of this trend line, provides a measure of rate of progress that can be compared to the slope of the aimline. If the trend line is steeper than the aimline, then the student is making a greater-than-expected pace of growth. If the trend line is flatter than the aimline, then the student is making a lower-than-expected pace of growth. If the trend line and aimline are parallel, then the student's growth rate is as expected based on the goal.

Rather than comparing the slope of the trend line to the aimline on an individual graph, another alternative, which is considered stronger for decision-making purposes, is to compare this slope to a designated expectation for growth rates at particular grade levels (Fuchs, 2003). These growth rates can be derived from the research literature (Fuchs et al., 1993), or developed locally based on local norms or specific local expectations. For example, in our buildings, we have set criterion-referenced targets for all GOM measures that predict success on our NCLB state tests. The growth rate represented as the difference between our fall and spring target scores divided by the number of weeks between fall and spring data collection becomes the expected level of growth per week for the grade level. Individual-student growth rates are compared to this expectation. If your system does not have criterion-referenced targets set up with which you could set these slope expectations, you can use normative comparisons instead. For this procedure, the team identifies the average slope of all students being monitored at a particular grade level and calculates one standard deviation below that average. Individuals with growth rates one standard deviation or more below the average growth rate for the grade level would be considered to be making insufficient growth. We note that it is very possible (and, indeed, not uncommon) for students who are significantly behind to show growth that is faster than the expected rate of growth as determined by the target scores. They can also demonstrate growth that is at least average among grade mates and yet not experience enough growth to meet the goal of grade-level expectations by the spring of the school year. When teams can evaluate growth from both vantage points, they are better able to decide whether the level of student growth is acceptable.

Progress Monitoring for Social Behavior Concerns

Curriculum-based measures have been preferred tools for monitoring progress of academic basic skills for students. For social and behavioral concerns, many of the logistical decisions made for monitoring growth in academics are parallel, including choosing students and picking frequency for data collection and review. The specific measures used for monitoring, however, must be unique to the set of behaviors. Often, direct observation of identified behaviors is used for progress monitoring. To do this, teams must carefully define the behavior in observable terms and then design a data collection plan that includes frequency and location of data collection efforts. Finally, the team needs to decide how data will be collected, considering whether a frequency count of the number of behavioral instances over a period of time, a duration measurement of the length of time a target behavior occurred within a set observation time, or a measure of latency between expected behavior and actual behavior is important for planning.

An example of a promising tool for progress monitoring of social and behavioral variables is direct behavior ratings (DBRs; Chafouleas, Riley-Tillman, & Christ, 2009). DBRs consist of direct observation of a specific behavior of concern. Following a specified observation period, observers provide a rating for student behavior. Research shows that DBRs have contextual and instructional relevance and can be reliably used by diverse practitioners within an RTI framework (Chafouleas, Riley-Tillman et al., 2009; Christ, Riley-Tillman, Chafouleas, & Boice, 2010). Further, research is emerging to support their technical adequacy (for example, Chafouleas et al., 2010; Riley-Tillman, Chafouleas, & Eckert, 2008) and their use for screening (Chafouleas, Kilgus, & Hernandez, 2009). In light of few standardized and empirically supported progress-monitoring tools for social and behavioral issues, DBRs are a good option to consider. Visit www.directbehaviorratings.org for more information.

Homework

Among behavior concerns at the secondary level, homework completion comes up over and over as one of the most common referral concerns. Given this, there is good rationale for thinking about the most efficient and effective method for collecting ongoing data. Teams commonly work on some sort of frequency count for monitoring progress on homework completion. That is, out of x opportunities each day to turn in an assignment (total count of assignments assigned for the day), how many assignments were turned in? Certain decisions must be made about how to categorize assignments for monitoring progress in this way. For example, does an assignment turned in late count as a completed assignment or not? Does an assignment turned in (on time or not) that contains incomplete or otherwise poor quality work count as a completed assignment or not?

There are not necessarily easy answers to these questions, but clear definitions need to be established prior to starting data collection in order to establish clarity in measurement decisions. Regarding logistics, considering that teams may reasonably be collecting homework completion data on a number of students, designing an efficient method for ongoing data collection across classes is helpful. For example, if a school is using an electronic gradebook system, is there an agreement about how soon after assignments are collected grades (or other notations of completion) are posted? Is there a method by which one person could access these data to compile a progress-monitoring graph? If paper-and-pencil gradebooks are collected, is there a method by which grade reports can be copied or otherwise shared with one person for compilation? As an example, two numbers might be collected for each class in which a student is enrolled one time per week or every other week—the total number of assignments expected to be turned in during the time frame and the total number of assignments that were actually turned in that met the quality indicators determined a priori (for example, does it have to be on time? accurate?).

We promote the standard that progress-monitoring information should be entered on a graph for each student; at first glance, it would appear that a straight percentage of assignments completed per day or per week or two weeks could be graphed over time. However, there are some limitations to this choice. In particular, consider the student who was given five assignments on day one, two assignments on day two, and four assignments on day three. If the student turned in two assignments the first day, two assignments the second day, and one assignment on the third day, then the percentages for completion would be 40 percent, 100 percent, and 25 percent, respectively. Figure 8.3 (page 120) illustrates what that would look like over time.

Although it seems to make sense at first, this method yields a graph that shows a lot of bounce and does not display trends well. This type of data is difficult to use because in most buildings there are not enough assignments given within a day and often even within a week that lend themselves to good percentage data. If only four assignments are offered, and the student completes two, this would represent a 50 percent completion rate. If the student completes three, the completion rate would jump to 75 percent. In this way, just one assignment causes a jump of 25 percent in completion rate.

As an alternative to this procedure, consider graphing the same data (fig. 8.4, page 120) using two lines. The first line shows a cumulative total number of assignments given over time. The second line shows the cumulative total number of assignments turned in over time.

Notice that each day shows the cumulative total of all assignments given since the start of the data collection. At any time, a team can determine the current percentage of total assignments turned in by dividing the total turned in assignments by the total number of assignments. Visually, as the two lines grow closer to each other, the student is catching up. As the two lines diverge, the student is falling farther behind. This visual display allows for more effective data-based decision making and provides more reliable data to describe the problem.

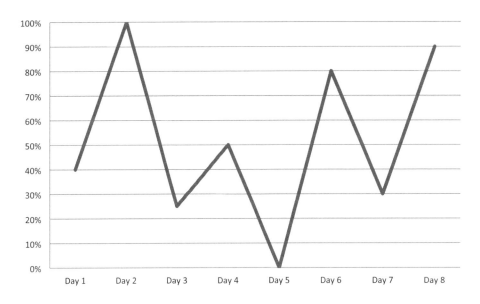

Figure 8.3: Progress monitoring for an irregular number of assignments over eight days.

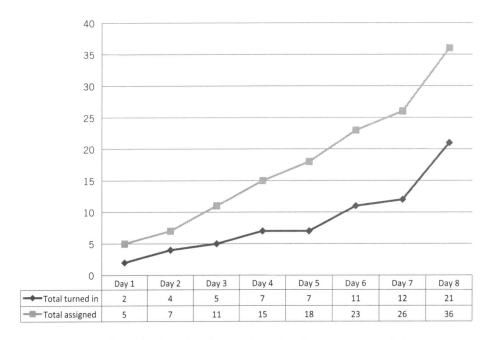

	Day 1	Day 2	Day 3	Day 4	Day 5	Day 6	Day 7	Day 8
Total turned in	2	4	5	7	7	11	12	21
Total assigned	5	7	11	15	18	23	26	36

Figure 8.4: Progress monitoring for eight days showing number of assignments separately.

Conclusion

In this chapter, we took a closer look at frequent monitoring of student progress for academics and social behavior. Selecting measures and target scores, deciding who to monitor and the logistics involved, and considering details related to monitoring homework completion are critical tasks for secondary schools seeking to implement and RTI framework. As we move forward, we turn our attention to supplemental instruction and problem solving for success.

Tier 2 Supplemental Instruction: Standard Treatment Protocol

Better is possible. It does not take genius. It takes diligence. It takes moral clarity. It takes ingenuity. And above all, it takes a willingness to try.

—Atul Gawande

Advance Organizer

✓ *The master schedule can be used as a tool for finding time for interventions.*

✓ *Choosing a few effective standard academic interventions will meet the needs of many.*

✓ *Think of and plan for behavioral interventions just as you would for academics.*

✓ *The CLHS Check & Connect intervention program is one successful example.*

Despite our best efforts to engage students with rigorous and relevant Tier 1 instruction, some students continue to need something more. We can't really be surprised that one common instructional program, even if well differentiated, will not fully meet the needs of the diversity of students served in our schools. In an RTI framework, the something more is referred to as Tier 2 supplemental instruction. Tier 2 is instruction delivered *in addition to* what students are receiving in Tier 1. This means that courses or intervention groups are provided to some but not all students in a particular grade on the basis of need. The most effective use of Tier 2 resources is to serve these students with sufficient intensity so they can transition back to entirely Tier 1 instruction after they have closed the identified discrepancy gap between themselves and their peers. The most efficient allocation of Tier 2 resources is to serve groups of students who share a similar skill or performance deficit with a limited number of common interventions. To make Tier 2 supplemental instruction happen in your building, courage, leadership, and creativity are needed. So, take a deep breath, and get ready to talk about adjusting the master schedule.

The Master Schedule

Of all the "sacred cows" in a high school, the master schedule ranks at the top—with good reason. To figure out a system by which several hundred (or thousand) students all move through the required and elective classes they need, as well as through the lunchroom, and all teachers have full course loads as well as lunch and prep time is quite an accomplishment. Once you have it figured out, heaven forbid you alter the student day in any way, shape, or form. Anyone who has spent time working in secondary education can attest to the panic that ensues if the period-ending bells are altered or, in a situation of true desperation, they don't go off at all. So, realizing the dynamics that are defined by a master schedule, how do you go about changing it?

Acceptance and Data

First, we must acknowledge that to implement the RTI framework you will need to disrupt the master schedule! Anyone who believes he can make such changes without doing so is fooling himself. The level of disruption or alteration can vary from school to school, and leadership teams should carefully consider all changes before implementing them. The rationale for why and how the master schedule is disrupted also needs to be carefully examined and communicated, so that leadership can maintain or build consensus. When we change the schedule, we are changing the daily work experience of our staff—hitting very close to home. Change can be hard, but it's much smoother if it is well thought out and rational.

We suggest you start by examining your data. No matter what form of registration you use—arena scheduling or student request format—the first step is to review your registration data and ask questions like the following:

▶ How many classes don't meet minimum enrollment requirements?

▶ What classes have high failure rates?

▶ What classes have a history of low overall enrollment?

Questions like these help administrators identify courses that may not be serving students in the best possible way. From that point, they can begin to formulate potential areas of change in the master schedule. The purpose of this inquiry is to identify room for movement or innovation.

While options that come out of this type of questioning can have controversial outcomes, it is important to consider them. Reviewing the data gives administrators a powerful tool. While an option can easily be challenged, documentation of a class having the highest failure rate for three years or meeting its enrollment capacity at the end of registration cannot be easily dismissed. As budgets get tighter and resources dwindle, reviewing these data is an essential process for identifying areas of change in the master schedule. Administrators must be willing to find that potential change, fight the battle for change, and know that in the long run it is better for kids.

Schedule Reorganization

In addition to reviewing your registration and class enrollment data, take time to consider other aspects of your current system to see if they might be reorganized or refined to support stronger outcomes for students.

Advisement

Most schools have a system for advising students, but is its purpose clearly defined? Schools can start with examining current structures already in place. Think about your current advisement system, and ask the following questions:

▶ How often do students and teachers see each other?

▶ What is the structure for their time together?

▶ Are there specific tasks or activities students need to complete each day, week, month, or term?

▶ How are academic supports fostered during this time?

▶ Is there, or could there be, time for remediation?

▶ How do students and staff build relationships during this time?

▶ What data or information do you have supporting the effectiveness of the current system? (Sometimes this is as easy as using a short survey to begin gathering some baseline data.)

Once you have the data, what do they tell you? Are students in need of work completion skills? Do they need skills development in the area of reading? Whatever the data may indicate, look to an already established time, like advisement, as a potential for delivering tiered services to your students. Advisement time can be used largely as a Tier 1 activity, providing additional relationship building and academic and social behavioral support to all students. In addition, specific plans can be made for a subgroup of students to address a unique need through this system. Figure 9.1 (page 124) shows a few options to consider for creatively using advisement time in middle or high school settings.

In order to build time for Tier 2 interventions, consider reallocating the number of advisements. For example, if you currently have twenty-five advisements with twenty kids, what would it look like if you now had twenty advisements with a few more kids in each one? If you could make that happen, you would have the five additional teachers available to deliver interventions during this time. Rather than having to add staff in order to add time, often the solution is about being creative with what you have.

Whatever your school decides, if there is a current advisement system in place, you can and should review the allotted time. The insight and buy-in for the teaching staff is another critical aspect to consider when examining how to best utilize an advisement system. When

---

Option A: Daily homeroom—Eighteen minutes a day

- **Each day has a purpose:**
    - Monday—Grade checks
    - Tuesday and Thursday—Academic supports
    - Wednesday—Group meetings
    - Friday—PBIS activities
- **Student organization:** Each teacher has approximately twenty students of mixed grades.

Option B: Once a week—Thirty-five minute-advisement

- Grade-level activities
- Student organization: Each teacher has approximately twenty student of one grade level.

Option C: Daily—Thirty-two minutes a day

- Monday: Grade checks
- Tuesday: Character-education activities
- Wednesday: Silent sustained reading
- Thursday: Antibullying Olweus activities
- Friday: Current events and homework time
- Student organization: Grade level

Figure 9.1: Options for using advisement time in middle and high school settings.

reviewing the current structure, it is important that administrators seek out insight from teachers. Of course, it is equally important to realize that 100 percent upfront buy-in for this or any change is unlikely.

Passing Time

All secondary schools have passing time. The need to transition students from class to class creates a potential opportunity to implement some interventions. The length of passing time can vary from school to school: some schools use three to four minutes, whereas block-schedule schools frequently use eight to ten minutes. Using this time for intervention may not be feasible in some settings, but in some schools, especially block-schedule schools, passing time is a valuable time slot that can be tapped into.

For example, schools that are implementing a check-in/check-out intervention may use passing time for more frequent check-ins with students. Some repeated reading interventions, for example, can take three to five minutes to complete. While that amount of time is not ideal, schools need to be creative and look at all time slots in the day as potential opportunities to implement an intervention. Note that attempting to implement an intervention during a passing time must have student buy-in. Passing time gives opportunity for social interactions with peers, so some students may see delivering the intervention then as a punishment. Staff must be willing to build a relationship with a student to make using this time work. The student and intervention staff must also have a clear agreement about where they will be meeting, because time is precious.

Study Halls

For students who are struggling with academic and organization skills, study halls are most often a complete waste of time. For students who lack the skills to maintain independent self-directed work, or the mastery of content needed to meaningfully do the work in the first place (even if they could keep themselves on task), study halls can be a recipe for disaster for those who are struggling. However, many secondary buildings do include study halls for students on a regular basis (often to get that master schedule to work out!). We encourage you to think about how this gold mine of time could be repurposed for the benefit of at-risk students. What if the only students who had study halls were those with the academic and organizational skills to make independent study time a valuable part of their day? Study halls have potential to deliver a variety of interventions to those for whom independent study is not yet possible. The students would not be missing valuable instructional time if they were pulled from a study hall to participate in an intervention! If schools are going to utilize study halls as a delivery model, potential ideas to structure this valuable time include teaching and practicing study skills, implementing a modified check-in/check-out, or delivering targeted instruction in a particular content area.

Longer (or Shorter) Lunches

If your school has thirty or more minutes allocated to lunch, this time could also be considered for interventions. Again, student buy-in, a positive relationship with the person delivering the intervention, and a specific, agreed-on meeting time and location are necessary. Because this is usually considered a social time for kids, lunches have the potential to be used for a modified check and connect.

On the other hand, what would happen if you reduced the amount of time for each lunch? What if you went from a thirty-minute lunch to a twenty-five-minute lunch? You would have five minutes to work with. Now, what if you adjusted other aspects of the school day—shorter passing times and maybe a minute or two reduction in class time? You could potentially come up with twelve to fifteen minutes to use creatively in providing interventions. Leadership teams must be willing to be creative. Every minute counts.

Before or After School Intervention

Commonly, there is time in the schedule at the end of the day, when staff are available but students are not in session. This is another possible time for intervention implementation. At the high school level, some students can drive. Even if the students themselves don't drive, occasionally parents are willing to either transport their children to school a bit early or pick them up from school a bit late. This may be especially true if implementing the intervention outside of the school day limits the impact of an intervention on other class choices for a student. Another option is to work with district transportation departments to determine whether an early or late bus route can be created to bring students in or take them home at different times. If a student is willing to commit to coming in before or after school, could you have some flexibility in the staff start time? Could it be altered ten to fifteen minutes? Before and after school are great times for a check-in/check-out intervention. Student buy-in and motivation to attend are essential to the success of before- and after-school interventions.

Graduation and Credit Recovery Options

Another common feature of high schools are graduation and credit recovery programs. While the organization and requirement for these types of programs varies by school and state, they have the potential to greatly assist struggling learners. Most credit recovery programs take place after school or on weekends, allowing students to accumulate time outside of the typical school day toward credit. Many credit recovery programs are based on accumulating a certain amount of time (minutes or hours) before credit is awarded. As students spend time outside of the school day working on improving their skills in the identified area, schools can consider how this time toward credit recovery can be allocated in students' best interests. Technology has become an increasingly efficient and cost-effective format to assist with this.

Additional Courses

If you have squeezed every opportunity out of the current structures available in your system, it may be time for more significant changes, such as adding or changing course offerings. When schools view their current structure and registration data to identify potential places for change, the conversation almost certainly turns to what else needs to be added to support additional courses. One option is to add staff, but given the current state of educational funding, that is not a practical solution to rely on. Think further outside the box, and don't equate additional courses with new staff. If we go back to our discussion earlier in this chapter, we discussed the need for the master schedule to be adjusted. What if you found four classes that had the lowest enrollment and chose to offer a specific class focused on improving reading comprehension (or any other skill identified through your data review) in its place? Yes, you may have staffing concerns to deal with or, in some states, licensing issues or restrictions to consider; but these ideas merit consideration in light of making more efficient resource allocations.

Same Courses With Extra Benefits

If additional courses are not an option, another possibility is to offer certain courses with extra time. What if you could take your typical core curriculum and add to it so more students would reach the intended outcomes?

Consider a school that was experiencing a high number of ninth-grade algebra I failures (substitute any class here—it could be biology or geography). Does this sound familiar? The school is already allocating course sections to the high number of students who are repeating the class. Since the sections are already being taught, the purpose of the class can be reconsidered. For example, let's say you currently have fourteen sections of algebra I for ninth-grade students. When you look at the data on the incoming ninth graders, you learn you really only need twelve. However, you have two additional sections due to the high number of students who need to repeat algebra I. What if you did something different with the sections of algebra I for those students needing to retake it? Perhaps students could be scheduled more strategically according to MAP math scores? Potentially organizing students this way would allow for a more fine-tuned structure of the curriculum offered to that group of students—for example, one or two strands.

Double Dosing: Investing in Time on the Front End

Sometimes the needs are best addressed with a double dose of instructional time. This usually comes at the cost of an elective or an allied arts class. However, the argument here is that investing in more time up front to address foundational reading, writing, or math deficits will benefit students greatly as they progress through their middle and high school careers. Further, students who don't have mastery in basic skills are more likely to struggle in *all* their courses—electives and core courses alike.

An effective example of double dosing is found at Chisago Lakes High School. Students who are identified as being in need of remedial reading and writing are placed in the RTI English 9 class. This class is team taught by a licensed English teacher and an intervention specialist, who is also a licensed teacher (in this case, a licensed Spanish teacher). Being a four-by-four block school with eighty-minute class periods, a typical English 9 class is one full block for one semester. A double dose means that students in the RTI English 9 class receive double the instructional time, which is a full school year of English.

The class is designed around research-based practices in literacy instruction for secondary students (for example, Allain, 2008; Diamond, 2004; Kamil, 2004). The course covers standards and content addressed in the core English 9 curriculum, but it is taught at a modified pace, with adaptations based on the instructional needs of the students. For example, all ninth-grade students study *Romeo and Juliet*, but RTI English 9 students may learn the play with the support of a parallel text. In the additional time allotted, remedial reading and writing interventions occur for about thirty to forty minutes daily, at the beginning of each block. The data collection plan includes weekly assessment with the CBM-Reading and twice monthly assessment with CBM-Written Expression (correct word sequences—CWS) for every student.

It is important to note how this intervention is not just the same class "slower and louder." Students get twice the instructional time to cover the expected content, with a smaller class and even smaller student-to-teacher ratio. Given twice the time, students cover all grade 9 ELA standards, plus work on remediation of missing skills in integrated fashion. The expectation and reality is that most students who were at-risk readers placed in this class for grade 9 are ready to succeed in a regular grade 10 English class. Far from tracking, this is intensive targeted remediation with the focused goal of catching kids up.

For the first quarter of the school year, goals of the RTI English 9 class are to build relationships with students, establish a regular cycle of CBM data collection and review, and begin problem solving for students who are not making progress within the first four to five weeks of school. The class does a Daily Oral Language (DOL) as a bell ringer (identifying and correcting grammar and spelling mistakes in given sentences), and the Six-Minute Solution to offer more oral reading practice time to all (Adams & Brown, 2003). This instruction is led by the intervention specialist.

At the end of the first quarter, teachers adapt supplemental instruction for students who require supports not addressed by the standard treatment protocols used for fluency and writing. These decisions are made based on performance on CBM and CWS, as well as on MAP assessments. Given the additional time in this course, the instructors are able to make changes to accelerate the progress of the enrolled students.

Data reviews on all students occur twice per quarter. These are facilitated by the school psychologist and attended by the assistant principal, school counselors, and RTI English staff. The RTI English 9 teacher and intervention specialist review data prior to the meetings to identify individual, small-group, or classwide issues. This advance preparation helps make the meeting time and problem solving very productive.

Choosing Interventions

Once administrators and staff in a building have found time to offer supplemental support to students, the question of what that time will be spent on must be addressed. In Tier 2, we promote the use of standard treatment protocols (STP). As defined by Ted Christ, Matt Burns, and Jim Ysseldyke, a standard treatment protocol is a standard set of empirically supported instructional approaches that are implemented to prevent and remediate academic problems (Christ, Burns, & Ysseldyke, 2005). STP can be intimidating, but we encourage you to think of it as well-planned and consistently implemented instruction that addresses the needs of a group of students. Rather than developing fully unique and individualized instructional plans for every student at risk, the STP format provides schools with the opportunity to develop a well-reasoned and -researched instructional plan that has a high probability of meeting the needs of a group of at-risk students at the same time. STP interventions are more efficient than those developed individually, an important feature for resource-strained systems. Systems are encouraged to use the data they have collected about at-risk students to help guide them in selecting specific foci for intervention.

Planning for Tier 2 STP in Secondary Settings

The following is a list of additional topics that staff need to take into account when developing Tier 2 STP instruction in middle or high school buildings. Our experience is that attention to these details helps ensure effective outcomes.

Gain Student Buy-In

Secondary students often need choice, independence, and buy-in to the instruction. No matter what form of tiered services a school might be considering implementing, the team must acknowledge and program for the intended audience. While giving many options and choices may not be a realistic outcome in all settings, giving smaller choices or having, at a minimum, a discussion with students about *why* they need the service or class is important. We suggest sharing the data with students. This allows for a discussion between students and staff concerning what the data tell us as adults, an opportunity to discuss a student's motivation or performance on the test, and a chance for the staff to share what benchmarks they are looking for and why. Think of the staff who seem to intrinsically understand the needs of secondary students. Find the staff who always seem to understand the behavior of the students they teach. These are the types of staff who fit well in an RTI system.

Build Relationships With Students

As emphasized in chapter 6, building relationships with students is probably one of the most essential aspects to implementing RTI in secondary settings, especially at Tiers 2 and 3. We all know that students who feel as if they belong in a school and who connect with at least one adult in the building tend to perform better. Think about it this way: students receiving Tier 2 or 3 instruction are already identified as most at risk for a variety of issues. Wouldn't it make sense that they also have a history of poor or neutral interactions with school staff? There are always exceptions; however, the importance of building positive relationships can't be overlooked.

If a student resents the person delivering the intervention and feels belittled or disrespected by staff, we will not see the outcomes we hope for. At this point, the data being collected really aren't a reflection of a student's ability, but rather of the type of relationship the student has with the person delivering the intervention. Administrators should look for the teacher or interventionist who can build positive relationships with kids—not the teacher who wants to be friends with students, but the teacher who makes kids want to come to school. These teachers exist in all schools! The challenge is to tap into their talents.

Award Credit for Tier 2 Instruction (High School)

All high school students must earn a certain number of credits to earn a diploma. What must be considered when implementing STP is that many, if not most, of the students identified for Tier 2 or 3 supports are either credit deficient already or at risk of not passing their current classes. When implementing Tier 2 instruction delivered in a class format, it is important to grant students credit. While the credit may be coded as an elective credit, awarding credit gives the class legitimacy within the system and helps with student buy-in.

Supplemental Interventions: Academics

Planning for buy-in for students is crucial, no doubt. But teams must also think clearly about exactly what the students involved in instruction will be learning and doing class. The following is a nonexhaustive list of ideas as a starting point.

Reading Interventions/STP Options

Reading interventions or reading skill development can be a foreign concept in a secondary school, especially a high school. By the time students reach sixth or seventh grade, reading is often no longer a part of the core curriculum. Rarely do high schools even employ designated reading teachers. The expectation is that by the time students enter the secondary level, they should know how to read. And truthfully, many do. However, if sufficient numbers of students have not mastered this skill, we need to think about how that need can be addressed.

At the elementary level, teachers are likely aware of the results of the National Reading Panel (NICHD, 2000), which identifies five big ideas for reading instruction: phonemic awareness, phonics, fluency, vocabulary, and comprehension. In 2008, Greg Roberts and colleagues (Roberts, Torgenson, Boardman, & Scammacca, 2008) provided a revised list of big ideas specific to secondary students: word study, fluency, vocabulary, comprehension, and motivation. We note the overlap among these two lists: fluency, vocabulary, and comprehension are listed in both places, and word study replaces phonemic awareness and phonics as a natural progression. Based on these lists, let's look at two of the common needs areas for Tier 2: fluency and comprehension.

Although for some students it is true that lack of reading fluency is really related to inadequately developed word-study skills (including phonemic awareness and phonics skills), for many students the issue is most closely related to the need for more eyes-on-print time to make their reading more automatic. In a word, they need practice. When formal reading instruction goes away in school, often the opportunities students have to practice reading quickly diminish. Because we can predict that those students who are not proficient readers may not be making the best, most concentrated use of their opportunities for silent sustained reading, we know they may actually be doing little if any independent reading during the school day. This can be corrected, and it takes little time to make a big impact (Anderson, Wilson, & Fielding, 1988).

There are a variety of standard treatment protocols that have the support of empirical research to address this issue. Repeated reading and variations on that theme, including additional modeling (as through a neurological impress method), additional cuing (for reading at the phrase or sentence level, or for reading with accuracy, for example), or additional explicit focus on reading for meaning can be implemented efficiently while providing important and effective practice for students.

A second area of need commonly identified in Tier 2 is comprehension skill. Specific activities related to active reading of text can be described, modeled, and practiced in order to increase student skills in gaining meaning from text. Skills such as effectively previewing text; making plausible predictions before reading and reflecting on their accuracy afterward; identifying the main points and providing a summary of the author's message; and making connections between the text and other texts, the reader, and the world are important—and they can be taught.

We encourage you to use these protocols and to adapt them to meet the needs of your students. Visit **go.solution-tree.com/rti** to find sample reading practice protocols. Notice the focus in each on maximizing student oral reading time, while providing explicit instruction, modeling, and feedback to promote student growth.

Know also that there are myriad published standard interventions in the area of reading as well, and that many of these are very good! Sources such as the What Works Clearinghouse (http://ies.ed.gov.ncee.wwc), Florida Center for Reading Research (www.fcrr.org), and the National Center on RTI (www.rti4success.org) offer helpful reviews on published materials. When selecting supplemental materials about what skills students need to learn, it is important to think very specifically. Collaborative Strategic Reading (Klingner, Vaughn, Dimino, Schumm, & Bryant, 2002; Vaughn, 2003) is a very effective group intervention to support use of comprehension strategies and active reading of text. It does not provide explicit instruction on decoding multisyllabic words, however. Interventions must be matched to need area to be successful in remediating the identified problem.

Math Interventions/STP Options

Less research has accumulated about math interventions than reading interventions, and we think it is fair to say that a smaller percentage of educators would self-identify as being experts in the area of math than language arts. These issues make identifying or designing math interventions more difficult. Still, there are some good models to follow as we work in this area. The National Council of Teachers of Mathematics (NCTM) and the National Common Core Standards in Mathematics provide detailed road maps for expected skills across grade levels. The What Works Clearinghouse and National Center for RTI offer reviews of math instructional programs. In our local schools, our math specialists have done work to develop instructional protocols that support explicit teaching of important mathematical procedures that involve intensive modeling and a gradual release of responsibility over many instructional sessions. Visit **go.solution-tree.com/rti** to view and download some of these protocols.

Supplemental Interventions: Social Behavior

Just as with academic options, targeted behavioral interventions such as social skills groups, school counseling programs, and peer tutoring must be provided for students at the secondary level. One of the most well-researched and empirically established interventions is a check-in/check-out program.

Check-In/Check-Out

This standard treatment protocol intervention is for students who are disengaged from school (Filter et al., 2007; Hawken & Horner, 2003; Todd, Campbell, Meyer, & Horner, 2008). There are numerous versions—for example, Check & Connect (Christenson et al., 2008); Check-In/Check-Out (CICO) (Crone, Horner, & Hawken, 2004); and student support work (described in Bowen et al., 2004). Fortunately, many secondary schools already are implementing elements of check-in/check-out programs.

Check-in/check-out interventions are designed to increase (1) proactive recognition of appropriate behavior, (2) positive, explicit adult feedback and connection, (3) structure throughout the school day, and (4) communication with families (Crone et al., 2004; Filter et al., 2007; Hawken & Horner, 2003). In order to make this type of intervention robust and effective, we recommend that secondary schools implement or refine these practices strategically with regard to structure, individualized instruction, and communication. This type of intervention typically includes:

- ▶ Regular, documented monitoring of student behavior

- ▶ Regular, documented feedback to students about their behavior

- ▶ Positive reinforcement of desirable behavior

- ▶ A home-school component

Students check in with school personnel in the morning, receive feedback throughout the day, and then check out with school personnel before they leave. Typically, the child earns points to receive some form of daily reinforcer.

The following are the core features of a CICO intervention:

- ▶ Program is supported by and complements already established Tier 1 PBS implementation.

- ▶ Target students are those who are reinforced by adult attention.

- ▶ Target students are those who demonstrate performance deficits (won't do) as their primary area of concern rather than those who have specific academic skill deficits (can't do) as the primary area of concern. If an academic area such as reading, math, or writing is identified as the primary area of concern, prioritize those skills first or in conjunction with a CICO intervention.

- ▶ The key to success is, again, the relationship with the student. The interventionist believes all kids can learn. He or she will persist and outlast the kids and their well-ingrained skills of not being engaged in school.

Choose the interventionist wisely. A master check-in/check-out interventionist knows how to balance and shape the student's tolerance for frustration with task completion and physical involvement. He or she knows how to establish a supportive relationship without causing student dependence on him or her for motivation. The interventionist also knows when to ask questions, when to teach directly, and when to remain silent.

The Chisago Lakes High School Check and Connect Program

To address student disengagement, a CLHS Check and Connect (CLHS C&C) intervention was developed from the research-based practices of Check & Connect (Christenson et al., 2008) and the Behavior Education Program (Crone et al., 2004). The story of how the CLHS C&C intervention was developed is told as it happened through application of the five-step problem-solving model.

Step 1: Problem identification
Answers the question: What is the discrepancy between what is expected and what is occurring?

During first couple of years of RTI implementation, there were consistently high numbers of ninth- and tenth-grade students (about twenty-five to thirty) who were referred, primarily for high class-failure rates to the building problem-solving team. At the time, Tier 1 universal supports in place through advisement and school counselors and special education were available for intensive services. This small group needed something else. What was developed continues to follow these steps for decision making.

The problem-solving team reviews a host of existing data on all these students, aggregated in an Excel spreadsheet:

▶ Current academic information—GPA, credits earned, state test scores, and NWEA MAP scores

▶ Historic academic information—grades, state test scores, CBM scores, and NWEA MAP scores

▶ Reports and records from middle school on prior interventions (for example, contracts and check-ins)

▶ Office discipline referrals

▶ Attendance

▶ Existing problem-solving information if available

▶ Student engagement inventory (Appleton, Christenson, Kim, & Reschly, 2006)

The list of students to be targeted was initially reduced by identifying which students appeared to have solid academic skills (but were not performing) and through counselor input. These students were referred to a different intervention. There were still about twenty students remaining. The CLHS Check & Connect program currently has the capacity to serve up to twenty students with fidelity.

Step 2: Problem analysis
Answers the question: Why is the problem occurring?

At this step, the team may or may not determine that additional data are needed on some students. If needed, those data are gathered. Problem analysis consists of using the RIOT/ICEL framework to identify students whose problem-identification data supports the hypothesis that they are reinforced by adult attention. In the first two years, ten students were initially selected. While the team wanted to include more, they decided to start small, so any implementation issues could be addressed effectively early on and fidelity of the intervention was more likely.

Step 3: Plan development
Answers the questions: What is the goal? What is the intervention plan to address this goal? How will progress be monitored?

What is the goal? The overarching goals of the program were:

▶ By spring of the current school year, students participating in the program will go from passing zero classes per quarter to passing 75–80 percent of their classes each quarter.

▶ By spring of the current school year, students participating in the program will receive no more than one office discipline referral per school year.

▶ By spring of the current school year, students participating in the program will arrive at class on time 100 percent of the time.

In addition, each participant has his or her own individualized goals that are developed with the program coordinator.

What is the intervention plan to address this goal? Before year two, the school psychologist conducted a research review to meet the identified need. From the review, two intervention programs emerged that appeared to have the instructional contents these disengaged students needed. The two programs were Check & Connect (Christenson et al., 2008) and the Behavior Education Program (Crone et al., 2004).

The first year the Behavior Education Program was implemented. While it was successful for some students, it was not for others. Problem analysis of this outcome revealed that (1) the intervention had not been consistently implemented with fidelity, and (2) not all of the instructional components were a good fit with CLHS staff and students.

During year two, CLHS received consultation and training from Sandra Christenson, professor in the educational psychology department at the University of Minnesota, who worked with the CLHS problem-solving team to blend the research-based elements and practical applications of both the Behavior Education Program and the Check & Connect program to create what is called CLHS Check & Connect.

The Basic CLHS Check & Connect Program

Component 1: Morning Check-In

▶ Student meets with C&C coordinator each morning before first block.

▶ Student enters name in raffle for checking in.

▶ Make sure student has supplies for day and check his or her planner.

▶ Decide whether missing work should be completed at tutoring center after school.

▶ Check student's mindset and attitude for the day.

▶ Send student off to class with positives.

▶ Do a brief check-in with students periodically throughout the school day as scheduling permits.

Component 2: Individual Problem-Solving Sessions

▶ Meet over student lunch periods biweekly.

▶ Provide students with a free lunch.

▶ Discuss specific skill deficits identified by the coordinator and student.

▶ Work through the problem-solving process (SODAS). SODAS has demonstrated effectiveness as a method of problem solving for both youth and adults (Kifer, Lewis, Green, & Phillips, 1974).

　　1. Situation

　　2. Options

　　3. Disadvantages

　　4. Advantages

　　5. Solution

Problem-Solving Lunch Session

The Check & Connect coordinator and individual student meet weekly or biweekly to discuss current issues regarding behaviors and academics. The coordinator works with the student on problem-solving techniques as they relate to these issues. The goal is to educate the student on how to work through issues using his or her own problem-solving process.

Component 3: Reinforcement System

▶ Weekly drawing for check-ins

▶ Small short-term rewards

▶ Lunch with coordinator

▶ Larger rewards for making progress toward term-end goals

The instructional goal behind the CLHS C&C program is to teach the link between effort and outcomes to disengaged students. A primary task of the CLHS C&C coordinator as it applies to all these components is to frequently call attention to the daily academic and social behaviors that affect long-term academic outcomes. The CLHS C&C coordinator is a twenty-hour per week position in the building. Student progress is monitored through data on the following basis:

▶ Classes passed or failed and student grades

▶ Discipline referrals

▶ School attendance—absences and tardies

Step 4: Plan implementation
Answers the question: How will implementation integrity be established?

Implementation integrity is established through direct observation. In most cases, the observations are conducted by the building school psychologist due to the flexibility in the schedule of that position to accommodate the multiple observation periods needed.

Step 5: Plan evaluation
Answers the questions: Did our plan work? Are we closer to the goal?

In order to answer these questions, CLHS C&C data reviews occur on the following time schedule:

▶ Weekly—by the coordinator

▶ Biweekly—by the CLHS C&C coordinator and school psychologist

▶ Monthly—by the CLHS problem-solving team

Overall, implementation of this standard Tier 2 intervention at CLHS has resulted in a decrease from fifty-four to twenty total tardies per term, a decrease from a high of twenty-eight to thirteen total office discipline referrals per term, and an increase from 68 percent to 89 percent of classes passed per term for participating students. Data like these tell us that efforts in implementing Tier 2 interventions are making meaningful differences for students.

Conclusion

Implementing Tier 2 supplemental instruction is often the biggest change and challenge for a secondary school on the journey to implementing an RTI framework. First, the master schedule must be adjusted to accommodate for the additional time that some students need in order close the gap in identified areas of educational need. Next, there must be research-based instruction that is well matched to the identified student needs and a system of progress monitoring established for each participating student. Finally, schools must schedule data reviews and establish clear decision-making rules for entrance and exit to ensure students don't become lifelong Tier 2 participants.

CHAPTER 10

Tier 2 Problem Solving: Managing Supplemental Interventions

Do not assume that there is a correspondence between talking and doing that produces change in behavior.

—Joseph C. Witt

Advance Organizer

✓ *Problem solving at Tier 2 focuses on how data-based decisions are made to move students across different tiers of service and what should happen instructionally when they are moved.*

✓ *Direct observation of interventions is the most reliable method of ensuring integrity of implementation.*

✓ *You can ensure problem-solving meeting productivity with the right team members, defined roles, a clear agenda, and solid facilitation.*

In chapter 7 (page 89), we looked at our five-step problem-solving process through the lens of Tier 1 or the core curriculum. In this chapter, we discuss the application of the same five-step process to support the subset of students who need supplemental intervention. Let's begin by considering the questions we ask at each step of the process, with respect now to Tier 2:

1. **Problem identification**—Which students are demonstrating discrepant performance?

2. **Problem analysis**—Why is the performance discrepant? What common needs are evident?

3. **Plan development**—What is our goal for closing this gap? What intervention do students need to meet this goal? How will we monitor student progress toward this goal?

4.   **Plan implementation**—How will we be sure our interventions are delivered with integrity or fidelity?

5.   **Plan evaluation**—Did our plan work? Are we closer to our goal?

Problem Identification

Here we once again see the intersection between our screening data collection and problem solving. The very same data that are used for screening to evaluate the health of our core curriculum are used here to identify the specific students whose pattern of performance suggests they are at risk for missing important outcomes. If you have gradewide data on reading skills from GOM assessments, other achievement tests (for example, NWEA, SAT10, state NCLB assessment, or PSAT), the list of students who scored below the score you have selected as the expected score should be considered for Tier 2 intervention.

Remembering the quality practice of seeking convergent evidence, our suggestion to your teams is to begin with a list of all students scoring below target on one assessment, then cross-reference this list with other data to help you rule each student in or out. For example, if you have state NCLB test data and a second local achievement test, you might look at students who scored below expectation on both assessments. You might also review the relevant classroom performance of students on this list, or interview teachers regarding these students to see whether they have seen evidence of the concern identified through screening. By seeking convergent evidence, you can shorten the list of students needing supplemental support by removing students who had a poor test score but who show satisfactory skills in other ways. You may also add some students to the list who scored above expectation on the screener but are of concern to teachers based on other data. Once the list is refined, you can move ahead to considering commonalities of need among these students.

Problem Analysis

In Tier 2, we are seeking solutions that are effective, but also make efficient use of our limited resources. To the extent that we can identify groups of students who are struggling for the same reason and who need the same type of support to close the gap, we are able to develop one intervention that meets the needs of many. This provides efficiency to our system.

Plan Development

The goal for which we advocate is grade-level performance for students served in Tier 2 interventions (unless a special education individualized education program [IEP] team had determined something else). Plans at the Tier 2 level are often standard treatment protocol group interventions. At the secondary level, they are sometimes actual courses, or additional time within courses, added to the schedule. Monitoring takes place monthly or twice monthly. Progress monitoring can look different depending on the type of intervention in place, but it needs to be happening with all interventions. Chapters 4, 7, and 10 contain more specific information regarding data and data collection.

Plan Implementation

Intervention fidelity is a big deal. If we do great screening work, identify all the right students, analyze thoroughly what the group needs, develop the perfect intervention to address these needs, and then don't implement our plan with fidelity, our work and our students' time is wasted. Let's carefully examine implementation fidelity and its related issues in order to provide strong support for this step.

What Is Implementation Integrity?

James Tibballs (1996) reports in the *Medical Journal of Australia* that only 12 percent of physicians in a pediatric intensive care unit washed their hands after patient contact. When another sample of doctors was surveyed about their behavior, they reported that they washed their hands 50–95 percent of the time, but when they were surreptitiously observed, their actual rate was as low as 9 percent. Commenting on this study, Pritchard and Raper (1996) wrote:

> It seems a terrible indictment of doctors that practices and protocols must be developed to take the place of something as simple as hand washing. Perhaps an even bigger concern for current medical practice, and one which should lead us all to do some soul searching, is that careful and caring doctors can be extraordinarily self-delusional about their behavior. (pp. 389–390)

A critical and often overlooked feature of implementing intervention at the system or individual level is ensuring that the there is integrity of implementation (Upah & Tilly, 2002). The terms *treatment*, *integrity*, and *treatment fidelity* are used interchangeably in the research literature (Gansle & Noell, 2007; Glover & DiPerna, 2007). The definition of *integrity of implementation* we use for this book is the degree to which planned instruction is implemented as designed (Gresham, Gansle, Noell, Cohen, & Rosenblum, 1993). Implementation integrity is established by adhering to a protocol for how instruction is delivered at the building, classroom, and individual levels (Glover & DiPerna, 2007; Johnson et al., 2006).

Why Should I Care About Implementation Integrity?

Consider the following real-life example.

A secondary-level problem-solving team designed a repeated reading intervention for three students not making progress in a remedial general education language arts class. After the intervention had been going on for several weeks, the school psychologist happened to be in the room and realized that the implemented plan had very little in common with the intended plan: the teacher was the one doing the repeated reading while the students followed along; a student textbook was being used for the reading material rather than an easier passage; and the intended correction procedure was not being used. One cause of the disparity in process was that, while the interventionist had been given written procedures of the intervention protocol, she did not receive explicit training, modeling, and practice before implementing the intervention with students. The school psychologist also discovered that students were not coming to participate in interventions on a regular basis, because they did not perceive the intervention as relevant to their needs. The school psychologist and the problem-solving team learned that fidelity of implementation was critical to ensure not only that high-quality instruction was provided but also that students were actually receiving it! The lesson learned is that *unless there is an intentional check of* implementation integrity, teams cannot be sure that interventions are being applied as designed (DuPaul & Stoner, 2003). Refer to the Implementation Status Checklist (page 39 and online).

How Can We Ensure Implementation Integrity?

The following are key proactive components of developing and implementing an intervention plan that has a high probability of implementation integrity:

▶ Select an intervention with a high probability of success.

▶ Communicate a clear plan to interventionists. Tell them exactly what you want!

▶ Ensure the intervention is acceptable and feasible to interventionists.

▶ Provide specific training and support to those implementing interventions.

▶ Ensure that the intervention is easy to implement. The more complex an intervention, the less likely it can be implemented with fidelity, no matter how talented the instructor (Lentz, Allen, & Erhardt, 1996).

▶ Emphasize increasing appropriate and prosocial skills as opposed to focusing on decreasing or punishing maladaptive skills (Clark & Elliott, 1988).

▶ Observe the intervention in action. Our guideline is to do the observation within forty-eight hours of an intervention starting.

▶ Make adjustments to the intervention plan when needed.

▶ Collect and graph data on the intervention goal.

▶ Ensure the intervention is compatible with the instructional environment. Can the intervention be implemented from a logistical, practical standpoint in the classroom or school environment?

What Is An Integrity Check?

An essential but frequently overlooked aspect to problem solving is completing an integrity check on an intervention. Although it is on our list, it deserves additional attention. An integrity check is an actual observation of the intervention in action to certify that it is being implemented as it was designed. While some may view this as an intrusive step, it's a critical component to the process. Teams must ask themselves, how do we know that the student is or isn't making progress due to the intervention and not some other outside influence? Teams must develop a system to ensure that integrity checks are being completed on the interventions being delivered. We suggest they be completed early (within forty-eight hours of implementation), so that if adjustments have to be made, they are done sooner rather than later.

The importance of ensuring implementation integrity across all practices within an RTI framework is noted in several publications (Gansle & Noell, 2007; Glover & DiPerna, 2007; Johnson et al., 2006), particularly in light of RTI being used as a process to identify learning disabilities. Lane, Bocian, MacMillian, and Gresham (2004) succinctly summarize the salience of ensuring treatment fidelity: "It is absolutely essential that treatment [fidelity] data be collected when conducting school-based interventions in order to draw accurate conclusions about the effectiveness of the intervention" (p. 37).

To make decisions about whether our practices and processes are influencing positive, negative, or stagnant outcomes, we need to know exactly how instruction is being implemented, how reliably data are being collected, and how well teams are using a problem-solving process for making decisions. For example, ensuring fidelity for a student receiving a supplemental intervention (Tier 2) and an intensive intervention (Tier 3) means that problem-solving teams can have increased confidence in making a referral to the special education team.

What Best Practices Ensure Treatment Fidelity?

Some resources suggest that a continuum of efforts directed at ensuring treatment fidelity be applied. These efforts include teacher self-report, interview, and record or permanent product review (Gansle & Noell, 2007). So far, research supports the use of direct observation as the most reliable and valid means by which to ensure treatment fidelity (Noell et al., 2005; Wickstrom, Jones, La Fleur, & Witt, 1998).

This method can pose very realistic challenges by requiring advanced planning and scheduling, and those efforts can be time intensive (Bollman et al., 2007).

While there is a continuum of methods by which treatment fidelity can be assessed, we advocate for districts and buildings to build capacity to support the use of direct observation, in order to ensure fidelity of implementation across all three tiers, especially RTI for special education entitlement. To do this, schools need to conduct targeted professional development focusing on what implementation integrity is, what instructional tools and strategies to use, how integrity will be established, and what decisions will be made using direct observation of instruction.

Is Direct Observation Necessary?

Let's go back to the study of handwashing by doctors (Pritchard & Raper, 1996; Tibballs, 1996). The U.S. Centers for Disease Control and Prevention (2002) estimated that about 1.7

million patients would contract a nosocomial (hospital-transmitted) infection every year. Of these, 20,000 patients would die directly from the infection, while the infection would contribute to the deaths of another 70,000 people. As noted earlier, part of the problem is cognitive: doctors and nurses *think* they wash their hands more frequently than they actually do. Handwashing is so 19th century, and 21st century medical technology may give doctors a false sense of security.

Educational research reveals a similar message: a participant report alone is too unreliable and should *not* be used to evaluate integrity (Moncher & Prinz, 1991; Noell et al., 2005; Wickstrom et al., 1998). Consider the costs in terms of student and teacher time and resources, assuming we are implementing our practices with fidelity without actually checking to ensure they are happening as intended. Consider the fiscal and socioemotional costs of misidentifying a student as needing more intensive instruction or as having a learning disability when the conclusions are not true. The decisions we make are too high stakes for our systems, our staff, and our students for us to neglect trying to ensure 100 percent implementation of our instruction and interventions. We serve our children best by being circumspect and not allowing confidence in our skills to translate into a sense of infallibility. You really do need to complete the direct observations.

A common and understandable concern with any use of direct observation is whether it will be used as part of staff evaluation. This is not what the observation is intended to be. In fact, we strongly discourage the use in any staff evaluation process of direct observation to document instructional integrity within this problem-solving process. The primary purpose this observation serves is to establish whether or not the intervention plan or curriculum is implemented as planned for the benefit of making decisions about instructional programming for an individual or for groups of students. Period. We find that once integrity checks through direct observation become part of a school's culture, accusations or concerns that these observations are being used to evaluate teachers rather than the intervention itself wane. In fact, we find that staff value them and appreciate the collaborative nature that accompanies the direct observations.

How Do I Create Intervention Scripts and Checklists?

Intervention scripts provide a step-by-step protocol to follow. Their use has been directly related to positive outcomes (Ehrhardt, Barnett, Lentz, Stollar, & Reifin, 1996; Hirallal & Martens, 1998). An intervention script can easily be translated into an intervention checklist, which is an observable task analysis of the major elements of the instruction or intervention.

One of the biggest challenges for administrators is finding someone who has flexible time to conduct the necessary observations. To that end, we offer the following suggestions:

▶ Utilize staff who have flexible schedules, such as school psychologists, Title I teachers, guidance counselors, school social workers, and administrators, to name a few.

▶ Allow certified staff to use their prep time for conducting direct observation fidelity checks on interventions in place of other duties, such as supervision, detention, lunch duty, or other such assignments.

Plan Evaluation

In Tier 2, we are asking whether the students who participated in supplemental interventions achieved expected grade-level outcomes as a result of the additional supports supplied. Remembering our 80-15-5 triangle, these interventions are supported for the 15 percent of students in the yellow, but our goal is for those students to score in the 80 percent–green area at least by the end of the year. If our intervention is not achieving this outcome for at least 50 percent of the students identified, the team must question whether the intervention was sufficiently robust, or if it was well matched to the needs of the students being served. This evaluation, in addition to evaluating the progress on each student's graph, helps buildings move forward on continuous improvement.

Next, we turn our attention to details related to making problem solving at Tier 2 happen in secondary buildings. We address questions related to who engages in this process and the organization of this collaborative work. We begin by discussing the team of staff who would manage the work of problem solving at this level in a building.

What Is the Role of the Problem-Solving Team?

In chapter 3, we discussed the idea of secondary buildings supporting several teams to conduct problem solving at various levels. We suggested an overall leadership team, a core team, a Tier 2 team, a problem-solving team, and a special education team. In a well-developed system, these teams all use the same problem-solving process to review the progress of their assigned students on an ongoing basis. Establishing clear delineation of roles and interaction points among multiple teams is critical to the efficiency of the system. Establishing consistency in utilization of the problem-solving structures is also critical to success. In this chapter, we discuss the role of the Tier 2 team in greater detail.

Problem-Solving Team Members Across Teams

All problem-solving teams exist to support the academic and behavioral progress of individual students and groups of students. Regardless of the specific role of a particular team, we offer guidelines about the structure of these teams and the meetings that occur to increase effectiveness. First, consider size and membership. Each problem-solving team consists of five to ten building staff members. This is not so small as to overburden individual staff, but not so large as to make meetings unwieldy. The membership of this group is specifically arranged to be representative of the group served by the team. This means the majority of problem-solving team members are general education teachers, except in an instance in which a problem-solving team is developed for the specific purpose of supporting students identified as needing special education.

The principal is always a member of all teams for several significant reasons. First, as an instructional leader of the building, the principal communicates values and expectations with regard to student service through his or her actions. Full participation in problem-solving teams establishes a data-based problem-solving orientation as the behavioral norm for all building staff. Second, the authority of the principal is needed to make decisions regarding allocation of resources. Problem-solving teams need this authority to design intervention plans that might utilize resources in new or different ways to meet student needs. Third, principals benefit from and appreciate active and ongoing knowledge of specific efforts supporting at-risk students in the building.

Other members to consider include a specials teacher (physical education, music, art), who brings the unique perspective of knowing referred students in a less traditional academic setting, often across multiple years. In addition, a special education teacher may participate as a consistent member of the teams. It is critical, however, that the majority of problem-solving team members are general education staff. Often, in secondary settings, school counselors are members of problem-solving teams. Administrators see such participation as a valuable part of the counselors' role. As a means of utilizing resources and staff time more efficiently, some buildings elect to train a large number of staff on the problem-solving process and then use different subsets of these members in an extended version of the problem-solving team, depending on the individual student of concern. This practice also serves to build common vocabulary and understanding of the thought process used to address the needs of all students in a building.

Logistics of Tier 2 Problem-Solving Meetings

Everyone acknowledges that reviewing data is a key aspect to successfully implementing RTI. As with many aspects of RTI, the details are of paramount concern. Who should be at the data review? What types of data will be reviewed? How frequently will we meet? How many data points do we need to make an instructional change? The answers to these and other similar questions are essential aspects to consider when performing data reviews.

Team Membership

In some buildings, particularly in middle schools, grade-level or core teams may be able to take on the responsibilities of monitoring student progress through standard Tier 2 interventions. A nice feature of this organization is that, by virtue of the team being the same for Tiers 1 and 2, there will likely be high levels of continuity between core instruction and interventions. At other times, particularly in buildings serving grades 9–12, we have found that operating separate teams that focus solely on students in Tier 2 interventions are needed. The membership of these teams should include the teachers who deliver the Tier 2 interventions, a building administrator, and if not already represented on the team, someone who delivers core instruction in the areas of concern for academics. In addition, you may consider including any paraprofessionals who are involved in intervention delivery. Often the school psychologist in the building acts as facilitator on many teams, including this one.

Some buildings' RTI teams have gone so far as to separate Tier 2 intervention monitoring into unique teams covering math, reading and language arts, and behavior. We've all sat at many meetings in our professional careers in which the purpose and content of the meeting had no correlation to our daily tasks. By streamlining the groups, the meetings can have a defined purpose, specific data to review, and identified team members—all essential components of an effective team meeting. The idea of having multiple teams also forces a school to have a strong leadership team whose role is to oversee the teams and serve as the moral compass of the process.

Scheduling

Meetings must be scheduled or they will not happen. When we say schedule the meetings, we mean schedule them at the beginning of the year so everyone knows the schedule for the entire year. Staff may have the best intentions, but the reality is, they're busy! By scheduling all meetings, you send the message that they are important. The key team members know to arrange their schedules around the assigned dates and times, and team members have built in accountability to the team. We advocate that the progress of every student involved in a Tier 2 intervention should be reviewed at least every eight weeks, with opportunity to review progress more often if growth is not adequate. We recommend setting up a longer meeting every other month, with a shorter meeting in the intervening months as a minimum.

Technology

The idea of working smarter, not harder, applies to RTI as well. In all aspects of implementing RTI, look to technology to assist in managing your student data. Teams should have a laptop computer and LCD projector available at meetings to make data displays easy to read for the entire team. Also, recording notes of decisions in electronic format during the meeting and making them accessible to all team members can assist with task completion and save time outside the meeting.

Facilitators

Who should facilitate the team meeting is always a good question. In many systems, the school psychologist has the training and background in RTI. We suggest that whoever facilitates should have completed problem-solving training and facilitator training and have a personality that can manage conflict and keep a team focused on the agenda. We also suggest you have a backup person if ever the primary facilitator cannot be at the meeting. Keep in mind, you have set the meeting dates for the entire year, so rescheduling will be difficult. It's better to hold the meetings, regardless of who is unavailable for a particular gathering, and keep the team moving forward.

Meeting Purpose

Each meeting should have a defined purpose. Most RTI teams meet to review the status of their standard Tier 2 intervention programming and students. The meetings should have an agenda that is distributed to the team at least three days before the scheduled meeting. This allows the team members time to organize and prepare the necessary materials. It is also important that team members take responsibility for reviewing the agenda and giving input to its content. Leadership should give teachers the responsibility to add specific student names they want reviewed to the agenda. This does two things: it allows the group to begin thinking about what specific students and data they need to discuss, and it also allows the meeting to be well organized and structured to keep the meeting moving forward.

Data Review

As shown in table 10.1, the types of data to be reviewed depend on the purpose of the meeting.

Table 10.1: Data to Review According to Meeting Topic

Type of Meeting	Data to Review
English	CBM-R, CBM-WE, CBM-Maze, class grades
Math	Math probes (new and old), class grades

Attendance

Who attends the meetings will be directly correlated to the purpose of the meeting. If the Tier 2 team supports both reading and math, and all students to be reviewed on a particular day are involved only in reading interventions, then the math teachers may choose not to attend. The team members should be committed to attending all the necessary meetings, as defined by the agendas. This makes meeting facilitation a smooth process.

Graph Review

In our buildings, we've set the local norm that all students are reviewed every eight weeks at minimum. A data review schedule helps those who are collecting, scoring, and entering progress-monitoring data into the system used for scoring the information to be sure that the graphs being reviewed on any given week are as up to date as possible.

In many of our buildings, the review of all graphs every eight weeks truly does mean that a team views and discusses every single graph on this schedule. Particularly in settings in which the only students being progress monitored are those enrolled in Tier 2 or Tier 3 supplemental interventions, this is a regular part of the Tier 2 problem-solving team's role. However, some of our larger buildings have run into logistical challenges with this schedule due to the volume of graphs for review, the total number of students involved in intervention, or their agreement to monitor every child below target, regardless of whether he or she is involved in a supplemental intervention. In these instances, the team must establish a prioritization plan to provide sufficient time to review the graphs of those in need on a regular basis.

For us, a gated review system has helped make this possible. Within this system, each grade level has identified one point person to facilitate graph reviews. Prior to the team meeting, this facilitator reviews all the student graphs and places them into one of three possible piles. The first pile is made up of graphs showing greater-than-expected progress. Graphs in this pile have at least the three most recent consecutive data points plotted above the aimline for the graph. The second pile is made up of graphs showing progress as expected. These have the most recent data points on both sides of the aimline, with no more than three in a row above or below it. The third pile is made up of graphs showing less-than-expected progress. These graphs have at least the three most recent consecutive data points plotted below the aimline for the graph. If adherence to data collection practices is a problem, a fourth pile of graphs that don't have enough current data for decision making can be made, and these issues can be discussed at the group meeting.

At the group meeting, following this plan, the facilitator first shares with the team the percentage of total graphs reviewed that show students making expected progress or greater (the total of piles one and two divided by the total number of graphs reviewed). This celebration of growth is a nice way to begin the meeting. Following this discussion, the team can focus on pile three—those students who are making below expected growth and may need an intervention change. At this point, the facilitator may ask the team for names of students not yet discussed who are a priority for discussion at the meeting. Students may be included based on team member concern that an intervention change may be warranted, even if the data criteria did not identify the student. Next, the team may determine whether pile one is appropriate for students who may be ready to fade or discontinue interventions. Finally, the team may review pile two as time allows. This gated system helps ensure that discussions related to students whose programs need to be changed are prioritized. In chapters 8 and 11, we share more information on instructional planning and decisions made by teams.

Roles and Responsibilities

Team members need to have specifically identified roles and responsibilities at the meetings. One common pitfall is that the meetings become reporting sessions, and some staff begin to have the expectation that administration or school counselors are there to solve all the problems or that they have absolved themselves of responsibility by just reporting problems. It is essential that all team members be trained in the problem-solving process, including the steps, the questions asked at each step, and the tasks involved in addressing each question. This training helps guide the team and keeps a focus on the problem as a means to assist in identifying a solution.

The team needs to always keep in mind it is a *team*. All team members need to be willing to step up and tackle student issues, be creative in their thinking, and support each other. All team members should walk out of a meeting with an identified list of tasks that are their responsibility, a date by which the tasks should be completed, and a knowledge of whom they should report them to. This internal accountability system allows individuals and teams to hold each other accountable.

Length of Meeting

For the team to feel effective, the meetings must be kept to a reasonable amount of time. In our experience, meetings that last much beyond seventy to seventy-five minutes become unproductive. As teams become more confident in their problem-solving skills, they are able to facilitate discussions and make decisions quickly. But in the beginning, expect the process to feel cumbersome. If the teams have done an effective job of planning, members have given prior feedback regarding the students they need to discuss, and they have collected data and prepared for review at the meeting, teams can reasonably determine how much time should be allocated to each student. It's not always feasible to accomplish this task, of course, so all team members must come to meetings with their calendars. If a student's case cannot be resolved at a regularly scheduled meeting, or if the team goes into the meeting knowing there is an extremely intense problem to solve, a separate meeting might be needed. There, the team may consist of the school psychologist, school counselor, administrator, and any regular education teacher who needs to support the student and plan. The process followed at this additional meeting is the same problem-solving process utilized throughout RTI programming—except the number of team members may be smaller.

Effective Behaviors Monitoring Form

Through the course of working with teams on data review meetings, we have developed an observation form that includes features of these meetings we have found to be important to the successful functioning of the team and quality decision making. This form, included as a reproducible on page 186 as well as online at **go.solution-tree.com/rti**, should be completed by a knowledgeable observer of the team—someone who has expert knowledge of RTI but is not a regular team member—who provides concrete feedback on team functioning. Discussions of the results of this observation form are intended to support teams in continuous improvement of their functioning.

Conclusion

At Tier 2, problem solving becomes more individualized to the needs of groups of students. We encourage holding planned data reviews with strategic agendas to maximize the effectiveness of intervention implementation. In addition, the importance of ensuring implementation integrity within an RTI framework cannot be overstated. Direct observation is the best means of documenting this.

Tier 3 Assessment: Data That Drive Instruction

Measurements are not to provide numbers but insight.

—Ingrid Bucher

Advance Organizer

✓ *Assessment in Tier 3 is more frequent and more diagnostic.*

✓ *There is power in the use of curriculum-based measurement (CBM).*

✓ *Curriculum-based evaluation (CBE) is a useful and highly relevant method of diagnosing why academic problems may be occurring.*

✓ *Functional behavior assessment (FBA) is a useful and highly relevant method of diagnosing why social and behavioral problems may be occurring.*

Every school setting seems to have students who don't make expected progress in basic academic skills areas even when provided with systematic supplemental supports. If teachers have crafted strong, comprehensive core instructional programs that provide differentiated instruction to thoroughly address grade-level standards and have carefully designed standard supplemental supports that focus on common areas of additional need for students, then the number of persistently low responders will be few. These students will require the best from us as educators so their progress can be accelerated. For these most challenging learners, a most intensive assessment system will help guide our decisions.

In chapter 4, we described a system of Tier 1 screening for secondary schools. This model included assessment of basic skills for all students through grade 8 three times per year, a comprehensive review of multiple data points in preparation for each building transition year (grades 6 and 9), and ongoing regular screening for students in grades 9–12 who have not met grade 8 expectations and for students who are new to the school.

In chapter 8, we described a more frequent data collection practice to monitor progress of students identified through Tier 1 screening as at risk. Curriculum-based measures of academic skills have been appreciated for their sensitivity to growth as well as their time and cost efficiencies for this purpose. Collecting monthly or twice monthly progress-monitoring data for at-risk students allows teams to understand the growth individual students are making—and by extension, the effectiveness of standard interventions that have been put in place.

In this chapter, we consider assessment practices that inform our work with students who have been persistent low responders to standard intervention efforts. We discuss both intensified progress monitoring efforts and diagnostic work to help teams understand and plan for the unique needs of these students. The discussion of these topics is intended to be an overview of the concept, not a comprehensive training on these techniques. See the references and resources section (page 203) for more information.

Progress Monitoring

For the Tier 3 level, we recommend an increase in frequency of monitoring. For some curriculum-based measures, weekly or twice weekly data collection becomes the norm at this level. One rationale for this increase in intensity is that fewer weeks elapse before a reliable trend line can be drawn. Research on growth on CBMs with younger students suggests that educators need twelve to fifteen data points before the resulting trend line representing a student's growth becomes stable (Christ, 2006). Although intervening for two to three months before deriving a reliable growth rate may seem reasonable, for many, waiting six months or more to begin an intervention is not. And so, the increased frequency of data collection allows RTI teams to make decisions at a pace that feels reasonable.

Some CBM assessments do not advise weekly or biweekly data collection—for example, the math applications assessments. Our analysis indicates that the standard error of measurement for this tool is greater than the expected weekly growth rate we have set based on predicting our state NCLB assessment on grade-level performance. In this instance, collecting these data weekly would not yield reliable information. For this measure, we collect data twice monthly on our most discrepant students, even though monthly data collection is completed for students in Tier 2 supplemental standard interventions. We uphold the concept of increasing frequency of data collection in this situation.

For some schools, the question of how often to collect these progress-monitoring data is not yet the pertinent question, because they are still grappling with whether these assessments are reliable and valid for secondary students; they are concerned about the use of fluency-based assessment, especially at secondary level. Their argument is that teachers, perceiving pressure to increase fluency scores for students, focus their instructional efforts on building student speed in basic skill areas rather than on rich instruction focused on developing deep understanding of concepts and critical and creative thinking about content. While research on acquisition of both math and reading skills supports the need and benefit for automaticity with basic skills such as math facts, letter identification, and word reading, quality instruction in math and reading cannot end with fluency alone. Believing that a low reading CBM score universally indicates the need for reading fluency training alone is a gross misinterpretation of the score. The idea that drilling students to increase speed in reading without paying attention to other instructional priorities such as word analysis, vocabulary, comprehension, and motivation for reading will create good readers is dangerously misinformed. Understanding that CBMs are much more robust indicators of reading skills, including rate, prosody, accuracy, and comprehension is paramount to preventing misuse and misinterpretation of the CBM results and countering the tendency to use fluency training to create speed at the cost of other important reading skills.

The Power of CBMs

Understanding the power that lies in the validity of CBMs is critical to supporting their use. Remember that oral reading fluency, for example, is highly correlated with other broad measures of total reading and has been shown to accurately predict student performance on measures of broad reading. So, rather than mistakenly thinking of CBMs as an end in and of themselves, we more accurately see them as indicators of broad knowledge in the content area.

When working with a student who has demonstrated poor performance on reading CBMs, the knowledgeable teacher understands that there is a strong indication that the student needs an intervention in the area of reading, but the type of instruction the student needs cannot be determined based on this assessment alone. Additional diagnostic information is needed to help focus instructional priorities. The teacher also understands that the reading CBM will act as a sensitive measure of growth and provide feedback on the student's growth in total reading skill.

A question of level is occasionally raised at this point. Specifically, what grade level of assessment materials should be used to monitor progress for these at-risk students? We maintain that use of enrollment-grade-level materials (through grade 8) makes the most sense for general education students. Our rationale is, in part, ideological. If we are monitoring progress, then we have set a goal for our desired student outcome. Our goal for general education students should be grade-level standards attainment within the school year from an efficacy perspective; after all, outside of those whom we have identified as needing special education support, for which students would we not have a goal of grade-level standards attainment?

Our argument is also practical. From a research perspective, we know how much growth we should expect on grade-level materials within progress-monitoring assessments. We don't have norms or standards of expectation for growth for students being monitored outside of grade-level materials. So, interpreting growth rates becomes difficult. This being said, despite strong efforts within a district, there may be several secondary students who have fallen quite far behind grade-level expectation. For those students, setting goals of grade-level proficiency may seem overly aggressive. However, setting such a goal sets the tone and expectation for the intensity of instructional intervention these students need to get on track.

As a note, progress-monitoring materials are commonly developed only through grade 8. This, of course, means that students in grades 9–12 will be using out-of-grade-level materials for progress monitoring. Because the purpose of the curriculum-based measures is to monitor progress of basic academic skills, it makes sense that high school probes would not be developed. These would need to be more challenging than what is typically considered a proficient level in basic academic skill areas, and thus working outside the accepted purpose of the measures. Students on target in grades 9–12 certainly continue to make growth in academic areas, but this growth is over and above their work to become basically proficient readers, writers, and mathematicians.

Diagnostic Assessment for Academic Skills

An important purpose of diagnostic assessment is to help educators understand why a student is experiencing difficulty. There are certainly formal standardized diagnostic assessments designed to do this. Although the assessments may be proven reliable and valid, they are often criticized, because their organization and common usage reinforce investigation of within-child problems or pathologies to explain student difficulty. Another concern about formal diagnostic assessments is that they may not contain content that is representative of or consistent with work representing the student's classroom experience. As such, the assessment may be less relevant to real school experiences, and may require educators to make inferences about how performance in one setting relates to performance in another. In addition, often diagnostic tests are not designed to be utilized repeatedly to monitor growth or change in learning over short periods of time.

Another option that holds appeal is the use of low-inference assessments that help educators analyze student performance on specific classroom expectations. One such method, curriculum-based evaluation, written about primarily by Ken Howell and Victor Nolet (2000) of Western Washington University, provides a process for hypothesis-driven inquiry regarding student challenges. Curriculum-based evaluations are best defined as "any set of measurement procedures that use direct observation and recording of a student's performance in a local curriculum as a basis for gathering information to make instructional decisions" (Deno, 1987, as cited in Shinn, 1989, p. 62).

For example, consider a student who is experiencing difficulty in his mathematics class, as evidenced by poor homework completion and test grades. Educators may be able to determine the root of this problem through a series of student interviews and informal assessment experiences: given a word problem, can the student set up a formula to calculate the solution? If not, can the student complete the procedure to solve a problem once it is written in mathematical language? If the student does not show proficiency with completing problems, is there evidence that the correct process was not used? Or was the process right, but a lack of basic-facts mastery caused the problem?

Talking with students about their thoughts as they complete schoolwork and observing them as they complete schoolwork, we argue, are viable alternatives to more formalized testing at this stage. Following the problem-solving model, hypotheses generated through this informal assessment model should be tested formally through a review of student growth rate on CBM progress-monitoring data. If the diagnostic information collected successfully points to an area of student need that, when addressed through intervention, meaningfully increases the student's rate of improvement, then it has served its purpose. In this hypotheses-driven model, we use informal assessments to help design interventions and formal standard assessments to measure the success of our intervention design.

The "Daly 5"

A second and somewhat related model that is useful to educators seeking to use good analysis skills to match instruction to student need consists of the five reasons for academic failure suggested by Ed Daly and his colleagues (Daly, Witt, Martens, & Dool, 1997). Within this model, teachers are asked to differentiate between problems caused by students who: (1) are not interested in doing the work, (2) need more practice to become fluent, (3) need more instruction to be proficient, (4) need support in generalizing across content, and (5) are missing prerequisite skills needed to perform the focus task.

Consider the problem analysis a team would use to determine which of these five hypotheses might be in play for a student. First, we could motivate the student to do his or her best work on a task by offering desirable incentives to see if work quality increases. If it improves substantially in the face of motivation, a team may reasonably suspect that Hypothesis 1 is accurate. Hypothesis 2 describes a student who can perform the expected task, but does so haltingly, or with great effort. If asked to think aloud through a task, these students eventually get to the correct response, but perhaps through a circuitous route or with some trial and error. Students who need more instruction (Hypothesis 3) display greater error rates on expected tasks, though they demonstrate the skills to complete any component task expectations.

In Hypothesis 4, the student may be able to complete a task following one specific method, but may not have enough mastery of the concept to work flexibly through different methods to attain the same result. Finally, Hypothesis 5 is often confirmed through analysis of permanent product in which a lack of the building-block skills can be seen inhibiting the student's ability to complete more complex tasks. Careful interviews with and observations of students as they complete work, with running commentary and reviews of permanent products, provide teachers important insight about what is causing difficulty for students—and by extension, what students need to make progress.

Diagnostic Assessment for Social and Behaviorial Skills

In chapters 3 and 7, we described screening and progress monitoring for social and behaviorial concerns, often in the form of frequency counts for office discipline referrals and frequent ongoing data collection on salient behaviors to monitor progress. As with academic concerns, progress monitoring continues in Tier 3, typically with increased frequency to yield a richer data set for decision making. Although the purpose of this book is not to provide in-depth training or information on diagnostic assessments in academics or social behaviors, we do want to say a word about this more intensive assessment system for social behavior here. Typically, when social behaviors rise to the level of concern of Tier 3, it means that the students are in the top 5 percent of most challenging behaviors in the school setting. A functional behavior assessment will be most useful to assist teams in understanding why the problem is occurring and determining what can be done to reduce or eliminate the problem behavior.

The following section is intended to offer an overview of the FBA process. Learning to conduct an FBA takes special training and many hours of practices to be proficient. The building school psychologists is a good resource to call on when this level of diagnostic assessment is needed. A good FBA should reveal the following information (O'Neill, Horner, Albin, Storey, & Sprague, 1997):

▶ Operational definition(s) of problem behavior(s)

▶ Identification of the contexts (locations, activities, routines, times of day, people) where the problem behaviors are most likely and least likely to occur

▶ Identification of the specific antecedent events, or triggers, that are most likely to predict the identified problem behaviors

▶ Identification of the consequences that maintain or reinforce the problem behavior

The sequence of steps for conducting an FBA are:

1. Identify the target behavior of concern.

2. Collect data to better understand the problem behavior using multiple data sources including a record review, functional assessment interviews, and functional assessment observations. Note that data that give examples of when the problem behavior occurs and when it does not occur are equally useful.

3. Create an observable, measurable definition of the target behavior.

4. Use the information from step two to build a sequence for the chain of events or a hypothesis statement explaining why the problem behavior occurs. A summary of this step is called a competing behavior pathway model (O'Neill et al., 1997). This includes identification of the setting events and antecedents and consequences and reinforcers.

5. Within this model, identify the appropriate behaviors that will be taught to replace the inappropriate behavior that is problematic.

6. Develop a positive behavior support plan that will provide intensive teaching of the appropriate skills, reinforce those skills through positive means, and detail consistent, logical consequences for demonstration of the inappropriate behavior.

Note that an FBA is different from a functional analysis. A *functional analysis* involves direct observation of problem behavior during experimental manipulations of environmental events. This allows systematic identification of the antecedent events that occasion problem behaviors and the consequences that reinforce them. A functional analysis must be conducted by someone with specialized training—for example, a behavior analyst. This type of analysis is not discussed in this text.

Table 11.1 provides two examples of problem behaviors with specific, observable definitions together with descriptions of behavior frequency, duration, and intensity.

Table 11.1: FBA Summary Table for Two Behaviors

Descriptive Name	Definition	Frequency	Duration	Intensity
Out of place	Subject will not remain seated in class; often gets up to sharpen pencils or throw things away. This may precede more disruptive behavior and typically escalates into arguing.	Daily—usually earns a referral after several redirections	Varies from a few minutes of each class to an entire class period	Moderate to intense
Arguing	When a redirection is given, student often argues with staff to delay the onset of a task—verbally refuses to work, refuses to remain seated, or has a disrespectful tone and may swear.	Daily—usually earns a referral after several redirections	Varies from a few minutes of each class to an entire class period	Moderate to intense

The team uses multiple sources of data to develop some hypotheses about why the problem behavior is occurring. The question the team is trying to answer is, What is the function or what purpose does the problem behavior serve? For example, does the student obtain attention from adults and peers when he is arguing? Does wandering around serve to delay the start of an undesirable task that might be too hard or not appealing? Four common functions of behavior include getting attention, escaping or avoiding, gaining a tangible (for example, a concrete reinforcer), or gaining sensory stimulation (Alberto & Troutman, 2009).

Given a reasonably well-supported hypothesis for the cause of the problem behavior, the team may then design a plan to address it. The key is to determine replacement behaviors that are incompatible with the problem behavior. That is, teach the student an appropriate social or behavioral skill that addresses the identified function of the behavior, and then positively reinforce them for using it.

Figure 11.1 provides a visual summary of a pattern of specific problem behaviors from start to finish, as well as desirable replacement behaviors. The purpose of summarizing the information from an FBA using this format is to communicate in a linear and succinct way what precedes the problem behavior and what reinforces or maintains it. This visual representation helps problem-solving teams identify what to include in the intervention plan to assist prior to the antecedents, what replacement behavior skills are needed for the problem behavior, and how to positively maintain the identified appropriate replacement behaviors.

As with more intensive diagnostic data collection for academic behaviors, this functional behavior assessment does take more time and energy on the part of the school staff. The outcome of this effort is the greater likelihood of defining an intervention that effectively addresses the identified student concern.

As with all aspects of a child's educational programming, it's critical that communication with families is a priority throughout. This is especially true when intensive problem solving is needed in order to figure out what instruction will work for a child. Parents are invaluable partners with schools. Early and ongoing communication and collaboration with them benefits everyone.

Note that the steps for conducting an FBA are parallel to those for conducting problem solving. Figure 11.2 illustrates this comparison.

Setting Condition	Antecedent/Predictor	Desired Alternative Behavior	Maintaining Consequence/Function
Classroom setting	Redirection or task demand	Ask for help.	
		Problem Behavior	**Maintaining Consequence/Function**
		Arguing	Escape/avoid
		Out of place	
		Replacement Behavior	
		Follow instructions.	
		Accept consequences or criticism.	
		Disagree appropriately.	
		Accept no for an answer.	
		Accept decisions of authority.	
		Use appropriate voice tone.	

Figure 11.1: Example of a competing behavior pathway model.

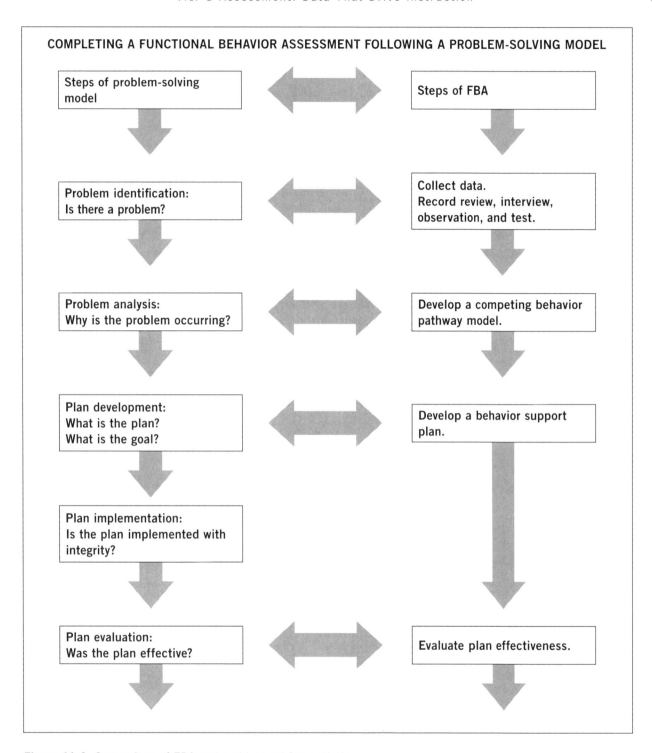

COMPLETING A FUNCTIONAL BEHAVIOR ASSESSMENT FOLLOWING A PROBLEM-SOLVING MODEL

Steps of problem-solving model ⟷ Steps of FBA

Problem identification: Is there a problem? ⟷ Collect data. Record review, interview, observation, and test.

Problem analysis: Why is the problem occurring? ⟷ Develop a competing behavior pathway model.

Plan development: What is the plan? What is the goal? ⟷ Develop a behavior support plan.

Plan implementation: Is the plan implemented with integrity?

Plan evaluation: Was the plan effective? ⟷ Evaluate plan effectiveness.

Figure 11.2: Comparison of FBA and problem-solving analysis.

Conclusion

Tier 3 assessment is defined as being more frequent and more diagnostic, so that specific skills are targeted for more intensive instruction. The diagnostic assessment for academics is curriculum-based evaluation. For social and behavioral issues it is functional behavior assessment. Implementation of these techniques requires more time and more training. Secondary systems will not address Tier 3 until screening and progress-monitoring procedures are already in place. It follows that a system will have the capacity to support Tier 3 assessment efforts when it is ready.

CHAPTER 12

Tier 3 Instruction: Intensive Support for Complex Learners

Effective teaching may be the hardest job there is.

—William Glasser

The task of the excellent teacher is to stimulate "apparently ordinary" people to unusual effort. The tough problem is not in identifying winners: it is in making winners out of ordinary people.

—K. Patricia Cross

Advance Organizer

✓ *Assessment in Tier 3 is more frequent and more diagnostic.*

✓ *There is power in the use of curriculum-based measurement.*

✓ *Curriculum-based evaluation is a useful and highly relevant method of diagnosing why academic problems may be occurring.*

✓ *Functional behavior assessment is a useful and highly relevant method of diagnosing why social and behavioral problems may be occurring.*

Considering the 80-15-5 resource allocation model for RTI, we anticipate that 5 percent of students in any building will need intensive, or Tier 3, instruction through general education even in the best case scenario. At this stage, intensive instruction is more individualized in both type and amount (Torgesen, 2004). Tier 3 instruction may be defined as instruction provided to a few students (in addition to core instruction) who need significant differentiation and greater intensity in their instruction.

A Shift in Focus

For instruction in Tier 2, one of our goals was to develop standard interventions that could be delivered efficiently to groups of students with similar needs in order to address our concerns for the groups of students, yet utilize the lowest level of resources possible. By the time students have reached the Tier 3 level, intervention teams have tried the standard group interventions and have been unsuccessful. At that point, we move to a more individualized, often more resource-intensive plan to address the unique and more significant needs of these students.

A Shift in Content

Tier 3 interventions in our model are individually developed by the building-based problem-solving team after a thorough examination of the student and his or her instructional needs. The student's program may include the implementation of a standard published curriculum, but will often also include some unique extension to personalize the program. It may be that the level of content needed is significantly below that of most other students in a particular grade level. Or, it may be that the number of models, practice repetitions, and type and amount of feedback that a student requires to learn the skills at hand are significantly greater than other students in the system.

You might, for example, assign a student to participate in a reading class using the Language! Curriculum for ninety minutes per day. You could then add an additional repeated reading fluency session for ten minutes each day, because you realize that the particular student needs more intense eyes-on-print practice time to generalize decoding skills and build automaticity. Note, importantly, that repeated reading to provide more practice might be an intervention that a team would implement with students falling in a Tier 2 designation as well. In other words, a particular intervention protocol might be used in less or more intensive interventions, with the difference depending on how the protocol relates to the whole program—and how it is implemented.

In Tier 3, we really see the connection between the data collection and hypothesis consideration processes in problem solving and intervention design. For example, if a team has collected specific diagnostic information in the problem-analysis step or tested student response to a series of competing interventions, finding the intervention that is most effective will lead directly to a discussion of continued implementation of that intervention. For behavioral concerns, knowing exactly what behaviors you are working on and what the desired replacement behaviors are—through a functional behavior assessment—gives teams a pretty good picture of what they need to do instructionally to affect progress. The better the understanding of the student's needs, the more perfectly the instruction can be designed. More details about these procedures can be found in chapter 13.

Instruction in Tiers 2 and 3 share many common features. The key here is to be clear about how *intensity of instruction* is defined. Distinguishing characteristics for Tier 3 instruction, relative to Tier 2, include instruction that is more precisely targeted at the right level, smaller instructional groups, more instructional time, clearer and more detailed explanations, more extensive opportunities for guided practice, more opportunities for error correction and feedback, and higher rigor.

Getting More Intense

Here's the big idea behind intensity of instruction:

1. **Problem identification**—You have a headache.

2. **Problem analysis**—This is because you are overtired from a poor night's sleep.

3. **Plan development**—Don't call the neurosurgeon when Tylenol would likely get rid of it.

When developing intervention plans, there should be a direct relationship between the severity of the problem and amount of resources being used to solve it (fig. 12.1).

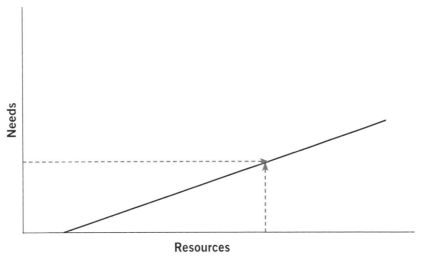

Figure 12.1: Needs versus resources.

When considering the intensity of instruction, teams should ask themselves, how severe is the problem or how great is the need? There are two important variables to consider when answering these questions:

1. **Level of student performance compared to peers or criteria**—This refers to how big the gap in performance is between the target student and his or her age or grade peers. This question also asks how big the gap is between the target student's performance and where the criterion for his or her performance is set.

2. **Convergence of multiple data sources to certify this discrepancy**—As stated in other parts of this book, teams should make decisions using multiple sources of information. They should not make important educational decisions about groups or individual students based on only one data point or one piece of information. The multiple information sources need to come together and converge on a particular hypothesis or reason for why the student's problem is occurring. This is all the more critical when teams are at a point where one or more interventions have been attempted without success.

What Does More Intensive Instruction Look Like?

Consider the following variables:

▶ More in-depth assessment or frequent progress monitoring (if needed)

▶ More precisely targeted at right level

▶ Smaller instructional groups

▶ More instructional time (frequency or length)

▶ Clearer and more detailed explanations

▶ More extensive opportunities for guided practice

▶ Higher rates of responding

▶ More opportunities for error correction and feedback

▶ Increased expertise of interventionist

How Intense Is Intense?

We know that one of the most powerful factors affecting student growth is engaged time. For this reason, the amount of time a student spends in interventions becomes a reasonable consideration when we think about intensity. There should certainly *not* be a one-size-fits-all requirement for the number of minutes a session lasts in order for the intervention to be considered Tier 3, or anything else for that matter. However, we can learn from published empirical research demonstrating that particular intervention models have been successful for students. Consider the following list of intervention schedules that have resulted in successful outcomes for small groups of students:

▶ Daily half-hour lesson for twelve to twenty weeks (D'Agostino & Murphy, 2004)

▶ Daily half-hour lessons for ten to twenty weeks (Vaughn et al., 2010)

▶ Sessions of thirty to fifty minutes, three times each week (O'Connor, Harty, & Fulmer, 2005)

▶ Sessions of thirty minutes, four times each week (Burns, Dean, & Foley, 2004)

▶ Sessions of twenty minutes, four times each week for two-and-a-half years (Torgesen et al., 1999)

▶ Sessions of fifty minutes, four times each week from October to May (Torgesen, Rashotte, Alexander, Alexander, & MacPhee, 2003)

Most of these interventions were implemented with students in elementary schools. We know that secondary students typically need more time in intervention. So, while we will not advocate for a specific rule related to time, there is a level of convergence that leads us to suggest that ten minutes every other day may not provide enough time to be effective. Teams really need to look at student data to answer the question of how intense is intense enough. If the student is making adequate progress, then the intervention is intense enough. If not, then the team needs to consider whether the intervention is not appropriately matched to the student's need, or, if it is well matched, whether an increase is required to accelerate growth. Time is one way to increase intensity.

Checking on Intensity: Asking the Right Question

We like to ask, as we are designing an intervention, will we be *surprised* if this intervention plan does not work? Think about it. Teams should be so confident in the interventions they design for students that they will actually be surprised if a student *doesn't* respond to the intervention. This sounds like a high standard, and it is. However, the alternative is really just wasting everybody's time. If your team cannot say with confidence that the intervention it designed will work to close the gap for the identified problem, you need to go back and reconsider whether the intervention is intensive enough. We work hard to avoid the perception (and the reality) that problem solving and interventions are just hoops to jump through in order to get to special education. If the team members don't honestly believe they are putting a plan in place that is going to be effective for the student, they need to do more planning.

Teaching Basic Skills at the Secondary Level

A long time ago in our schools, we made an agreement that we would not provide resource rooms to drag students through instructional content that was too hard for them to do on their own in other classes. Instead, we agreed to provide continued instruction in basic skills at the secondary level so that these students would gain the skills they need to access content across classes. This is not a universal stance in secondary buildings, especially among students receiving special education services (often considered Tier 3 interventions). A question to consider, for example, is whether your secondary building offers reading instruction to students in grades 6 to 12 using a research-based, explicit core curriculum. We would encourage you to consider this. Of course, all students deserve access to grade-level standards, which may be accomplished by adding a supplemental reading course to a core English course within students' schedules, or by implementing a replacement course that provides explicit systematic instruction in reading as well as content covering grade-level English and language arts standards. Realistically, this replacement course will require longer class periods per day to do a quality job and maintain a reasonable pace to close the gap for participating students.

Conclusion

At Tier 3, we use the best of what we know about effective instruction to create individualized plans and implement related interventions to address the needs of our students with the most challenging learning needs. By thoughtfully using our problem-analysis data, and by responding to ongoing progress-monitoring data of student growth, we can implement effective instruction to accelerate student growth. We can both teach missing basic skills and address grade-level standards through strategic planning.

CHAPTER 13

Tier 3 Problem Solving: Managing Intense Interventions

The significant problems we face cannot be solved at the same level of thinking at which we created them.

—Albert Einstein

A problem well stated is a problem half solved.

—John Dewey

Advance Organizer

✓ *Tier 3 consists of more resource-intensive and skill-specific targeted instruction provided through general education.*

✓ *With solid implementation of a problem-solving process, staff should be surprised if Tier 3 instruction does* not *remediate a problem.*

✓ *You can teach missing basic skills and address grade-level standards with wise and creative resource allocation and planning.*

At Tier 3, we use a building-based problem-solving team that addresses the individual needs of students who have not made sufficient progress within the general education curriculum alone, or with the additional supports that Tier 2 standard interventions provide. This small number of learners consists of our most discrepant, most complex, most challenging students within the general education setting. Our powerful five-step problem-solving process remains the best method for considering supports for these students. (See table 13.1, page 166.)

Problem Identification

If there is a challenge with Tier 3 problem identification, we find that it is in prioritizing the problem to be solved. It is no surprise that students referred for this level of problem solving present multiple complex issues that are often interwoven. Citing well-intentioned platitudes about considering the whole child, teams can make attempts to intervene in multiple areas simultaneously with a given student. We urge you to resist this temptation. Our

Table 13.1: The Five-Step RTI Problem-Solving Process

Problem Identification	What is the discrepancy between what is expected and what is occurring?
Problem Analysis	What is the performance discrepant?
Plan Development	What is our goal for closing this gap? What is the intervention plan for addressing the identified problem? How will we monitor student progress toward this goal?
Plan Implementation	How will be sure our interventions are delivered with integrity and fidelity?
Plan Evaluation	Did our plan work?

rationale is both practical and results oriented. Time and time again, we have witnessed teams who have tried to implement intense, multifaceted interventions across multiple areas for particular students all at one time. Predictably, these efforts fail. Most schools do not have the coordinated resources to pull all that off at one time. Teams become overwhelmed by the tasks they have set up for themselves, nothing gets done, and nothing changes for the student. Instead, we suggest that teams select one area for problem solving at a time, and work to develop a plan they believe has a high likelihood of success for the student. For the other areas of concern, allow whatever current supports are in place to continue. We have found that very often, if teams have developed an effective plan that results in improvement in the prioritized area of concern, these effects are generative. That is, the gains made in the prioritized area also positively affect performance in other areas of concern. Even if they don't, having already developed an effective plan for the first area, a team will have good momentum as it seeks to address a second.

A second reminder for teams in problem identification is to be broad and comprehensive in the collection of data. The acronym RIOT (review, interview, observe, and test) serves as a reminder of the main sources of data a team might access in order to understand the unique needs of an individual student.

Problem Analysis

At the individual student level, techniques such as curriculum-based evaluation, as discussed in chapter 11, are invaluable for determining the cause or function of the identified concern. The admonition to work within the realm of hypotheses that are within the control of school personnel continues to be critical at Tier 3. That is to say that, within-child deficits, while possibly present, are not a fertile ground for problem solving. Daly's five hypotheses (Daly et al., 1997) are a strong alternative starting point for teams. We also encourage teams to use the acronym ICEL (instruction, curriculum, environment, learner) as a prompt to think broadly about the interactions that may be resulting in difficulty for students. If we see problems as mismatches between the student's needs and the current resources offered, then we can think more strategically about what we can alter for a student to help create a more effective instructional match. To determine the best starting point, teams should ask if there is something in the instructional delivery that is problematic for the student (insufficient modeling), something about the content or curriculum being covered (less practice than is needed included in the materials), something related to the environment (nonoptimal seating arrangements), or finally something related to the learner (need for glasses) that could be the primary cause of the identified problem. To help you understand possible causes for student difficulty organized around ICEL, we offer a nonexhaustive list of examples. Take note that the examples are all situations that a school team could address.

Instruction

Instruction consists of the *methods and strategies* in which the curricula are delivered. What about the instruction is not meeting the student's need? Examples could be:

- ▶ Opportunities to respond

- ▶ Opportunities for positive practice

- ▶ Opportunities for generalization

- ▶ Instructional pacing

- ▶ Frequency of feedback and reinforcement

- ▶ Particular reinforcement and correction strategies

- ▶ Classroom management

- ▶ Format of instruction (teacher led, cooperative, computer)

- ▶ Instructional delivery (whole or small group)

- ▶ Opportunities for breaks

- ▶ Specificity or amount of modeling

- ▶ Level of consistency in instruction

- ▶ Particular approach or combination of approaches

- ▶ Total allocated time and engaged time

- ▶ Adaptations or accommodations

- ▶ Perceived relevance of the curriculum

- ▶ Nature of instructional demands

Curriculum

Curriculum is the *informational content* covered. What about the curriculum is not meeting the student's need? Examples could be:

- ▶ Focus of class is different from student's instructional need

- ▶ Content of class assumes knowledge of prerequisite skill student has not mastered

- ▶ Materials are insufficiently explicit

- ▶ Materials are not well aligned with curricular goals

- ▶ Task-related skills for displaying learning within curriculum

- ▶ Scope and sequence of content

- ▶ Insufficient repetition of new concepts

- ▶ Insufficient review of previously taught concepts

Environment

Environment is the *physical and social space* in which education is occurring. What about the environment is not meeting the student's need? Examples could be:

- ▶ Teacher : student ratio or class size

- ▶ Opportunities for practice and feedback outside of school

- ▶ Student's seating arrangement or classroom positioning

- ▶ Level of supervision

- ▶ Schedule of activities

- ▶ Length of bus ride

- ▶ Temperature, lighting, or noise level

- ▶ Disciplinary procedures

- ▶ Availability of resources and materials

- ▶ Opportunities for movement

- ▶ Visual appearance of classroom

- ▶ Accessibility of environment

- ▶ Peers as inadequate or inappropriate models

- ▶ Conflict with student instigated by peers

Learner

Learner is the *individual characteristics* of the student of focus. What about the learner is not meeting the student's need? Examples could be:

- ▶ Particular pattern of errors noted

- ▶ Apparent lack of motivation for task

- ▶ Physical impairment limiting task completion

- ▶ Utilization of strategies

- ▶ Distractibility

- ▶ Social skills

- ▶ Self-monitoring skills

- ▶ Nutrition

- ▶ Sleep patterns

- ▶ Attendance

- ▶ Language, speech, and communication

- ▶ Anger management

- ▶ Medication

- ▶ Health, vision, and hearing

- ▶ Adaptive and self-help skills

- ▶ Chemical use

- ▶ Mental health concerns

There is a high-quality and growing body of research on the topic of brief experimental analysis (BEA) that extends Daly's five hypotheses work and can inform quality practices in problem analysis at this most intensive level (Barnett, Daly, Jones, & Lentz, 2004; Daly & Martens, 1994; Daly et al., 1997). In BEA, specific interventions based on each of the five hypotheses are attempted in a hypothesis-testing model with a student to determine which one results in the greatest increase in performance. For example, after taking a baseline measure of reading, an examiner might try to elicit improved performance from the student through pure motivational techniques (testing Hypothesis 1, that the student is not interested in performing the desired task). Next, the examiner might try to elicit improved performance from the student by providing quality practice (testing Hypothesis 2, that the student needs additional practice with the task). By trying each of the five hypotheses and comparing the effects on student performance, the evaluator can identify which set of circumstances led to the greatest gain in performance. Knowing the type of intervention that causes the greatest performance increase provides explicit direction for plan development. The reader who is familiar with the differences between behavior assessment and behavior analysis will see the parallel here to behavior analysis, in that particular antecedents are implemented in order to trigger the target behavior so the behavioral responses can be measured to inform decision making. For example, the evaluator might try implementing two different conditions to trigger corrected reading: one might be using a small, desirable toy that a reader can earn if they demonstrate zero reading errors. Another might be asking the child to read the same sentences several times with the goal of increasing their fluency with each reading.

Plan Development

Goal setting for Tier 2 problem solving and Tier 3 problem solving are virtually identical. Intervention planning is done at the individual student level rather than for groups with similar needs. In developing an individual intervention, it is useful for teams to analyze the student's performance in the previous unsuccessful intervention, asking what it was about this previous intervention that was not ideally matched to the student's needs and how a new intervention could address this problem in a more suitable way. In developing a new intervention, the following questions must also be addressed:

▶ What is the intervention?

▶ Who will implement the intervention?

▶ Where will the intervention occur?

▶ When will the intervention occur?

▶ How often will the intervention occur?

Progress monitoring is often more frequent at Tier 3, occurring weekly or twice weekly or even more often for some measures.

Plan Implementation

All we shared about integrity checks at Tier 2 in chapter 10 is also true at Tier 3. Because interventions are typically individualized for these students, the need for a clear script is evident for managing consistency and integrity of intervention delivery. However, at the Tier 3 level we introduce a bit more give and take with integrity checks. In Tier 2, many times the interventions that are implemented are standard purchased programs. If you have purchased a standard intervention program that is supported by empirical research, then implementing it as designed by the publisher is only reasonable. In addition, as these interventions are delivered commonly to groups of students together, individualization is less possible. However, at Tier 3 we seek to be ultimately responsive to the needs of the individual student receiving the intervention. In addition, following a problem-solving model, it is possible that, rather than choosing an off-the-shelf scripted intervention, we may have less of a sense that the publisher is always right, and the team may develop a protocol with the student's unique needs in mind.

Consider for example, a repeated reading intervention implemented for a particular student. The team uses an intervention script previously developed that reflects four repetitions of the same piece of text, with different comprehension activities in between each activity.

Suppose that the teacher begins to implement this intervention and notes over a few sessions that the student's reading rate plateaus after the third repetition and that the error rate increases significantly during the fourth reading. The student's best read is consistently the third one. It would be desirable for the intervention implementer to be able to make an adjustment to the intervention based on these data and, following this, an adjustment to the intervention script so that the written record of the intervention that was actually implemented is accurate.

We also encourage teams to consider two aspects of implementation integrity. The first is completing an observation to certify that the intervention was implemented as intended (at least once). The second refers to intervention dosage—that is, whether the student has received as much of the intervention as planned. Problems with attendance or transition to or from the intervention time may result in the student receiving less than the planned support. Knowing this will assist teams in evaluating the plan.

So in summary, for plan implementation, we are still highly focused on establishing that we have implementation integrity with our planned intervention and an accurate record of what the implemented intervention actually looked like.

Plan Evaluation

In this step, teams are reviewing student data and determining whether there has been sufficient growth on the part of the student involved in the intervention. Decision-making guidelines described in chapter 8 are applicable here as well. In the plan evaluation step, we see the ongoing cyclical nature of this process.

Teams may determine that the student is making good progress toward the goal but that the plan should be continued for additional time (staying on Step 4). Or teams may decide that the identified problem was entirely solved and move on to problem identification of another problem the student is experiencing (back to Step 1). Alternately, the student's problem may not be solved, and a team may decide to stay with the same problem identification statement but create a new hypothesis (back to Step 2). Some teams may feel they still need to work on the problem, that their analysis of the problem was correct but they need a new plan to support the student (back to Step 3). Finally, a team may continue to focus on the same problem with the same hypothesis and intend to correct a problem with integrity in order to move forward (back to Step 4). This continuous look through the five-step problem-solving process has potential stopping and re-entry points all along the way.

Given this theoretical (and practical) overview of the steps of problem solving as they relate to Tier 3, we now turn our attention to some of the logistics of operation for the problem-solving team.

Problem–Solving Team Roles

Any problem-solving team needs to have a designated *facilitator*, a person in a leadership position whose charge is to ensure the integrity of the overall problem-solving process, consult and assist with the completion of specific steps, ensure any documentation is kept current, and so on. We say more about this role at the end of this chapter.

In addition to a facilitator for each team, an additional member takes on the role of note taker. The note taker is responsible for making sure that any problem-solving paperwork is completed for all students in a timely manner, with decisions of the team documented during the course of each meeting. Some buildings have computers and LCD projectors dedicated to the problem-solving teams so that electronic copies of student graphs as well as the problem-solving paperwork can be accessed easily and displayed for the team during meetings. We strongly recommend that the roles of facilitator and note taker are practiced by two different members of the team if meetings are to run efficiently. There are several other common member roles and tasks beyond these two, summarized in table 13.2.

Table 13.2: Roles, Tasks, and Skills for Problem-Solving Team Members

Role	Tasks	Skills Needed	Additional Comments
Time Keeper	Keeps team on track by setting time limits publicly	Assertive	May have another role in the meeting Sets time limits before meeting
Referring Teacher	Attends all meetings and collects data when necessary Responsible for intervention development and implementation	Aware of **who** does what at a problem-solving meeting	Has role only during the meeting
Data Manager or Content-Area Representative	Communicates with parents and staff Makes sure all tasks are completed prior to the next meeting and the intervention is implemented Assists referring teacher with the process for referral	Organized Comfortable with data	Helps to have written guidelines Best to rotate role
Team Members	Participate during meetings Responsible for data collection and intervention implementation	Trained in problem-solving process	Not necessary to know the student All members committed to problem solving

Role	Tasks	Skills Needed	Additional Comments
Principal	Assures implementation of the problem-solving process and the importance of the initiative Responsible for resource allocation Monitors staff climate	Willing to take risks Prioritizes student needs	May have another role on team
Note Taker	Responsible for documentation standard forms Verbally summarizes information for the team Records assigned tasks Records main problem-solving decisions	Detail and task oriented Fluent in the problem-solving steps	Uses forms and technology to communicate publicly
Facilitator	Ensures integrity of the process Supports effective communication Keeps the team on track Is able to generalize problem-solving skills and knowledge of the process	Knowledge of the problem-solving process Assertive Strong leader	Carefully selected; not every member makes a good facilitator

Meeting Logistics

Teams typically meet one time per week for approximately forty-five minutes each meeting. For buildings that elect to have part-time members that function as part of an as-needed extended problem-solving team, all members agree to keep the pre-established time open in their schedules with the understanding that they may not participate in every meeting.

Once we have the five steps of the theoretical problem-solving model internalized, it is helpful to think about how these steps relate to a common meeting format. First, it is important to understand that many of the activities related to problem solving happen outside of the formal meeting time. Let us consider a specific case as it might relate to problem-solving meetings.

We begin with a referral to the problem-solving team, which in this instance is made by the Tier 2 team regarding a student who is not making expected progress. This student is enrolled in grade 7 communications, the core language arts course for the grade level, in addition to a supplemental class using Corrective Reading C (direct instruction curriculum from SRA/McGraw-Hill) and Rewards (direct instruction curriculum from Sopris-West) to build needed decoding and word attack strategies to improve reading skills. The referring team fills out a brief referral form, such as the Teacher Request for Assistance Form (see the reproducible on page 178 and online at **go.solution-tree.com/rti**), and submits this form to the building school psychologist, who is the facilitator of the problem-solving team.

At the next meeting, the team places this student on the agenda for a brief discussion for initial planning. One member is identified to gather records related to this student's past history and current progress (grades, AIMSweb graph, history of MAP and state test scores). Another team member is identified to work with the referring group to gather additional information about the current interventions, the identified problem, and possible hypotheses for the cause of the problem. This task may be accomplished through interviews or observations.

This information is gathered over the course of a week, and the team places the student on the agenda at the next meeting so the process can continue. At this meeting, the first step is to agree on a problem identification statement that reflects the current discrepancy in the prioritized area of concern. Once this statement is recorded (see the Problem Identification Screening Summary on page 79 and online), the team members consider the information they currently have available to determine if they have a reasonable hypothesis for why the problem is occurring. If the team does not have good evidence supporting a hypothesis, then plans for collecting the additional needed information are made at this time. For example, it may be determined that additional diagnostic information through CBE is needed to understand the pattern of skills the student is demonstrating. Alternatively, the team may decide to conduct a BEA to try out a few competing hypotheses in order to better understand the student's needs. Under these circumstances, hypothesis selection will be completed at the next meeting.

Once the team is able to identify a well-supported hypothesis (meeting two or three), this is recorded (see the sample Problem-Solving Team Analysis Form, page 181 and online), and the team moves on to plan development. The team begins by stating a goal for the student. General outcomes measures are well-suited for statements of discrepancy, goal writing, and progress monitoring because of their technical features—so we use them whenever possible. The level of aggressiveness of the goal will drive the level of intensity of the intervention. It is at this time that the team will work to determine the new intervention for the student, as well as to articulate the progress-monitoring plan. The plan development section of the problem-solving process should take the greatest amount of time and utilize the greatest variety of expertise on the team. It is important that those who will be implementing this intervention be present at the design meeting whenever possible. The details of the intervention are determined at the level of specificity that allows the development of a step-by-step written plan (see the sample Problem-Solving Team Intervention Form on page 182 and online at **go.solution-tree.com/rti**). Before leaving this meeting, the team must make plans to provide training to the interventionist and check on implementation integrity. A follow-up meeting for data review should be set for no more than eight weeks in the future, with an agreement that if problems arise before that time the student will be put back on the agenda sooner.

After the intervention has been implemented for eight weeks, assuming no intermediate meetings have been needed, the team places the student on the team meeting agenda for an intervention review. The team first reviews the integrity of implementation by examining the results of the observation and participation records for the student (see the sample Problem-Solving Team Plan Implementation Review form on page 183 and online). Having determined that the intervention was delivered as planned and that the student received the planned dosage, the team reviews the student progress monitoring graph to evaluate the rate of growth since the implementation of the current intervention. The team will decide if the data warrant continuation of the plan or alteration in some way. These decisions are recorded, and next steps in the problem-solving process are pursued (see the sample Problem-Solving Team Plan Evaluation Form on page 184 and online).

Notice that with the exception of the meeting in which the plan was developed, each of the other meetings involved only a brief activity on the problem-solving team's agenda. Five minutes or so should be all it takes at the meeting to plan for problem identification or problem analysis work. Perhaps in the most complex cases ten minutes may be needed to agree on a hypothesis. Plan evaluation is quick as well, because the data are available to tell the story. So, if a team has forty-five minutes to an hour for each weekly meeting, it can review several students within that time.

Facilitation of Quality Problem Solving

A common pitfall of problem-solving teams is expending a great deal of energy documenting process rather than product. By this we mean that during the meeting, many people take notes about what student issues are and what each person is going to do next. For example, Mr. Jones is going to conduct an interview with the parent, Mrs. Smith is going to gather permanent products to bring to the next meeting, and so on. What will often happen, then, is that a well-meaning facilitator will take time outside of the meeting to rewrite these process notes into a more formal document for distribution to team members. It is not that this is poor practice necessarily, but the problem comes when so much attention is paid to documenting process that attention is not paid to documenting product. By *product* we mean answers to the questions at each step of the problem-solving process. What was the prioritized area of concern? What was the discrepancy statement, and what converging evidence supports this? What is the team's main hypothesis about the cause of the problem? What is the goal? What is the plan? How will progress be monitored? Nailing down concrete and specific answers to these questions is a hallmark difference between a strong problem-solving team and a more common student-assistance team.

A critical role of the facilitator is to make the steps of the process, as well as the decisions that are made, explicit to all meeting participants. The statements made by the facilitator to do this will help the team keep on track and not get lost in assigning tasks. One way to do this is through the written agenda. Listing the name of each student who will be discussed in the meeting, along with the step of the process the team hopes to complete, will send a clear message of purpose to all team members. Table 13.3 provides a sample meeting agenda.

Table 13.3: Problem-Solving Agenda

Time	Student	Step
7:45	Lila	New referral: Plan to gather needed information for problem identification.
7:50	Gregory	Plan development: Set a goal, develop a plan, and determine progress-monitoring logistics.
8:20	Skyler	Plan evaluation: Review integrity, determine outcome of intervention, and plan next steps.
8:25	Bethany	Problem identification: Review data and converging evidence to prioritize area of concern, develop a discrepancy statement, and begin hypothesis generation.

A second way to do this is by posting a visual of the problem-solving process in the room or having it on the agenda. Third, facilitators can use anchor statements to communicate decisions and guide next steps. These may feel unauthentic or stiff, but they work wonders at keeping teams on track. Consider these sample statements:

▶ "It sounds like as a group we are prioritizing the area of math for Matthew at this time. Our next step is to decide what measure we will use to quantify a discrepancy between our expectations and his current performance."

▶ "Our problem identification statement is that Jodi engages in fights involving screaming on the bus four out of each ten bus rides on average, although the expectation is that this behavior would never occur. Now let's think about what we know already to generate hypotheses about why these screaming fights may be occurring."

▶ "We've agreed that Jeff's problem in reading appears to be occurring mostly because of careless errors in reading, which he does not seem to recognize. Now we will move on to develop a plan to address this concern. Let's begin by setting a goal for Jeff."

Evaluating Quality Problem-Solving Practices

In consideration of continuous improvement in problem-solving practice, we have developed and implemented an observational progress-monitoring feedback form for teams. This Problem-Solving Team Effective Behaviors Monitoring Form (page 186 and online) has two parts. The first poses questions related to general team functioning: active participation, presence of the administrator, timely completion of agenda items, and so on. Items were included in this list based on our observation of characteristics that appeared to be consistent with effective teams. The second lists all the different meeting sections that could take place, followed by a list of observable actions or decisions that should be present in each meeting section. For example, for a new referral, we have listed activities the team should complete for a student who is on the agenda as a new referral.

To complete this form, the observer must determine what section(s) of the problem-solving process will be addressed for each student on the agenda. The observer awards one point for each behavior listed that is observed by the team for each student. At the end of the meeting, the observer can add up the points from the top section as well as all points collected from the bottom section for a final score.

This form has been beneficial to our problem-solving teams in a number of different ways. Certainly having a quantitative score to compare across observations has provided a unique form of feedback related to growth of a team that may otherwise be difficult to measure. We have tried not to put too much stock in this score, given the experimental nature of our form. What has been more helpful is its use as a regular, explicit reminder of the actions and decisions that should be present at each step of the problem-solving process. Like the use of a rubric for feedback on student's written work, this form of feedback provides detailed examples of the expected behavior. Finally, this form has helped to increase consistency of feedback given to teams by those in the instructional coach role.

Conclusion

Problem solving at Tier 3 is a big project involving definite resources. We use this intensive process for our most discrepant students—those who need the best we have to get them back on track toward successful grade-level outcomes attainment. It is significant to note that as many as 85 percent of students involved in problem solving did not need evaluation for special education in one study (Hartmann & Fay, 1996). For some students, however, the pattern of performance in school or other information provided to the school may suggest that the student could be entitled to receive special education services. We argue strongly that quality problem solving should occur regardless of special education identification status. In the next chapter, we discuss the issues related to the entitlement decision within an RTI framework.

Teacher Request for Assistance Form

Use this form to document referral of a student by a teacher, general education team, or parent and describe the nature of the problem for which the referral is being made to the building-based problem-solving team.

School or District: _____

Student Information:

Name: _____

Grade: _____

DOB: _____

Parent Information:

Name: _____

Address: _____

Phone: _____

☐ Parent   ☐ Guardian   ☐ Noncustodial parent   ☐ Relative   ☐ Foster parent   ☐ Nonrelative

Teacher Information:

Name: _____ Best time to meet: _____

I contacted parents on _____ by ☐ phone   ☐ letter   ☐ note home   ☐ email   ☐ at conference

Result: ☐ Supports intervention   ☐ Other:

Reason for request for assistance: ☐ Academic   ☐ Behavior   ☐ Speech/Language

☐ Other: _____

Comments: _____

_____

_____

Student strengths: _____

_____

_____

Interventions attempted: _____

_____

_____

Form completion and turn-in date: _____

Problem Identification Screening Summary Form

Use this form to document and summarize all of the problem identification data that have been collected to determine what problem the problem-solving team will target. Problem-solving teams should be sure to use the data indicated on this form to develop their discrepancy statements.

School or District: _____

Student: _____ Date Form Completed: _____

CUMULATIVE FOLDER REVIEW

Health Information

☐ Vision concern
☐ Hearing concern
☐ ADHD
☐ Asthma
☐ Other diagnosis: _____

Attendance

\# Days absent last year: _____
\# Days absent current year: _____
Other concerns:

Previous Schools/Services

☐ Prereferral interventions—Dates: _____
☐ Title 1—Dates: _____
☐ SPED Eval/Services—Dates: _____
☐ Out of district—Dates: _____
☐ Retained—Dates: _____
☐ Home schooled—Dates: _____
☐ Other

Grades

Elementary

	Math	Reading	Writing
Above			
Meets			
Below			

Other concerns:

Secondary

GPA: _____
Credits earned: _____

INTERVIEW SUMMARY

	Parent	Student	Teacher
Date:			
Type of Interview:			

☐ Attach completed interview notes

CLASSROOM OBSERVATION

Date:		By:	
Type:	☐ Interval ☐ Frequency	☐ Latency ☐ Duration	☐ Other: _____ ☐ Other: _____

TESTING RECORDS

☐ Attach historical record of all local district and state testing results

PROBLEM IDENTIFICATION SUMMARY

Team met to review these data on: _____

Prioritized area of concern:

Discrepancy statement:

List at least two sources of convergent data that support this discrepancy:

☐ Baseline data are plotted on the attached graph

Disposition: ☐ Level 1: Grade-level team   ☐ Level 2: Consultation from support staff: _____
☐ Level 3: Problem-solving team   ☐ Level 4: Special education

Team members:

Team member responsible for follow-up:

How RTI Works in Secondary Schools • © 2012 Solution Tree Press • solution-tree.com
Visit **go.solution-tree.com/rti** to download this page.

Problem-Solving Team Analysis Form

Use this form to document the hypotheses and RIOT/ICEL data used by problem-solving teams to support or refute each identified hypothesis. Problem-solving teams should indicate their chosen hypothesis on this form.

School or District: _____

Student: _____ Date Form Completed: _____

Step 1: List all hypotheses regarding cause or function of prioritized problem.

Step 2: List all relevant data to support or refute each hypothesis listed.

	Hypotheses	R Review	I Interview	O Observe	T Test
I Instruction					
C Curriculum					
E Environment					
L Learner					

Step 3: Indicate selected hypothesis. Selected hypothesis must have convergent data to support including quantitative data.

Problem-Solving Team Intervention Form

Use this form to articulate the measurable, observable goal for the student, the specific details of the intervention to be implemented, and the progress monitoring of that intervention. Problem-solving teams should complete each piece of information to promote fidelity of implementation of the both intervention and progress monitoring. Finally, teams will need to document what criteria will be used to determine if the student is responding to the intervention and indicate when the team will review student progress.

School or District: _____

Student: _____ **Plan Development Date:** _____

Intervention #: ☐ 1 ☐ 2 ☐ 3 ☐ _____

Area of concern: ☐ Reading ☐ Math ☐ Writing ☐ Behavior

Goal: _____

_____

_____

INTERVENTION
Brief description:
Description of needed materials:
Intervention implementer:
When:
Where:
How often:
MEASUREMENT SYSTEM
Data-collection system:
Data collector:
What will be recorded?
Frequency of data collection:
When will data be collected?
DECISION-MAKING RULE
☐ Slope/trend analysis ☐ Consecutive data-point rule ☐ Level of performance ☐ Other: _____

Intervention Start Date: _____ Review Date: _____ Time: _____ Place: _____

Problem-Solving Team Plan Implementation Review

Use this form to document whether or not the intervention plan described on the Problem-Solving Team Intervention Form was implemented as described. A member of the problem-solving team should complete a direct observation of the intervention using an intervention checklist and attach the completed form to this form. Teams then use the observation information to document the implementation status of the intervention.

School or District: _____

Student: _____ Review Date: _____

Intervention #: ☐ 1 ☐ 2 ☐ 3 ☐ _____

☐ Attach completed, dated, intervention script observation form from initial observation

INTERVENTION PROTOCOL INTEGRITY
☐ Team agrees that the written intervention script fully matched the implemented intervention.
☐ Team agrees that the written intervention script did not fully match the implemented intervention from the initial observation.
Describe all revisions made to the intervention script:
☐ Attach completed, dated intervention script observation form after revisions were made documenting intervention integrity.

PLAN LOGISTICS INTEGRITY
☐ Team agrees that the intervention occurred for the number and duration of sessions as designed on the plan development form.
☐ Team agrees that the intervention did not occur for the number and duration of sessions as designed on the plan development form.
Describe differences between planned and actual intervention session number and length:

Problem-Solving Team Plan Evaluation Form

This form is used to summarize the achievement outcome of the intervention described on the Problem-Solving Team Intervention Form. Note whether or not the intervention plan was implemented as designed and progress monitoring data were collected as planned. Attach the graph of student progress data collected per the Problem-Solving Team Intervention Form to this form. Then use the decision-making rule identified on the Problem-Solving Team Intervention Form to decide on the outcome of the intervention plan.

School or District: _____

Student: _____ **Review Date:** _____

Intervention #: ☐ 1 ☐ 2 ☐ 3 ☐ _____

Midintervention Checks Resulting in No Change of Plan:

Date	# Data Points	Comments

Plan Evaluation:

Date: _____ Attach graph of student progress data.

This intervention began on _____ and continued through _____.

Total # of sessions received: _____

Total # of data points being considered: _____

1. As a result of this intervention implementation:
   ☐ *Goal was met*
   ☐ *Trend line shows student on track to meet or exceed goal*
   ☐ *Consecutive data points show student on track or meet or exceed goal*
   ☐ *Trend line shows student is not on track to meet or exceed goal*
   ☐ *Consecutive data points show student is not on track to meet or exceed goal*

2. For the academic concern for which student is not on track (or skip to item 3):
   ☐ *Trend line shows student making at least one year's growth in one year's time*
   ☐ *Consecutive data points show growth, with data points not far from aimline.*
   ☐ *Trend line shows student making less than one year's growth in one year's time*
   ☐ *Consecutive data points show scores far below aimline with very flat growth*

3. Optional comments regarding plan evaluation decision:

4. The next steps for the team will be to:
   ☐ *Discontinue intervention—goal met*
   ☐ *Maintain or generalize current plan*
   ☐ *Select a new problem (New Problem Identification form)*
   ☐ *Select a new hypothesis for the same problem (New Problem Analysis form)*
   ☐ *Retain current hypothesis, but modify the intervention plan (New Student Intervention Plan form)*

5. Is a referral for a special education evaluation being considered at this time?

   ☐ *Yes*   ☐ *No*

Next Meeting Date: _____

(If none is needed, information should be placed in the student's cumulative record.)

Problem-Solving Team Effective Behaviors Monitoring Form

Recorder:_____ Team:_____ Date: _____

	YES	NO		YES	NO
Today's meeting started on time.			The agenda for today was clearly communicated including goals and tasks.		
All members were present and actively participated.			Facilitator or Note taker reports that paperwork is complete and up to date.		
We got through our entire agenda.			Most of our meeting was spent developing specific solutions for students.		
Homeroom teachers/primary interveners were present.			Communication with teachers and parents regarding decisions was planned.		
SUBTOTALS:					

STEP	HIGH-QUALITY INDICATOR	STUDENT NAME				
New Referral	Concrete plans made to collect needed information for problem ID (who, what, when)					
Problem Identification	A discrepancy statement has been made using objective and empirical data					
	Converging evidence in support of discrepancy statement was identified					
Problem Analysis	Discussion of how problem is affected by all domains (ICEL) as appropriate					
	Evidence that team collected data from multiple sources (RIOT)—no obvious missing					
	Discussions related to multiple alterable hypotheses across RIOT/ICEL is observed					
	Evidence that team used data to determine skill versus performance function of problem					
	Evidence that team used data to differentiate between Daly's other four hypotheses					
	Discussions including specifics regarding student skills and needs are observed					
	A clear hypothesis was made that is supported by convergent data					
	Discussion of inalterable factors is minimized					

Plan Development	A goal statement has been made					
	The intervention is research based					
	The intervention appears sufficiently robust and connected to hypothesis					
	A clear implementation plan (script) is designed for the chosen intervention					
	A plan for monitoring progress using objective and empirical data was made					
	A plan to conduct an integrity observation was made					
Plan Implementation	A solution to a problem with implementation integrity was found					
Plan Evaluation	A direct observation of intervention integrity was reviewed					
	Decisions were recorded about both intervention integrity and dosage					
	Some quantitative data were reviewed—even if in raw form					
	A graph was reviewed by the team					
	Decisions were made about the quality of match between problem and intervention					
	Decisions were made about the effectiveness of the intervention					
	Decisions were made about next steps for the student					
	SUBTOTAL					
	TOTAL					

CHAPTER 14

RTI and Special Education Entitlement Under SLD

In an effective RTI system, special education is neither the placement to be avoided at all costs nor is it the catch-all for any student who is difficult to teach. Rather it operates as an integral part of the system.

—Evelyn S. Johnson, Lori Smith, & Monica L. Harris

Advance Organizer

✓ *IDEA provides the legal basis for connecting RTI with special education entitlement.*

✓ *There are some critical considerations before and during the establishment of decision-making rules for level and slope of growth.*

✓ *There exists a unique, research-based model of learning disability (LD) identification using criterion-referenced target scores.*

In considering students who are most discrepant and who need the greatest intensity of resources to make progress in our schools, it is natural to think about special education services and the interface those services have with system efforts to improve instructional outcomes. Indeed, special education can and should be a well-integrated resource within the total cascade of services offered by a school to meet the needs of the diversity of the student body. Those who work in special education know well that students must qualify to receive special education services. There are thirteen specific disability labels under which students could potentially qualify to receive these services, as defined in the federal special education law, IDEA. Nationally, over 6.5 million children are served under this law. While definitions of these categories are provided at the federal level, it is the job of each state to determine the specific criteria that students must meet in order to qualify for services under each category. As you might imagine, there is inconsistency across states related to criteria for each of the special education categories (Reschly & Hosp, 2004). Of all the categories, specific learning disability (SLD) is the most common, meaning that the greatest percentage of students identified to receive special education services are identified as meeting eligibility requirements under this category. It has also been among the most controversial categories, in part due to challenges with systems for determining that eligibility.

Decades of research have consistently questioned the validity of the most commonly used model for establishing the presence of a learning disability, the IQ-achievement discrepancy model. Despite decades of research proving the lack of validity of this model, it continues to persist in practice. Research has found that the model does not differentiate students with a learning disability from low-achieving students, is not consistently implemented, lacks adequate psychometric properties, and most importantly, does not inform instruction (Aaron, 1997; Fletcher, Coulter, Reschly, & Vaughn, 2003; Gresham & Witt, 1997; Vellutino, Scanlon, & Lyon, 2000). It is clear that a new approach is needed for making SLD eligibility and placement decisions.

The 2004 reauthorization of IDEA marked a significant change in entitlement practices for the special education category of specific learning disability. The revised law specifies that states must allow local education agencies to use "a process that determines if the child responds to scientific, research-based intervention," as part of a comprehensive evaluation in order to determine if a student is eligible for special education services under the category of specific learning disability. Specific language follows:

§300.307 Specific learning disabilities.

(a) General. A State must adopt, consistent with §300.309, criteria for determining whether a child has a specific learning disability as defined in §300.8. In addition, the criteria adopted by the State—

    (1) May prohibit the use of a severe discrepancy between intellectual ability and achievement for determining whether a child has a specific learning disability as defined in §300.8;

    (2) May not require the use of a severe discrepancy between intellectual ability and achievement for determining whether a child has a specific learning disability as defined in §300.8;

    (3) Must permit the use of a process that determines if the child responds to scientific, research-based intervention as part of the evaluation procedures described in §300.304; and

    4) May permit the use of other alternative research-based procedures for determining whether a child has a specific learning disability as defined in §300.8.

(b) Consistency with State criteria. A public agency must use the State criteria adopted pursuant to paragraph (a) of this section in determining whether a child has a specific learning disability. (Individuals with Disabilities Act, Volume Source § 300.307, 2004)

The federal regulation governing the full and individual evaluation can be found at 34 CFR 300.301–306. Following this change in federal special education law, states were required to revise state law to remove any conflict with the new federal language. For most states, this meant writing new criteria to specify how a student would qualify for special education services under the category of SLD without using an IQ-achievement discrepancy model, and using RTI data instead. It is important to note that school-based special education evaluation teams must address their own state criteria in making determinations of eligibility for SLD. Most state criteria for SLD include exclusionary factors, such as ruling out vision impairment as the cause for the academic difficulty. Student RTI data alone will typically not address all aspects of the SLD criteria in most states. What follows in this chapter is a series of considerations that help teams in decision making related to measuring student growth.

Necessary Conditions for RTI as an Eligibility Process

First, in order to effectively establish a process by which RTI can be used for SLD eligibility, it is imperative that the tasks associated with problem solving across all tiers of instruction prior to consideration for SLD eligibility are completed with a high degree of fidelity. RTI in general education systems must be implemented in a quality way before special education decision making can be layered on top. First, all students are provided with scientifically based core instruction in academic skill areas. Next, students participate in universal screening to identify those at risk for academic failure. Once students are identified as at risk, they are provided with scientifically based interventions of sufficient intensity that supplement, not supplant, core instruction. Interventions are accompanied by frequent (for example, weekly) progress monitoring using reliable and valid measures and implementation integrity checks in the form of direct observations. We advocate for checks to document 100 percent implementation integrity—with no exceptions.

We provide those students who on a first-intervention attempt continue to demonstrate performance well below target and insufficient rates of growth a second intervention designed with greater attention to problem analysis and diagnostic assessment, and with greater intensity, and we continue weekly progress monitoring and integrity checks. We complete all of these tasks through the use of general education resources and general education teams, which employ a structured, documented problem-solving process. Communication to all building staff members and parents regarding the procedures for proactive identification of students in need of assistance, as well as implementation of additional support to students at risk must be ongoing. Clearly, before a school can begin to utilize data from the RTI system to make entitlement decisions, there is much work to be done in getting these systems up and running smoothly.

Establishing that the problem-solving and intervention process has been implemented with fidelity prior to referral for special education entitlement consideration helps ensure that the evaluation team has the quality of data it needs to adequately evaluate whether the student meets eligibility criteria. A primary benefit to quality problem solving is that buildings find they have fewer referrals for special education evaluation. A side benefit is that it tends to increase the percentage of special education evaluation referrals that result in an entitlement decision.

A New Definition Through Dual Discrepancy

Data collected through general education interventions and progress monitoring allow teams to make determinations related to unexpected underachievement, one of the defining features of SLD. In essence, rather than measuring a student's IQ and academic achievement and noting that the achievement level is unexpectedly low given the student's IQ score, an RTI process provides intense interventions to students and notes unexpected underachievement if the student fails to demonstrate sufficient growth given these intensive supports. Most commonly, teams investigate the student's current level of performance and the student's slope, or rate of growth, over the course of intensive intervention. Students may be identified as dually discrepant if they demonstrate both low levels of performance and low rates of growth over time (Fuchs & Fuchs, 1998).

Using GOM Data to Determine Dual Discrepancy

The use of consistent targets allows educators to formatively evaluate student progress at each benchmark period to determine whether an individual student is on track to pass the upcoming state test. Targets at each benchmark period provide a benchmark of expected growth. For example, students who fell below the fall cut score at fall testing but score above the winter cut score at winter testing have grown faster than the cut scores and have caught up with the level of progress necessary to succeed on the outcome measure, in this case the state test. Conversely, scores for a student who was above the cut score during previous benchmark periods that fall below the most recent cut score are an indication that this student has begun to fall behind.

The use of consistent target scores has significant implications for the use of CBM-R within an RTI framework. Fuchs and Fuchs (1998) identify RTI as a process involving three phases for establishing a student's disability. Phase I involves tracking progress for all students within the mainstream classroom setting to determine, first, whether that instruction is generally effective. Fuchs and Fuchs (1998) suggest the use of local, or perhaps national, normative data to make decisions about the effectiveness of group progress. However, using established cut scores based on the probability of success on an upcoming state-mandated assessment, as described previously, is a useful alternative to normative data for making these decisions. If greater than 25 percent of students in the general education environment are not growing at the pace of the target scores or the rate of growth necessary to maintain grade-level standards, then a strong argument can be made that the environment is not generally effective.

If the classroom instruction is generally effective, Phase II involves a child-find process in which both the level of performance and rate of improvement for an individual student are compared to some established criterion that has typically been based on normative data (Fuchs & Fuchs, 1998). Again, cut scores based on probability of success on state tests are an alternative to normative data. For students who are identified by level of performance, rate of improvement can be compared to the rate of improvement of the target scores. A rate below that of the increasing targets would indicate that the child is not growing adequately as a result of his or her current educational environment.

Phase III, which involves tracking student progress during intervention, uses these same established criteria for rate of improvement, either within a problem-solving or standard treatment protocol approach. However, Phase III bases decisions on the students' being below the bottom of a 95 percent confidence interval, to ensure that the student is truly discrepant from the criterion. Decisions about exiting special education are based on students' being above the top of the 95 percent confidence interval, to ensure that the student is truly exceeding the rate of progress of the criterion and therefore catching up to grade-level standards.

SLD Decision-Making Guidelines Within RTI: St. Croix River Education District

The St. Croix River Education District (SCRED) developed guidelines related to dual discrepancy to assist teams and ensure more consistent decision making across teams and districts related to SLD entitlement decisions. These guidelines include benchmarks for both level and slope of performance to aid in making decisions about the need for and effectiveness of interventions.

Establishing Discrepancy

The guidelines, developed by the RTI leadership team at SCRED and published by Silberglitt and Gibbons (2005), use a norm-based score for establishing that a student is discrepant on level of performance, while simultaneously using a criterion-based score for establishing that a student is discrepant on slope. In Minnesota, students must achieve a score at or below the fifth percentile on a state or nationally normed test of achievement in order to qualify for special education services under the SLD category. This requirement addresses the *level* piece of the dual discrepancy model.

The Minnesota criteria are not specific with regard to slope. IEP teams are given the authority to determine whether student growth is insufficient. SCRED guidelines are provided to assist teams with this decision. Specifically, expected growth rates (slope) are determined based on the rate of increase of the fall, winter, and spring benchmark target scores on curriculum-based measures. These target scores were developed using methods described by Silberglitt and Hintze (2005), which link performance at each benchmark period to the desired outcome, in this case reaching grade-level standard on the statewide assessment. This linking process provides a consistent method for establishing the target scores and gives us a reasonable estimation of the growth necessary to maintain on-track status, or a year's growth in a year's time. After determining expected growth rates for each measure at each grade level, we placed a 95 percent confidence interval around the slope score in order to provide teams with a range of slope values that we are reasonably confident represent not less than (or more than) one year of expected growth. Students who fall below this confidence band are not making adequate progress in their current curriculum.

The graph in figure 14.1 visually represents the three data points provided in the slope table for a specific grade level. The dark line is the slope of the benchmark target, the targeted growth rate for students at a specific grade level in a specific measure. The gray area represents the 95 percent confidence interval for that growth line. That is, we are 95 percent confident that a year's growth would be any line of progress within the gray area. The bottom of the gray area is the minimum growth rate, and the top of the gray area is the maximum growth rate. A student whose growth line is below that gray area is definitely not making a year's growth in a year's time.

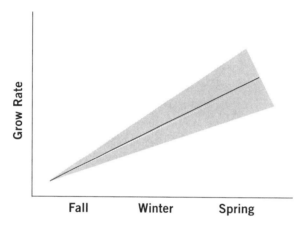

Figure 14.1: Slope table for a specific grade level showing the 95 percent confidence area.

Using criterion-referenced target scores is a fairly unique feature of the SCRED model. Other models have sought to define discrepant slope normatively instead. Two significant advantages of our criterion-based approach are that all involved know the slope goal at the beginning of the year, and the slope is relevant to the student. Slope goals based on normative information do *not* possess these characteristics. If the slope goal is to be based on the growth rates of the student's current cohort, then the goals cannot be established until that cohort has completed at least two benchmark assessments (fall and winter), and preferably all three. An alternative is to base the slope goals on the norms of previous cohorts or on national or state norms, but this reduces the relevance of the goal. Previous cohorts or other districts may have meaningfully different instructional experiences, such as not having all-day, everyday kindergarten or using less current versions of curricula, which would make their norms less applicable to the current local cohort.

Matthew Burns, Benjamin Silberglitt, Ted Christ, and Kim Gibbons (2007) explored the efficacy of various guidelines for LD incidence and found that the Silberglitt and Gibbons's (2005) model yielded the greatest consistency across grades, with higher LD rates in the early grades than with other models. This seems to support the usefulness of this model for early intervention and prevention of later learning difficulties, particularly in the area of reading.

Evaluating Exit

SCRED guidelines suggest that teams use level and slope information to assist with decisions to exit special education services as well as for entitlement purposes. Students whose growth rates are above the top end of the confidence interval for slope and those whose level of performance has increased normatively may be candidates for exit from services.

RTI and the Number of Students Referred to SLD

There is some concern in the education community that the use of an RTI method for determining SLD eligibility will cause a rapid increase in the rate of special education referrals (Hale, Naglieri, Kaufman, & Kavale, 2004). However, the data from SCRED run counter to this notion. Figure 14.2 displays the LD rate at SCRED as compared with the state of Minnesota and, more specifically, SCRED's geographic region (Region 7) within the state. SCRED data were not removed from the Region 7 or state totals. The figure illustrates that the LD rate at SCRED has dropped dramatically over the past decade by more than 40 percent. We feel this is primarily because special education referrals are not the only means for getting effective interventions in place for students, particularly for students with reading difficulties.

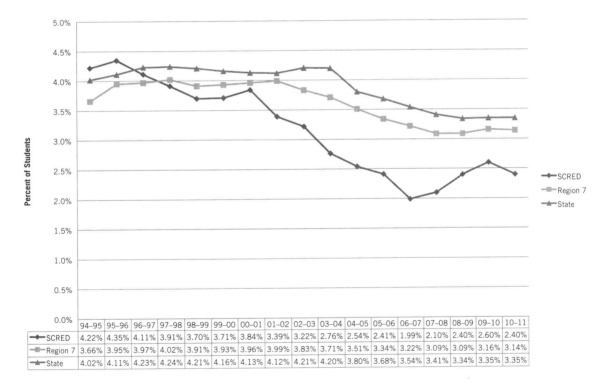

	94–95	95–96	96–97	97–98	98–99	99–00	00–01	01–02	02–03	03–04	04–05	05–06	06–07	07–08	08–09	09–10	10–11
SCRED	4.22%	4.35%	4.11%	3.91%	3.70%	3.71%	3.84%	3.39%	3.22%	2.76%	2.54%	2.41%	1.99%	2.10%	2.40%	2.60%	2.40%
Region 7	3.66%	3.95%	3.97%	4.02%	3.91%	3.93%	3.96%	3.99%	3.83%	3.71%	3.51%	3.34%	3.22%	3.09%	3.09%	3.16%	3.14%
State	4.02%	4.11%	4.23%	4.24%	4.21%	4.16%	4.13%	4.12%	4.21%	4.20%	3.80%	3.68%	3.54%	3.41%	3.34%	3.35%	3.35%

Figure 14.2: Percentage of students receiving services for specific learning disabilities in the St. Croix Education District, Region 7, and Minnesota.

When to Consider Referral to the Special Education Team

Special education is the most intensive instructional option for students, and it might be a consideration for students who are not making progress through intensive general education instruction. In deciding whether a referral for special education evaluation is appropriate, the problem-solving team may consider the following:

▶ Is there evidence that the student's achievement is significantly below that of other same-grade peers?

▶ Has the student had access to effective core instruction?

▶ Did the student participate in intense interventions with good research support?

▶ Were these interventions carried out with fidelity?

▶ Were the interventions implemented for an adequate length of time to expect growth?

▶ Is there evidence that good problem-analysis practice led to appropriate changes in interventions to meet student needs?

▶ Has student growth on progress-monitoring measures continued to be insufficient despite these efforts?

Be careful. Do not delay evaluation for special education entitlement if the problem-solving team has reason to suspect a disability. A strong RTI implementation that includes screening for all students and progress monitoring and interventions for students performing below expectation will ensure that teams have data they need to evaluate for SLD without delay.

Conclusion

To be more intense instructionally means to apply more individualized problem solving and resources in order to solve a learning problem. Since a foundation of robust Tier 1 and Tier 2 instruction has been established, Tier 3 will not be needed for more than 5–10 percent of students in the building.

There are many considerations before a secondary school should shift to using an RTI process for special education entitlement decisions under SLD. One important understanding is that Tier 3 interventions are not the same thing as special education. All systems will have students who need Tier 3 services but do not meet state criteria for special education entitlement. All systems will have special education identified students who do not need Tier 3 levels of service in all areas. So, the intensive instructional options must be built for an RTI system, and decisions to serve students with this level of service must be based on their instructional need for that service and not on special education eligibility. A high degree of integrity in the problem-solving process is paramount.

When an RTI framework is structurally in place, secondary schools will likely not see a sudden increase in students identified as SLD through the RTI process. Furthermore, special education will become part of the seamless system of educational services available for learners in a building and will serve those students who truly do have the most intense, unique, or complex instructional needs.

Epilogue

Q: What would you like other secondary schools to know about implementing RTI?

A: That it's not as difficult as it might seem. I think as educators we tend to think, "Oh, it's going to be a lot of work." But, honestly, it's things that we should be doing anyway. We're looking at how to help students achieve more, and that's what our goal is as educators. RTI is a way of measuring that.

—Bridget Budig, ninth-grade RTI English teacher,
Chisago Lakes High School

Advance Organizer

✓ *Building administrators must lead RTI implementation.*

✓ *Implementation integrity is paramount.*

✓ *The master schedule must be changed.*

✓ *A clear process for decision is needed.*

✓ *Student involvement and relationships must be created.*

✓ *Teachers must be given time and tools.*

The big ideas that have been covered throughout this text can be summarized succinctly by revisiting the five steps for implementation:

1. Establish ongoing commitment.

2. Establish an RTI and building-based leadership team.

3. Implement assessment—screening and progress monitoring. Get a database.

4. Implement instruction based on the data.

5. Implement a problem-solving process and organization.

Research and practice suggest that by following these steps to implement RTI—and doing them with fidelity—programs in secondary schools will have sustainability and experience success. That doesn't mean the journey will not be without setbacks and frustrations or that meaningful programs will happen quickly. Those are natural occurrences in systems when human behavior and school culture change is occurring.

Consider this analogy: suppose you are part of a family that eats dinner at 6:00 p.m. each night. Imagine that one day someone (maybe you) decided that dinner would be served every night at 8:00 p.m. What are some of the positive responses you might receive from family members? What are some of the complaints or concerns you might hear? What would be some potential barriers to implementation? How would this change be positively reinforced? How long would it take before the routine was changed and everyone fully motivated to implement it? A month? A year?

While this seemingly simple change appears straightforward, there are numerous considerations and a potentially more complex impact than initially anticipated. The point is that it takes time for a system—any system—and a culture to change. There will certainly be questions—sometimes very tough ones—and unanticipated outcomes that may be positive or negative. Honor that this is all part of the change process, but don't accept not changing as an option, especially if current practices are not leading to successful outcomes—in this case, for all learners.

It is our hope and intention that in following the practices explained throughout the text under these five steps, your school will take an RTI journey that features more success and celebration than lessons learned on what not to do. When the "what not to do" lessons happen, view and use them as growth opportunities rather than setbacks. Such an attitude will help you persevere in your efforts to implement RTI.

RTI on a Desert Island

While the big ideas are the essentials, what are some underlying practices—take-home messages—we would share from the journey of implementing RTI in secondary settings? Think about it like this: if we were stranded on a desert island and were asked to implement RTI in a secondary setting, what are the keys we would want to have to make it happen—and make it happen with excellence?

The obvious disclaimer here is that, just because these items are identified as essentials doesn't mean that other practices and procedures aren't relevant or important for overall effectiveness. It just means that we have lived and learned, and we would like to emphasize some key points that might be easily lost or forgotten. Remember these, and RTI implementation in your secondary building will avoid some of the mistakes we made and achieve results and sustainability more efficiently and effectively.

Here is the list of survival items that we believe are the essentials for RTI implementation in your secondary building.

Have Administrative Leadership for Implementing an RTI Framework in Secondary Settings

Hasn't this been mentioned several times already? Why would we bring this up again? To be frank, it is because RTI implementation really, truly won't happen—and won't be sustainable—without building and district leadership on board. It will become another passing fad or initiative. We, unfortunately, have witnessed the cycle of grassroots efforts that happen over and over again and burn out because there isn't administrative support.

School administrators! This section is for you.

Martin Maehr and Carol Midgley (1991) write that "teachers alone cannot carry the burden of significant school change; one must also engage school leaders in school change if the deepest structure of teaching and learning is to change (pp. 405–406). In our secondary schools, in order to educate all our diverse learners, the deepest structure of teaching and learning must change. As an administrator, you must lead that change.

Three key skills are needed by administrators for effective RTI implementation:

1. School administrators must think outside the box. Need we say more than how else is the master schedule going to be changed without creative and wise thinking?

2. School administrators must be instructional leaders. This doesn't mean knowing everything about every content area. It means having a working knowledge of what constitutes excellence in teaching and learning for secondary students, and articulating that to your staff.

3. School administrators must be data-driven decision makers. No exceptions.

Ensure Integrity of Implementation Across All Practices and Tiers

A well-known Russian proverb, "Trust, but verify," summarizes this whole concept. Do not underestimate the importance of establishing whether RTI practices are occurring with fidelity. It is easy to overlook this in the hustle of the school day. Practices happening without fidelity is a common reason for interventions ending up not working as planned. Attending to implementation integrity early and often will prevent setbacks, miscommunication, and unintended outcomes on numerous levels.

Adjust the Master Schedule for Data Reviews, Meetings, and Instruction

The first step in making talk turn into walk is getting a date and time on the calendar. When the meeting time arrives, do nothing else other than discuss whatever the meeting was originally intended to cover. Have an agenda, even if it's one item. Stick to it. Decide what the protocol will be for meetings. Make that protocol explicit, if that is needed.

Also, remember when we said school leaders need to think outside the box? As noted earlier, changing the master schedule is necessary and a challenge. Creative and wise thinking is needed in revising the master schedule. Create a timeline with meeting dates specifying when conversations will happen in the winter and early spring to discuss, draft, and then make these master schedule changes. Eventually, the practices that you originally needed to think carefully about and insert into the calendar and schedule will become a habitual part of the school day, schedule, and culture.

Have a Process for Decision Making

Numerous SCRED secondary practitioners across diverse content areas and roles have acknowledged that they don't know how they ever made effective decisions until they had a problem-solving model to guide the process. Having a specific process and a way to document the process will ensure that practices are actually happening as designed with good data use, good hypothesis development, and instruction that is well matched to student needs and implemented with fidelity. While it may seem as if the process exists to meet the needs of documentation-driven, micromanaging administrators or bureaucrats, there is a purpose being served that is relevant to us. Remember the statement, trust, but verify? Believe us, as busy educators, the extra minutes you spend following your process and documenting your decisions will pay dividends in the clarity of communication and consistency in follow-through that occurs as a result of these tasks. This prevents disgruntled teams and burnout from what some might consider "another initiative that doesn't work." Whatever decision-making or problem-solving process your building or team chooses, have the steps clearly defined. Include documentation of whether the process was implemented with fidelity. Apply the process literally and explicitly so information and outcomes are clear to all participants.

Ensure Student Involvement and Build Relationships

When educators are attending to getting student buy-in and building relationships with them, RTI implementation will happen. If students are left out of the planning and implementation, there is less chance that lasting change in student behavior will happen. Also, for students identified as at risk for school failure, content design, delivery, and relationship are intertwined. Consider how relationship building and student voices will be incorporated into each aspect of RTI. We have learned that the effort to build in these ideas will significantly increase successful and smooth implementation. Besides that, it's fun to work side by side with students. This is another great opportunity to do what we love.

Give Teachers the Tools to Implement RTI

Interestingly, many people assume that teachers will just know how to implement RTI. It is a best practice for serving kids, so educators must have learned how to implement RTI in their training programs. To assume this is inconsiderate and (often) inaccurate. Just as in any profession, educators must have the materials and the knowledge of how to use those materials in order to implement and develop their craft as practitioners. It is imperative to provide time and resources for innovation if we expect it to happen.

Professional development needs to be thoughtfully targeted at supporting secondary teachers in implementing all the RTI practices, as well as in understanding the nuances of implementation across the tiers. This means professional development activities must also be embedded in teachers' jobs and an ongoing process. Avoid the "sit and get" or drive-by workshops with an outside expert from at least fifty miles away (we have heard this referred to as the "train and hope" model). Professional development done in this manner is not a beneficial use of time or resources and will frustrate staff who already have a lot on their plates.

A Final Note

Our main purpose in writing this book was to share with fellow colleagues that implementing an RTI framework in a secondary school can be done! We truly wish you the best of luck on your journey of RTI implementation.

References and Resources

Aaron, P. G. (1997). The impending demise of the discrepancy formula. *Review of Educational Research, 67*(4), 461–502.

Ainsworth, L. (2003a). *Power standards: Identifying the standards that matter the most.* Denver, CO: Advanced Learning Press.

Ainsworth, L. (2003b). *"Unwrapping" the standards: A simple process to make standards manageable.* Denver, CO: Advanced Learning Press.

Ainsworth, L. (2007). Common formative assessments: The centerpiece of an integrated standards-based assessment system. In D. Reeves (Ed.), *Ahead of the curve: The power of assessment to transform teaching and learning* (pp. 79–101). Bloomington, IN: Solution Tree Press.

Alberto, P. A., & Troutman, A. C. (2009). *Applied behavior analysis for teachers* (8th ed.). Upper Saddle River, NJ: Merrill/Pearson.

Allain, J. K. (2008). *The logistics of literacy intervention: A planning guide for middle and high schools.* Boston: Sopris West.

Allen, D. (1989). Periodic and annual reviews and decision to terminate special education services. In M. R. Shinn (Ed.), *Curriculum-based measurement: Assessing special children* (pp. 182–201). New York: Guilford Press.

Allen, S. J., & Graden, J. L. (2002). Best practices in collaborative problem solving for intervention design. In A. Thomas & J. Grimes (Eds.), *Best practices in school psychology IV* (pp. 565–582). Washington, DC: National Association of School Psychologists.

Alliance for Excellence in Education. (2004). *Reading next—A vision for action and research in middle and high school literacy: A report to Carnegie Corporation of New York.* Accessed at www.all4ed.org/files/ReadingNext.pdf on June 10, 2006.

Alliance for Excellence in Education. (2005). *Adolescent literacy: Opening the doors to success.* Accessed at www.all4ed.org/files/AdolescentLiteracyOpeningDoors.pdf on July 11, 2009.

Alliance for Excellence in Education (2008). *Using early-warning data to improve graduation rates: Closing cracks in the education system.* Accessed at www.all4ed.org/files/EWIl.pdf on September 17, 2011.

Anderson, R. C., Wilson, P. T., & Fielding, L. G. (1988). Growth in reading and how children spend their time outside of school. *Reading Research Quarterly, 23*(3), 285–303.

Appleton, J. J., Christenson, S. L., Kim, D., & Reschly, A. L. (2006). Measuring cognitive and psychological engagement: Validation of the Student Engagement Instrument. *Journal of School Psychology, 44,* 427–445.

Ardoin, S. P., & Christ, T. J. (2008). Evaluating curriculum-based measurement slope estimates using triannual universal screenings. *School Psychology Review, 37*(1), 109–125.

Ardoin, S. P., & Christ, T. J. (2009). Curriculum-based measurement of oral reading: Standard errors associated with progress monitoring outcomes from DIBELS, AIMSweb, and an experimental passage set. *School Psychology Review, 38*(2), 266–283.

Balfanz, R. (2009). *Putting middle grades students on the graduation path: A policy and practice brief.* Westerville, OH: National Middle School Association. Accessed at www.nmsa.org/portals/0 /pdf/research/Research_from_the_Field/Policy_Brief_Balfanz.pdf on August 30, 2010.

Barnett, D. W., Daly, E. J., Jones, K. M., & Lentz, F. E. (2004). Response to intervention: Empirically based special service decisions from single-case designs of increasing and decreasing intensity. *Journal of Special Education, 38*(2), 66–79.

Barth, R. S. (2002). The culture builder. *Educational Leadership, 59*(8), 6–11.

Batsche, G., Elliott, J., Graden, J. L., Grimes, J., Kovaleski, J. F., Prasse, D., et al. (2005). *Response to intervention: Policy considerations and implementation.* Alexandria, VA: National Association of State Directors of Special Education.

Batsche, G. M., & Knoff, H. M. (1995). Best practices in linking assessment to intervention. In A. Thomas & J. Grimes (Eds.), *Best practices in school psychology III* (pp. 569–586). Washington, DC: National Association of School Psychologists.

Bergan, J. R. (1977). *Behavioral consultation.* Columbus, OH: Merrill.

Bergan, J. R., & Kratochwill, T. R. (1990). *Behavioral consultation and therapy.* New York: Plenum Press.

Boardman, A. G., Roberts, G., Vaughn, S., Wexler, J., Murray, C. S., & Kosanovich, M. (2008). *Effective instruction for adolescent struggling readers: A practice brief.* Portsmouth, NH: RMC Research Corporation, Center on Instruction.

Bohanon-Edmonson, H., Brigid Flannery, K., Eber, L., & Sugai, G. (Eds.). (2005). *Positive behavior support in high schools: Monograph from the 2004 Illinois High School Forum of Positive Behavioral Interventions and Supports.* Accessed at www.pbis.org/files/PBSMonographComplete.pdf on August 28, 2007.

Bollman, K. A., Silberglitt, B., & Gibbons, K. A. (2007). The St. Croix River Education District model: Incorporating systems-level organization and a multi-tiered problem-solving process for intervention delivery. In S. R. Jimerson, M. K. Burns, & A. M. VanDerHeyden (Eds.), *Handbook of response to intervention: The science and practice of assessment and intervention* (pp. 319–330). New York: Springer.

Bowen, J. M., Jenson, W. R., & Clark, E. (2004). *School-based interventions for students with behavior problems.* New York: Kluwer Academic/Plenum.

Brophy, J. (2004). *Motivating students to learn.* Mahwah, NJ: Erlbaum.

Brunner, M. S. (1993). *Reduced recidivism and increased employment opportunity through research-based reading instruction* (NCJ Publication No. 141324). Washington, DC: Office of Juvenile Justice and Delinquency Prevention.

Bui, K. T. (2005). Middle school variables that predict college attendance for first-generation students. *Education, 126*(2), 203-220.

Burns, M. K., Dean, V. J., & Foley, S. (2004). Preteaching unknown key words with incremental rehearsal to improve reading fluency and comprehension with children identified as reading disabled. *Journal of School Psychology, 42*(4), 303–314.

Burns, M. K., & Gibbons, K. (2008). *Implementing response-to-intervention in elementary and secondary schools: Procedures to assure scientific-based practices.* New York: Routledge.

Burns, M. K., Silberglitt, B., Christ, T. J., & Gibbons, K. A. (2007). Comparing norm- and criterion-referenced criteria for non-response (Manuscript in submission).

Busch, T. W., & Espin, C. A. (2003). Using curriculum-based measurement to prevent failure and assess learning in content areas. *Assessment for Effective Intervention, 28*(3–4), 49–58.

Bush, G. W. (2005). *Transcript of State of the Union.* Accessed at www.cnn.com/2005/ALLPOLITICS /02/02/sotu.transcript.2/index.html on July 11, 2011.

Caplan, G. (1964). *Principles of preventive psychiatry.* New York: Basic Books.

Caplan, G., & Grunebaum, H. (1967). Perspectives on primary prevention: A review. *Archives of General Psychiatry, 17*(3), 331–346.

Centers for Disease Control. (2002). Health-care associated infections. Accessed at www.cdc.gov /HAI/burden.html on October 4, 2011.

Chafouleas, S. M., Briesch, A. M., Riley-Tillman, T. C., Christ, T. J., Black, A. C., & Kilgus, S. P. (2010). An investigation of the generalizability and dependability of direct behavior rating single item scales (DBR-SIS) to measure academic engagement and disruptive behavior of middle school students. *Journal of School Psychology, 48*(3), 219–246.

Chafouleas, S. M., Kilgus, S. P., & Hernandez, P. (2009). Using direct behavior rating (DBR) to screen for school social risk: A preliminary comparison of methods in a kindergarten sample. *Assessment for Effective Intervention, 34*(4), 214–223.

Chafouleas, S. M., Riley-Tillman, T. C., & Christ, T. J. (2009). Direct behavior rating (DBR): An emerging method for assessing social behavior within a tiered intervention system. *Assessment for Effective Intervention, 34*(4), 195–200.

Christ, T. J. (2006). Short-term estimates of growth using curriculum-based measurement of oral reading fluency: Estimating standard error of the slope to construct confidence intervals. *School Psychology Review, 35*(1), 128–133.

Christ, T. J., & Ardoin, S. P. (2009). Curriculum-based measurement of oral reading: Passage equivalence and probe-set development. *Journal of School Psychology, 47*(1), 55–75.

Christ, T. J., Burns, M. K., & Ysseldyke, J. E. (2005). Conceptual confusion within response-to-intervention vernacular: Clarifying meaningful differences. *Communiqué, 34*(3). Accessed at www.nasponline.org/publications/cq/cq343rti.aspx on August 20, 2011.

Christ, T. J., Riley-Tillman, T. C., Chafouleas, S. M., & Boice, C. H. (2010). Direct behavior ratings (DBR): Generalizability and dependability of across raters and observations. *Educational and Psychological Measurement, 70*(5), 825–843.

Christenson, S. L., Sinclair, M. F., Lehr, C. A., & Hurley, C. M. (2000). Promoting successful school completion. In K. M. Minke & G. C. Bear (Eds.), *Preventing school problems—promoting school success: Strategies and programs that work* (pp. 211–257). Bethesda, MD: National Association of School Psychologists.

Christenson, S. L., Thurlow, M. L., Sinclair, M. F., Lehr, C. A., Kaibel, C. M., Reschly, A. L., et al. (2008). *Check & connect: A comprehensive student engagement intervention manual.* Minneapolis: University of Minnesota, Institute on Community Integration.

Clark, L., & Elliott, S. N. (1988). The influence of treatment strength information on knowledgeable teachers' evaluation of two social skills training methods. *Professional School Psychology, 3,* 241–251.

Commission on Chronic Illness. (1957). *Chronic illness in the United States.* Cambridge, MA: Harvard University Press.

Cooper, M. (2005). *Bound and determined to help children with learning disabilities succeed.* Weston, MA: Learning Disabilities Worldwide.

Covey, S. (1998). *Seven habits of highly effective teams.* New York: Simon & Schuster.

Crone, D. A., Horner, R. H., & Hawken, L. S. (2004). *Responding to problem behavior in schools: The behavior education program.* New York: Guilford Press.

Cunningham, A. E., & Stanovich, K. E. (1998). What reading does for the mind. *American Educator, 22*(1–2), 8–15.

D'Agostino, J. V., & Murphy, J. A. (2004). A meta-analysis of reading recovery in United States schools. *Educational Evaluation and Policy Analysis, 26*(1), 23–38.

Daly, E. J., & Martens, B. K. (1994). A comparison of three interventions for increasing oral reading performance: Application of the instructional hierarchy. *Journal of Applied Behavior Analysis, 27*(3), 459–469.

Daly, E. J., Witt, J. C., Martens, B. K., & Dool, E. J. (1997). A model for conducting a functional analysis of academic performance problems. *School Psychology Review, 26*(4), 554–574.

Danielson, C. (2007). *Enhancing professional practice: A framework for teaching* (2nd ed.). Alexandria, VA: Association for Supervision and Curriculum Development.

Deal, T. E., & Peterson, K. D. (1999). *Shaping school culture: The heart of leadership.* San Francisco: Jossey-Bass.

Deno, S. L. (1985). Curriculum-based measurement: The emerging alternative. *Exceptional Children, 52*(3), 219–232.

Deno, S. L. (1986). Formative evaluation of individual student programs: A new role for school psychologists. *School Psychology Review, 15*(3), 358–374.

Deno, S. L. (1989). Curriculum-based measurement and special education services. In M. R. Shinn (Ed.), *Curriculum-based measurement: Assessing special children* (pp. 1–17). New York: Guilford Press.

Deno, S.L. (n.d.). Ongoing student assessment. Accessed at www.rtinetwork.org/essential/assessment/ongoingassessment on September 8, 2011.

Deno, S. L. (2002). Problem solving as "best practice." In A. Thomas & J. Grimes (Eds.), *Best practices in school psychology IV* (pp. 37–56). Bethesda, MD: National Association of School Psychologists.

Deno, S. L., Espin, C. A., & Fuchs, L. S. (2002). Evaluation strategies for preventing and remediating basic skill deficits. In G. Stoner, M. R. Shinn, & H. M. Walker (Eds.), *Interventions for achievement and behavior problems* (pp. 213–241). Washington, DC: National Association of School Psychologists.

Deno, S. L., & Fuchs, L. S. (1987). Developing curriculum-based measurement systems for data-based special education problem solving. *Focus on Exceptional Children, 19*(8), 1–16.

Deno, S., Mirkin, P., & Wesson, C. (1984). How to write effective data-based IEPs. *Teaching Exceptional Children, 12*(2), 99–104.

Deshler, D. D., & Kovaleski, J. F. (2007). *Secondary applications of RTI: A guided discussion* [Presentation notes]. Accessed at www.nrcld.org/about/presentations/2007/DDSummitNotes.pdf on November 29, 2009.

Diamond, L. (2004). *Implementing and sustaining a middle and high school reading intervention program.* Berkeley, CA: Consortium on Reading Excellence.

Doll, B., Zucker, S., & Brehm, K. (2004). *Resilient classrooms: Creating healthy environments for learning.* New York: Guilford.

Donegan, B. (2008). The linchpin year. *Educational Leadership, 65*(8), 54–56.

DuFour, R., DuFour, R., Eaker, R., & Karhanek, G. (2004). *Whatever it takes: How professional learning communities respond when kids don't learn.* Bloomington, IN: Solution Tree Press.

DuFour, R., DuFour, R., Eaker, R., & Many, T. (2006). *Learning by doing: A handbook for professional learning communities at work.* Bloomington, IN: Solution Tree Press.

DuFour, R., & Eaker, R. (1998). *Professional learning communities at work: Best practices for enhancing student achievement.* Bloomington, IN: Solution Tree Press.

Duhon, G. J., Noell, G. H., Witt, J. C., Freeland, J. T., Dufrene, B. A., & Gilbertson, D. N. (2004). Identifying academic skill and performance deficits: The experimental analysis of brief assessments of academic skills. *School Psychology Review, 33*(3), 429–443.

DuPaul, G. J. & Stoner, G. D. (2003). *ADHD in the schools: assessment and intervention strategies.* New York: Guilford Press.

Eaker, R., DuFour, R., & DuFour, R. (2002). *Getting started: Reculturing schools to become professional learning communities.* Bloomington, IN: Solution Tree Press.

Eber, L., Sugai, G., Smith, C. R., & Scott, T. M. (2002). Wraparound and positive behavioral interventions and supports in the schools. *Journal of Emotional and Behavioral Disorders, 10*(3), 171–180.

Edelman, M. W. (2009, February 9). The cradle to prison pipeline: America's new apartheid. *Huffington Post.* Accessed at www.huffingtonpost.com/marian-wright-edelman/the-cradle-to-prison-pipe_b _165163.html on September 15, 2011.

Ehrhardt, K. E., Barnett, D. W., Lentz, F. E., Jr., Stollar, S. A., & Reifin, L. H. (1996). Innovative methodology in ecological consultation: Use of scripts to promote treatment acceptability and integrity. *School Psychology Quarterly, 11*, 149–168.

English Forums.com. (n.d.). *Mahatma Gandhi quotes.* Accessed at www.englishforums.com/English /MahatmaGandhiBeliefsBecomeThoughts/llhgc/post.htm on September 8, 2011.

Erickson, L. (2010). Conceptual designs for curriculum and higher-order instruction. In R. J. Marzano (Ed.), *On excellence in teaching* (pp. 169–192). Bloomington, IN: Solution Tree Press.

Espin, C. A., Busch, T. W., Shin, J., & Kruschwitz, R. (2001). Curriculum-based measures in the content areas: Validity of vocabulary-matching measures as indicators of performance in social studies. *Learning Disabilities Research and Practice, 16*(3), 142–151.

Espin, C. A., De La Paz, S., Scierka, B. J., & Roelofs, L. (2005). The relationship between curriculum-based measures in written expression and quality and completeness of expository writing for middle school students. *Journal of Special Education, 38*(4), 208–217.

Espin, C. A., & Deno, S. L. (1993a). Content-specific and general reading disabilities of secondary-level students: Identification and educational relevance. *Journal of Special Education, 27*(3), 321–337.

Espin, C. A., & Deno, S. L. (1993b). Performance in reading from content area text as an indicator of achievement. *Remedial and Special Education, 14*(6), 47–59.

Espin, C. A., & Deno, S. L. (1994/1995). Curriculum-based measures for secondary students: Utility and task specificity of text-based reading and vocabulary measures for predicting performance on content-area tasks. *Diagnostique, 20*(1–4), 121–142.

Espin, C. A., & Foegen, A. (1996). Validity of three general outcome measures for predicting secondary students' performance on content-area tasks. *Exceptional Children, 62*(6), 497–514.

Espin, C. A., Scierka, B. J., Skare, S., & Halverson, N. (1999). Criterion-related validity of curriculum-based measures in writing for secondary school students. *Reading and Writing Quarterly, 15*(1), 5–27.

Espin, C. A., Shin, J., & Busch, T. (2000). A focus on formative evaluation. *Current Practice Alerts, 3*, 1–4.

Espin, C. A., Shin, J., & Busch, T. W. (2005). Curriculum-based measurement in the content areas: Vocabulary-matching as an indicator of social studies learning. *Journal of Learning Disabilities, 38*(4), 353–363.

Espin, C. A., Shin, J., Deno, S. L., Skare, S., Robinson, S., & Brenner, B. (2000). Identifying indicators of growth in written expression for middle-school students. *Journal of Special Education, 34*(3), 140–153.

Espin, C. A., & Tindal, G. (1998). The use of curriculum-based measurement for secondary students. In M. R. Shinn (Ed.), *Advanced applications of curriculum-based measurement* (pp. 214–253). New York: Guilford Press.

Espin, C. A., Wallace, T., Campbell, H., Lembke, E. S., Long, J. D., & Ticha, R. (2008). Curriculum-based measurement in writing: Predicting the success of high-school students on state standards tests. *Exceptional Children, 74*(2), 174–193.

Espin, C., Wallace, T., Lembke, E., Campbell, H., & Long, J. D. (2010). Creating a progress-monitoring system in reading for middle-school students: Tracking progress toward meeting high-stakes standards. *Learning Disabilities Research and Practice, 25*(2), 60–75.

Espin, C. A., Weissenburger, J. W., & Benson, B. J. (2004). Assessing the writing performance of students in special education. *Exceptionality, 12*(1), 55–66.

Filter, K. J., McKenna, M. K., Benedict, E. A., Horner, R. H., Todd, A., & Watson, J. (2007). Check in/check out: A post-hoc evaluation of an efficient, secondary-level targeted intervention for reducing problem behaviors in schools. *Education and Treatment of Children, 30*(1), 69–84.

Flannery, K. B., & Sugai, G. (Eds.). (2009). *School-wide PBS implementation in high schools: Current practice and future directions.* Eugene: University of Oregon. Accessed at www.pbis.org/school/high _school_pbis.aspx on July 24, 2010.

Fletcher, J. M., Coulter, W. A., Reschly, D. J., & Vaughn, S. (2004). Alternative approaches to the definition and identification of learning disabilities: Some questions and answers. *Annals of Dyslexia, 54*(2), 304–331.

Flowers, N., Mertens, S. B., & Mulhall, P. F. (1999). The impact of teaming: Five research-based outcomes. *Middle School Journal, 31*(2), 57–60.

Foegen, A. (2007, February). *Progress monitoring measures in algebra: Potential applications in a three-tiered system* [PowerPoint slides]. Paper presented at The Pacific Coast Research Conference, Coronado, CA. Accessed at www.ci.hs.iastate.edu/aaims/docs/.../2007%20Foegen%20PCRC.pdf on October 4, 2011.

Foegen, A., Jiban, C., & Deno, S. (2007). Progress monitoring measures in mathematics: A review of the literature. *Journal of Special Education, 41*(2), 121–139.

Foegen, A., Olson, J. R., & Impecoven-Lind, L. (2008). Developing progress monitoring measures for secondary mathematics: An illustration in algebra. *Assessment for Effective Intervention, 33*(4), 240–249.

Fritschmann, N. S., Deshler, D. D., & Schumaker, J. B. (2007). The effects of instruction in an inference strategy on the reading comprehension skills of adolescents with disabilities. *Learning Disability Quarterly, 30*(4), 245–262.

Fuchs, D., Fuchs, L. S., Benowitz, S., & Barringer, K. (1987). Norm-referenced tests: Are they valid for use with handicapped students? *Exceptional Children, 54*(3), 263–271.

Fuchs, L. S. (n.d.). *Progress monitoring within a multi-level prevention system.* Accessed at www.rtinetwork .org/essential/assessment/prrogress/mutlilevelprevention on July 11, 2010.

Fuchs, L. S. (1986). Monitoring progress among mildly handicapped pupils: Review of current practice and research. *Remedial and Special Education, 7*(5), 5–12.

Fuchs, L. S. (1989). Evaluating student progress. In M. R. Shinn (Ed.), *Curriculum-based measurement: Assessing special children* (pp. 153–181). New York: Guilford Press.

Fuchs, L. S. (1993). Enhancing instructional programming and student achievement with curriculum-based measurement. In J. Kramer (Ed.), *Curriculum-based assessment: Examining old problems, evaluating new solutions* (pp. 74–148). Hillsdale, NJ: Erlbaum.

Fuchs, L. S. (2003). Assessing intervention responsiveness: Conceptual and technical issues. *Learning Disabilities Research and Practice, 18*(3), 172–186.

Fuchs, L. S., & Deno, S. L. (1991). Paradigmatic distinctions between instructionally relevant measurement models. *Exceptional Children, 57*(6), 488–501.

Fuchs, L. S., & Deno, S. L. (1994). Must instructionally useful performance assessment be based in the curriculum? *Exceptional Children, 61*(1), 15–24.

Fuchs, L. S., Deno, S. L., & Mirkin, P. K. (1984). The effects of frequent curriculum-based measurement and evaluation on student achievement, pedagogy, and student awareness of learning. *American Educational Research Journal, 21*(2), 449–460.

Fuchs, L. S., & Fuchs, D. (1998). Treatment validity: A unifying concept for reconceptualizing the identification of learning disabilities. *Learning Disabilities Research and Practice, 13*(4), 204–219.

Fuchs, L. S., & Fuchs, D. (2003). Can diagnostic reading assessment enhance general educators' instructional differentiation and student learning? In B. R. Foorman (Ed.), *Preventing and remediating reading difficulties: Bringing science to scale* (pp. 325–354). Baltimore: York Press.

Fuchs, L. S., Fuchs, D., & Hamlett, C. L. (1989a). Effects of alternative goal structures within curriculum-based measurement. *Exceptional Children, 55*(5), 429–438.

Fuchs, L. S., Fuchs, D., & Hamlett, C. L. (1989b). Effects of instrumental use of curriculum-based measurement to enhance instructional programs. *Remedial and Special Education, 10*(2), 43–52.

Fuchs, L. S., Fuchs, D., & Hamlett, C. L. (1989c). Monitoring reading growth using student recalls: Effects of two teacher feedback systems. *Journal of Educational Research, 83*(2), 103–111.

Fuchs, L. S., Fuchs, D., Hamlett, C. L., & Allinder, R. M. (1989). The reliability and validity of skills analysis within curriculum-based measurement. *Diagnostique, 14*(4), 203–221.

Fuchs, L. S., Fuchs, D., Hamlett, C. L., & Allinder, R. M. (1991a). The contribution of skills analysis to curriculum-based measurement in spelling. *Exceptional Children, 57*(5), 443–452.

Fuchs, L .S., Fuchs, D., Hamlett, C. L., & Allinder, R. M. (1991b). Effects of expert system advice within curriculum-based measurement on teacher planning and student achievement in spelling. *School Psychology Review, 20*(1), 49–66.

Fuchs, L. S., Fuchs, D., Hamlett, C. L., & Ferguson, C. (1992). Effects of expert system consultation within curriculum-based measurement using a reading maze task. *Exceptional Children, 58*(5), 436–450.

Fuchs, L. S., Fuchs, D., Hamlett, C. L., & Stecker, P. M. (1990). The role of skills analysis in curriculum-based measurement in math. *School Psychology Review, 19*(1), 6–22.

Fuchs, L. S., Fuchs, D., Hamlett, C. L., Thompson, A., Roberts, P. H., Kubek, P., et al. (1994). Technical features of a mathematics concepts and applications curriculum-based measurement system. *Diagnostique, 19*(4), 23–49.

Fuchs, L. S., Fuchs, D., Hamlett, C. L., Walz, L., & Germann, G. (1993). Formative evaluation of academic progress: How much growth can we expect? *School Psychology Review, 22*(1), 27–48.

Fuchs, L. S., & Shinn, M. R. (1989). Writing CBM IEP objectives. In M. R. Shinn (Ed.), *Curriculum-based measurement: Assessing special children* (pp. 130–152). New York: Guilford Press.

Gansle, K. A., & Noell, G. H. (2007). The fundamental role of intervention implementation in assessing response to intervention. In S. Jimerson, M. K. Burns, & A. M. VanDerHeyden (Eds.), *Handbook of response to intervention: The science and practice of assessment and intervention* (pp. 244–251). New York: Springer.

Gansle, K. A., Noell, G. H., VanDerHeyden, A. M., Slider, N. J., Hoffpauir, L. D., Whitmarsh, E. L., et al. (2004). An examination of the criterion validity and sensitivity of alternate curriculum-based measures of writing skill. *Psychology in the Schools, 41*(3), 291–300.

Germann, G., & Tindal, G. (1985). Applications of direct and repeated measurement using curriculum based assessment. *Exceptional Children, 51,* 110–121.

Gersten, R., Vaughn, S., Deschler, D., & Schiller, E. (1997). What we know about using research findings: Implications for improving special education practice. *Journal of Learning Disabilities, 30*(5), 466–476.

Gettinger, M., & Ball, C. (2008). Best practices in increasing academic engaged time. In A. Thomas & J. Grimes (Eds.), *Best practices in school psychology V* (pp. 1043–1058). Bethesda, MD: National Association of School Psychologists.

Glover, T. A., & DiPerna, J. C. (2007). Service delivery for response to intervention: Core components and directions for future research. *School Psychology Review, 36*(4), 526–540.

Good, R. H., Simmons, D. C., & Kame'enui, E. J. (2001). The importance and decision-making utility of a continuum of fluency-based indicators of foundational reading skills for third-grade high-stakes outcomes. *Scientific Studies of Reading, 5*(3), 257–288.

Greenberg, E., Dunleavy, E., & Kutner, M. (2007). *Literacy behind bars: Results from the 2003 National Assessment of Adult Literacy Prison Survey* (NCES 2007–473). Washington, DC: National Center for Education Statistics.

Gresham, F. (2002). Responsiveness to intervention: An alternative approach to the identification of learning disabilities. In R. Bradley, L. Danielson, & D. P. Hallahan (Eds.), *Identification of learning disabilities: Research to practice* (pp. 467–519). Mahwah, NJ: Erlbaum.

Gresham, F. M., Gansle, K. A., Noell, G. H., Cohen, S., & Rosenblum, S. (1993). Treatment integrity of school-based behavioral intervention studies: 1980–1990. *School Psychology Review, 22*(2), 254–272.

Gresham, F. M., Macmillian, D. L., Beebe-Frankenberger, M. E., & Bocian, K. M. (2000). Treatment integrity in learning disabilities intervention research: Do we really know how treatments are implemented? *Learning Disabilities Research and Practice, 15*(4), 198–205.

Gresham, F. M., & Witt, J. C. (1997). Utility of intelligence tests for treatment planning, classification, and placement decisions: Recent empirical findings and future directions. *School Psychology Quarterly, 12*(3), 249–267.

Hale, J. B., Naglieri, J. A., Kaufman, A. S., & Kavale, K. A. (2004). Specific learning disability classification in the new Individuals with Disabilities Education Act: The danger of good ideas. *School Psychologist, 58*(1), 6–13, 29.

Hall, B. (1985). Survey of the technical characteristics of published educational achievement tests. *Educational Measurement: Issues and Practice, 4*(1), 6–14.

Hartman, W. T., & Fay, T. A. (1996). *Cost-effectiveness of instructional support teams in Pennsylvania* (Center for Special Education Finance Policy Paper No. 9). Palo Alto, CA: Center for Special Education Finance, American Institutes for Research.

Hasbrouck, J., & Tindal, G. A. (2006). Oral reading fluency norms: A valuable assessment tool for reading teachers. *The Reading Teacher, 59*(7), 636–644.

Hawken, L. S., & Horner, R. H. (2003). Evaluation of a targeted intervention within a schoolwide system of behavior support. *Journal of Behavioral Education, 12*(3), 225–240.

Haynes, M. C., & Jenkins, J. R. (1986). Reading instruction in special education resource rooms. *American Educational Research Journal, 23*(2), 161–190.

Horner, R. (2010). *RTI as a framework for improving behavior and literacy supports* [PowerPoint presentation]. Accessed at www.pbis.org/presentations/default.aspx on July 25, 2010.

Howell, K. W. (1986). Direct assessment of academic performance. *School Psychology Review, 15*(3), 324–335.

Howell, K. W., & Nolet, V. (2000). *Curriculum-based evaluation, teaching and decision making* (3rd ed.). Scarborough, Ontario: Wadsworth/Thompson Learning.

Hughes, C., & Dexter, D. D. (n.d.). Universal screening within a response-to-intervention model. Accessed at www.rtinetwork.org/learn/research/universal-screening-within-a-rti-model on July 12, 2011.

Ikeda, M. J., Rahn-Blakeslee, A., Niebling, B. C., Gustafson, J. K., Allison, R., & Stumme, J. (2007). The Heartland Area Education Agency 11 Problem-solving approach: An overview and lessons learned. In S. R. Jimerson, M. K. Burns, & A. M. VanDerHeyden (Eds.), *Handbook of Response to Intervention* (pp. 255–268). New York: Springer.

Individuals With Disabilities Education Act (IDEA) § 300.307 (2004).

Ingham, J., Seidman, A., Yao, T. J., Lepore, J., & Portenoy, R. (1996). An exploratory study of frequent pain measurement in a cancer clinical trial. *Quality of Life Research, 5*(5), 503–507.

IRIS Center. (2007). Two approaches to response to intervention. Accessed at www.rti4success.org/index.php?option=com_content&task=blogcategory&id=40&Itemid=105 on July 11, 2010.

Irvin, L. K., Tobin, T. J., Sprague, J. R., Sugai, G., & Vincent, C. G. (2004). Validity of office discipline referral measures as indices of school-wide behavioral status and effects of school-wide behavioral interventions. *Journal of Positive Behavior Interventions, 6*(3), 131–147.

Jerald, C. D. (2006). *School culture: "The hidden curriculum."* Accessed at www.centerforcsri.org/files/Center_IB_Dec06_C.pdf on August 1, 2010.

Jinks., & Morgan, V. (1999). Children's perceived academic self-efficacy: An inventory scale. *The Clearing House, 72*(4), 224–230.

Jitendra, A. K., & Kame'enui, E. J. (1988). A design-of-instruction analysis of concept teaching in five basal language programs: Violations for the bottom up. *Journal of Special Education, 22*(2), 199–219.

Johnson, E., Mellard, D. F., Fuchs, D., & McKnight, M. A. (2006). *Responsiveness to intervention (RTI): How to do it.* Lawrence, KS: National Research Center on Learning Disabilities.

Johnson, E. S., Smith, L., & Harris, M. L. (2009). *How RTI works in secondary schools.* Thousand Oaks, CA: Corwin Press.

Jones, E. D., & Krouse, J. P. (1988). The effectiveness of data-based instruction by student teachers in classrooms for pupils with mild learning handicaps. *Teacher Education and Special Education, 11*(1), 9–19.

Kamil, M. L. (2004). *Adolescents and literacy: Reading for the 21st century.* Washington, D.C.: Alliance for Excellence in Education.

Kamil, M. L., Borman, G. D. , Dole, J., Kral, C. C., Salinger, T., & Torgesen, J. (2008). *Improving adolescent literacy: Effective classroom and intervention practices: A practice guide.* Washington, DC: National Center for Education Evaluation and Regional Assistance, Institute of Education Sciences, U.S. Department of Education. Accessed at http://ies.ed.gov/ncee/wwc/pdf/practiceguides/adlit_pg_082608.pdf on July 12, 2011.

Kay, D. (2005). A team approach to positive behaviors. *ASCA School Counselor, 42*(5), 16–21.

Kifer, R. E., Lewis, M. A., Green, D. R., & Phillips, E. L. (1974). Training predelinquent youths and their parents to negotiate conflict situations. *Journal of Applied Behavior Analysis, 7*(3), 357–364.

Klingner, J. K., Arguelles, M. E., Hughes, M. T., & Vaughn, S. (2001). Examining the schoolwide "spread" of research-based practices. *Learning Disabilities Quarterly, 24*(4), 221–234.

Klingner, J. K., Vaughn, S., Dimino, J., Schumm, J. S., & Bryant, D. (2002). *Collaborative strategic reading: Strategies for improving comprehension.* Longmont, CO: Sopris West.

Kratochwill, T. R., & Bergan, J. R. (1990). *Behavioral consultation in applied settings.* New York: Plenum Press.

Knoff, H. M. (2002). Best practices in facilitating school reform, organizational change, and strategic planning. In A. Thomas & J. Grimes (Eds.), *Best practices in school psychology IV* (pp. 235–253). Bethesda, MD: National Association of School Psychologists.

Knutson, N., & Shinn, M. R. (1991). Curriculum-based measurement: Conceptual underpinnings and integration into problem-solving assessment. *Journal of School Psychology, 29*(4), 371–393.

Lane, K. L., Bocian, K. M., MacMillan, D. L., & Gresham, F. M. (2004). Treatment integrity: An essential—but often forgotten—component of school-based intervention. *Preventing School Failure, 48*(3), 36–43.

Larson, J. (1994). Violence prevention in the schools: A review of selected programs and procedures. *School Psychology Review, 23*(2), 151–164.

Lassen, S. R., Steele, M. M., & Sailor, W. (2006). The relationship of school-wide positive behavior support to academic achievement in an urban middle school. *Psychology in the Schools, 43*(6), 701–712.

Lehr, C. A. (2004). Increasing school completion: Learning from research-based practices that work. *Research to Practice Brief, 3*(3). Accessed at www.ncset.org/publications/viewdesc.asp?id=1646 on July 25, 2010.

Leithwood, K., Louis, K. S., Anderson, S., & Wahlstrom, K. (2004). *Review of research: How leadership influences student learning.* Accessed at www.wallacefoundation.org/WF/KnowledgeCenter /KnowledgeTopics/Education Leadership/HowLeadershipInfluencesStudentLearning.htm on January 24, 2006.

Lentz, F. E., Allen, S. J., & Ehrhardt, K. E. (1996). The conceptual elements of strong interventions in school settings. *School Psychology Quarterly, 11,* 118–136.

Lentz, F. E., & Shapiro, E. S. (1986). Functional assessment of the academic environment. *School Psychology Review, 15*(3), 346–357.

Lewis, C., Enciso, P., & Moje, E. B. (2007). *Reframing sociocultural research on literacy: Identity, agency, and power.* Mahwah, NJ: Erlbaum.

Lewis, T. J. (2009). Connecting school-wide positive behavior supports to the academic curriculum in PBIS high schools. In B. Flannery & G. Sugai (Eds.), *School-wide PBS implementation in high schools: Current practice and future directions* (pp. 57–80). Eugene: University of Oregon.

Lortie, D. C. (1975). *Schoolteacher: A sociological study.* Chicago: University of Chicago Press.

Maehr, M. L., & Midgley, C. (1991). Enhancing student motivation: A schoolwide approach. *Educational Psychologist, 26*(3–4), 399–427.

Marston, D. B. (1989). A curriculum-based measurement approach to assessing academic performance: What it is and why do it. In M. R. Shinn (Ed.), *Curriculum-based measurement: Assessing special children* (pp. 18–78). New York: Guilford Press.

Marston, D., Lau, M., & Muyskens, P. (2007). Implementation of the problem-solving model in the Minneapolis Public Schools. In S. R. Jimerson, M. K. Burns, & A. M. VanDerHeyden (Eds.), *Handbook of response to intervention: The science and practice of assessment and intervention* (pp. 279–287). New York: Springer.

Marston, D., Muyskens, P., Lau, M., & Canter, A. (2003). Problem-solving model for decision making with high-incidence disabilities: The Minneapolis experience. *Learning Disabilities Research & Practice, 18,* 187–200.

Marzano, R. J. (2009). Setting the record straight on "high-yield" strategies. *Phi Delta Kappan, 91*(1), 30–37.

Marzano, R. J. (2010). *Formative assessment and standards-based grading.* Bloomington, IN: Marzano Research Laboratory.

Marzano, R. J., Pickering, D. J., & Pollock, J. E. (2001). *Classroom instruction that works: Research-based strategies for increasing student achievement.* Alexandria, VA: Association for Supervision and Curriculum Development.

McIntosh, K., Horner, R. H., Chard, D. J., Boland, J. B., & Good, R. H. (2006). The use of reading and behavior screening measures to predict nonresponse to school-wide positive behavior support: A longitudinal analysis. *School Psychology Review, 35*(2), 275–291.

McKinsey & Company. (2003). *The economic impact of the achievement gap in America's schools.* Accessed at www.mckinsey.com/app_media/images/page_images/offices/socialsector/pdf/achievement _gap_report.pdf on August 1, 2011.

McManus, S. (2008). *Attributes of effective formative assessment.* Accessed at www.dpi.state.nc.us/docs /accountability/educators/fastattributes04081.pdf on August 1, 2011.

McMaster, K., & Espin, C. (2007). Technical features of curriculum-based measurement in writing. *Journal of Special Education, 41*(2), 68–84.

Merrell, K. W., & Walker, H. M. (2004). Deconstructing a definition: Social maladjustment versus emotional disturbance and moving the EBD field forward. *Psychology in the Schools, 41*(8), 899–910.

Mogel, W. (2001). *The blessing of a skinned knee: Using Jewish teachings to raise self-reliant children.* New York: Scribner.

Moje, E. B. (2000). *"All the stories we have": Adolescents' insights about literacy and learning in secondary school.* Newark, DE: International Reading Association.

Moje, E. B., & O'Brien, D. G. (Eds.). (2001). *Constructions of literacy: Studies of teaching and learning in and out of secondary schools.* Mahwah, NJ: Erlbaum.

Moncher, F. J., & Prinz, R. J. (1991). Treatment fidelity in outcome studies. *Clinical Psychology Review, 11*(3), 247–266.

Moretti, E. (2007). Crime and the costs of criminal justice. In C. Belfield & H. Levin (Eds.), *The price we pay: Economic and social consequences of inadequate education* (pp. 142–159). Washington DC: Brookings Institution Press.

Morrone, A. S., & Schutz, P. A. (2000). Promoting achievement motivation. In K. M. Minke & G. C. Bear (Eds.), *Preventing school problems—promoting school success: Strategies and programs that work* (pp. 143–169). Bethesda, MD: National Association of School Psychologists.

Muhammad, A. (2009). *Transforming school culture: How to overcome staff division*. Bloomington, IN: Solution Tree Press.

National Center for Educational Statistics. (2006). The Condition of Education. Accessed at http://nces.ed.gov/pubs2006/2006071.pdf on September 15, 2011.

National Governors Association Center for Best Practices and Council of Chief State School Officers. 2010). *Common Core Standards*. Accessed at www.corestandards.org on October 4, 2011.

National Institute for Literacy. (2008). *Developing early literacy: Report of the National Early Literacy Panel*. Accessed at www.nifl.gov/nifl/NELP/NELPreport.html on January 12, 2009.

National Institute of Child Health and Human Development. (2000). Report of the National Reading Panel. *Teaching children to read: An evidence-based assessment of the scientific research literature on reading and its implications for reading instruction* (NIH Publication No. 00-4769). Washington, DC: U.S. Government Printing Office.

Noell, G. H., Freeland, J. T., Witt, J. C., & Gansle, K. A. (2001). Using brief assessments to identify effective interventions for individual students. *Journal of School Psychology, 39*(4), 335–355.

Noell, G. H., Witt, J. C., LaFleur, L. H., Mortenson, B. P., Ranier, D. D., & LeVelle, J. (2000). Increasing teacher intervention implementation in general education following consultation: A comparison of two follow-up strategies. *Journal of Applied Behavior Analysis, 33*(3), 271–284.

Noell, G. H., Witt, J. C., Slider, N. J., Connell, J. E., Gatti, S. L., Williams, K. L., et al. (2005). Treatment implementation following behavioral consultation in schools: A comparison of three follow-up strategies. *School Psychology Review, 34*(1), 87–106.

Obama, B. H. (2009). Inaugural address. Accessed at www.whitehouse.gov/blog/inaugural-address on July 11, 2011.

O'Connor, R. E., Fulmer, D., & Harty, K. (2003, December). *Tiers of intervention in kindergarten through third grade*. Paper presented at the NRCLD Responsiveness-to-Intervention Symposium, Kansas City, MO. Accessed at www.nrcld.org/symposium2003/oconnor/index.html on March 19, 2011.

O'Connor, R. E., Harty, K. R., & Fulmer, D. (2005). Tiers of intervention in kindergarten through third grade. *Journal of Learning Disabilities, 38*(6), 532–538.

OSEP Technical Assistance Center on Positive Behavioral Interventions and Supports. (n.d.). SWPBS for beginners. Accessed at www.pbis.org/school/swpbs_for_beginners.aspx on July 10, 2010.

Patrikakou, E. (2004). *Adolescence: Are parents relevant to students' high school achievement and post-secondary attainment?* Accessed at www.hfrp.org/publications-resources/browse-our-publications /adolescence-are-parents-relevant-to-students-high-school-achievement-and-post-secondary -attainment on November 29, 2009.

Perlman, C. L., & Redding, S. (Eds.). (2009). *Handbook on effective implementation of school improve-ment grants.* Accessed at www.centerii.org/handbook/Resources/Handbook_on_Effective_Implementation_of_School_Improvement_Grants on August 29, 2010.

Peterson, C. A., & McConnell, S. R. (1996). Factors related to intervention integrity and child outcome in social skills intervention. *Journal of Early Intervention, 20*(2), 146–164.

Peterson, K. D. (2002). Positive or negative? *Journal of Staff Development, 23,* 10–15.

Pritchard, R. C., & Raper, R. F. (1996). Doctors and handwashing: Instilling Semmelweis' message. *Medical Journal of Australia, 164*(7), 389–390.

Quint, J. (2008). Lessons from leading models. *Educational Leadership, 65*(8), 64–68.

Reeves, D. B. (2008). Improving student attendance. *Educational Leadership, 65*(8), 90–91.

Renchler, R. (1992). *School leadership and student motivation.* Eugene, OR: ERIC Clearinghouse on Educational Management. (ERIC Document Reproduction Service No. ED346558)

Reschly, D. J., & Hosp, J. L. (2004). State SLD identification policies and practices. *Learning Disability Quarterly, 27*(4), 197–213.

Riley-Tillman, T. C., Chafouleas, S. M., & Eckert, T. L. (2008). Daily behavior report cards and sys-tematic direct observation: An investigation of the acceptability, reported training and use, and decision reliability among school psychologists. *Journal of Behavioral Education, 17*(4), 313–327.

Roberts, G., Torgesen, J. K., Boardman, A., & Scammacca, N. (2008). Evidence-based strategies for reading instruction of older students with learning disabilities. *Learning Disabilities Research and Practice, 23*(2), 63–69.

Rock, M. L., & Thead, B. K. (2009). Promote student success during independent seatwork. *Intervention in School and Clinic, 44*(3), 179–184.

Salvia, J., Ysseldyke, J., & Bolt, S. (2010). *Assessment: In special and inclusive education* (11th ed.). Florence, KY: Cengage Learning.

Sandomierski, T., Kincaid, D., & Algozzine, B. (2007). Response to intervention and positive behavior support: Brothers from different mothers or sisters with different misters? *PBIS Newsletter, 4*(2). Accessed at www.pbis.org/pbis_newsletter/volume_4/issue2.aspx on November 1, 2007.

Scanlon, D., Deshler, D. D., & Schumaker, J. B. (1996). Can a strategy be taught and learned in second-ary inclusive classrooms? *Learning Disabilities Research aand Practice, 11*(1), 41–57.

Schmoker, M. (2006). *Results now: How we can achieve unprecedented improvements in teaching and learn-ing.* Alexandria, VA: Association for Supervision and Curriculum Development.

Scott, T. M., & Barrett, S. B. (2004). Using staff and student time engaged in disciplinary procedures to evaluate the impact of school-wide PBS. *Journal of Positive Behavior Interventions, 6*(1), 21–27.

Shapiro, E. S. (1987). Behavioral assessment of academic skills: Conceptual framework and overview. In E. S. Shapiro (Ed.), *Behavioral assessment in school psychology* (pp. 63–81). Mahwah, NJ: Erlbaum.

Shapiro, E. S., & Lentz, F. E. (1985). Assessing academic behavior: A behavioral approach. *School Psychology Review, 14*(3), 325–338.

Shaywitz, S. (2003). *Overcoming dyslexia: A new and complete science-based program for reading problems at any level.* New York: Knopf.

Shaywitz, S. E., Fletcher, J. M., Holahan, J. M., Shneider, A. E., Marchione, K. E., Stuebing, K. K., et al. (1999). Persistence of dyslexia: The Connecticut longitudinal study at adolescence. *Pediatrics, 104*(6), 1351–1359.

Sherman, L. W., Gottfredson, D. C., MacKenzie, D. L., Eck, J., Reuter, P., & Bushway, S. D. (1998). *Preventing crime: What works, what doesn't, what's promising* (NCJ Publication No. 165366). Washington, DC: U.S. Department of Justice, National Institute of Justice. Accessed at www .ncjrs.gov/pdffiles/171676.pdf on July 13, 2009.

Shinn, M. R. (1989). Case study of Ann H: From referral to annual review. In M. R. Shinn (Ed.), *Curriculum-based measurement: Assessing special children* (pp. 79–89). New York: Guilford Press.

Shinn, M. R. (2002). Best practices in using curriculum-based measurement in a problem-solving model. In A. Thomas & J. Grimes (Eds.), *Best practices in school psychology IV* (pp. 671–698). Bethesda, MD: National Association of School Psychologists.

Shinn, M. R., & Baker, S. K. (1996). The use of curriculum-based measurement with diverse learners. In L. A. Suzuki, P. J. Meller, & J. G. Ponterro (Eds.), *Handbook of multicultural assessment: Clinical, psychological, and educational applications* (pp. 179–222). San Francisco: Jossey-Bass.

Shinn, M. R. & Bamonto, S. (1998). Advanced applications of curriculum-based measurement: "Big ideas" and avoiding confusion. In M. R. Shinn (Ed.), *Advanced applications of curriculum-based measurement* (pp. 1–31). New York: Guilford Press.

Shinn, M. R., & Curriculum-Based Assessment leadership training participants. (1998). *Using curriculum-based measurement in a problem-solving framework: A comprehensive training manual.* Eugene: University of Oregon.

Shinn, M. R., & Good, R. H. (1993). CBA: An assessment of its current status and a prognosis for its future. In J. Kramer (Ed.), *Curriculum-based assessment: Examining old problems, exploring new solutions* (pp. 139–178). Lincoln, ND: Buros Institute.

Shinn, M. R., & Habedank, L. (1992). Curriculum-based measurement in special education problem identification and certification decisions. *Preventing School Failure, 36*(2), 11–15.

Shinn, M. R., Habedank, L., Rodden-Nord, K., & Knutson, N. (1993). Use of curriculum-based measurement to identify potential candidates for reintegration into general education. *Journal of Special Education, 27*(2), 202–221.

Shinn, M. R., & Hubbard, D. D. (1992). Curriculum-based measurement and problem-solving assessment: Basic procedures and outcomes. *Focus on Exceptional Children, 24*(5), 1–20.

Shinn, M., Phillips, M., & March, R. (2008). *School-wide behavior support: Proactive strategies for creating effective learning environments* [NASP workshop presentation materials]. Accessed at http:// schools.nyc.gov/documents/d75/EBS_overview.pdf on July 13, 2009.

Shinn, M. R., Tindal, G. A., & Stein, S. (1988). Curriculum-based measurement and the identification of mildly handicapped students: A research review. *Professional School Psychology, 3*(1), 69–85.

Silberglitt, B., & Gibbons, K. A. (2005). *Establishing slope targets for use in a response to intervention model* [Technical manual]. Rush City, MN: St. Croix River Education District.

Silberglitt, B., & Hintze, J. (2005). Formative assessment using CBM-R cut scores to track progress toward success on state-mandated achievement tests: A comparison of methods. *Journal of Psychoeducational Assessment, 23*(4), 304–325.

Simeonsson, R. J. (Ed.). (1994). *Risk, resilience and prevention: Promoting the well-being of all children.* Baltimore: Brookes.

Snow, C. (2002). *Reading for understanding: Toward an R&D program in reading comprehension.* Santa Monica, CA: RAND.

Sousa, D. A. & Tomlinson, C. A. (2011). *Differentiation and the brain: How neuroscience supports the learner-friendly classroom. Bloomington, IN: Solution Tree.* Sprick, R. S. (2006). *Discipline in the secondary classroom: A positive approach to behavior management* (2nd ed.). San Francisco: Jossey-Bass.

Stanovich, K. E. (1986). Matthew effects in reading: Some consequences of individual differences in the acquisition of literacy. *Reading Research Quarterly, 21*(4), 360–407.

Stecker, P. M., & Fuchs, L. S. (2000). Effecting superior achievement using curriculum-based measurement: The importance of individual progress monitoring. *Learning Disabilities Research & Practice, 15*(3), 128–134.

Stewart, R. M., Benner, G. J., Martella, R. C., & Marchand-Martella, N. E. (2007). Three-tier models of reading and behavior: A research review. *Journal of Positive Behavior Interventions, 9*(4), 239–253.

Strom, T. (2010). *Minnesota school finance: A guide for legislators.* Minnesota House of Representatives, St. Paul Research Department.

Sugai, G. (2007). *SWPBS coaching: Functions & fidelity of implementation.* Paper presented at the Maryland PBIS Summer Institute in Ellicott City, MD. Accessed at www.pbis.org/presentations/default.aspx on September 8, 2011.

Sugai, G., Flannery, B., & Bohanon-Edmonson, H. (2004). School-wide positive behavior support in high schools: What will it take? In H. Bohanon-Edmonson, K. B. Flannery, L. Eber, & G. Sugai (2004). *Positive Behavior Support in High Schools: Monograph from the 2004 Illinois High School Forum of Positive Behavioral Interventions and Supports.* Accessed at www.pbis.org/google_search.aspx?keyword=sugai,%202004 on September 15, 2011.

Sugai, G., & Horner, R. (2002). The evolution of discipline practices: School-wide positive behavior supports. In J. K. Luiselli & C. Diament (Eds.), *Behavior psychology in the schools: Innovations in evaluation, support, and consultation* (pp. 23–49). New York: Hawthorne Press.

Swanson, H. L., Hoskyn, M., & Lee, C. (1999). *Interventions for students with learning disabilities: A meta-analysis of treatment outcomes.* New York: Guilford Press.

Thinkexist.com. (n.d.). *Francis Bacon, Sr., quotes.* Accessed at http://thinkexist.com/quotation/it-s-not-what-we-eat-but-what-we-digest-that/397509.html on September 8, 2011.

Tibballs, J. (1996). Teaching hospital medical staff to handwash. *Medical Journal of Australia, 164*(7), 395–398.

Ticha, R., Espin, C. A., & Wayman, M. M. (2009). Reading progress monitoring for secondary-school students: Reliability, validity, and sensitivity to growth of reading aloud and maze-selection measures. *Learning Disabilities Research and Practice, 24*(3), 132–142.

Tilly, W. D. (2003, December). *How many tiers are needed for successful prevention and early intervention? Heartland Area Education Agency's evolution from four to three tiers.* Paper presented at the National Research Center on Learning Disabilities Responsiveness-to-Intervention Symposium, Kansas City, MO. Accessed at www.nrcld. org/symposium2003/tilly/index.html on March 19, 2011.

Todd, A. W., Campbell, A. L., Meyer, G. G., & Horner, R. H. (2008). The effects of a targeted intervention to reduce problem behaviors: Elementary school implementation of check in—check out. *Journal of Positive Behavior Interventions, 10*(1), 46–55.

Tomlinson, C. A. (2010). Differentiating instruction in response to academically diverse student populations. In R. J. Marzano (Ed.), *On excellence in teaching* (pp. 247–268). Bloomington, IN: Solution Tree Press.

Tomlinson, C. A., & Eidson, C. C. (2003). *Differentiation in practice: A resource guide for differentiating curriculum, grades K–5.* Alexandria, VA: Association for Supervision and Curriculum Development.

Torgesen, J. K. (2002). The prevention of reading difficulties. *Journal of School Psychology, 40*(1), 7–26.

Torgesen, J. K. (2004). Lessons learned from research on interventions for students who experience difficulty learning to read. In P. McCardle & V. Chhabra (Eds.), *The voice of evidence in reading research* (pp. 355–382). Baltimore: Brookes.

Torgesen, J., Rashotte, C., Alexander, A., Alexander, J., & MacPhee, K. (2003). Progress toward understanding the instructional conditions necessary for remediating reading difficulties in older children. In B. R. Foorman (Ed.), *Preventing and remediating reading difficulties: Bringing science to scale* (pp. 275–297). Baltimore: York Press.

Torgesen, J. K., Wagner, R. K., Rashotte, C. A., Rose, E., Lindamood, P., Conway, T., et al. (1999). Preventing reading failure in young children with phonological processing disabilities: Group and individual responses to instruction. *Journal of Educational Psychology, 91*(4), 579–593.

Upah, K. R. F., & Tilly, W. D. (2002). Best practices in designing, implementing, and evaluation quality interventions. In A. Thomas & J. Grimes (Eds.), *Best practices in school psychology IV* (pp. 483–502). Bethesda, MD: National Association of School Psychologists.

U.S. Department of Education. (1999). *Start early, finish strong: How to help every child become a reader.* Washington, DC: Author.

Vaughn, S. (2003, December). *How many tiers are needed for Response to Intervention to achieve acceptable prevention outcomes and to achieve acceptable patterns of LD identification?* Paper presented at the

National Research Center on Learning Disabilities Responsiveness-to-Intervention Symposium, Kansas City, MO. Accessed at www.nrcld.org/symposium2003/index.html on October 8, 2008.

Vaughn, S., Bos, C. S., & Schumm, J. S. (1997). *Teaching mainstreamed, diverse, and at-risk students in the general education classroom.* Boston: Allyn & Bacon.

Vaughn, S. R., Bos, C. S., & Schumm, J. S. (2004). Teaching students who are exceptional, diverse, and at risk in the general education classroom (4th ed.). Boston: Allyn & Bacon.

Vaughn, S., Cirino, P. T., Wanzek, J., Wexler, J., Fletcher, J., Denton C. D., et al. (2010). Response to intervention for middle school students with reading difficulties: Effects of a primary and secondary intervention. *School Psychology Review 39*(1), 3–21.

Vaughn, S., Linan-Thompson, S., Mathes, P. G., Cirino, P. T., Carlson, C. D., Pollard-Durodola, S. D., et al. (2006). Effectiveness of Spanish intervention for first-grade English language learners at risk for reading difficulties. *Journal of Learning Disabilities, 39*(1), 56–73.

Vaughn, S., Moody, S. W., & Schumm, J. S. (1998). Broken promises: Reading instruction in the resource room. *Exceptional Children, 64*(2), 221–225.

Vellutino, F. R., Scanlon, D. M., & Lyon, G. R. (2000). Differentiating between difficult-to-remediate and readily remediated poor readers: More evidence against the IQ-achievement discrepancy definition of reading disability. *Journal of Learning Disabilities, 33*(3), 223–238.

Vellutino, F. R., Scanlon, D. M., Sipay, E. R., Small, S. G., Pratt, A., Chen, R., et al. (1996). Cognitive profiles of difficult-to-remediate and readily remediated poor readers: Early intervention as a vehicle for distinguishing between cognitive and experimental deficits as basic causes of specific reading disability. *Journal of Educational Psychology, 88,* 601–638.

Walker, B., Cheney, D., Stage, S., Blum, C., & Horner, R. H. (2005). Schoolwide screening and positive behavior support: Identifying and supporting students at risk of school failure. *Journal of Positive Behavior Interventions 7*(4), 194–204.

Walker, H. M., Horner, R. H., Sugai, G., Bullis, M., Sprague, J. R., Bricker, D., et al. (1996). Integrated approaches to preventing antisocial behavior patterns among school-age children and youth. *Journal of Emotional and Behavioral Disorders, 4*(4), 194–209.

Wesson, C. L. (1990/1991). Curriculum-based measurement and two models of follow-up consultation. *Exceptional Children, 57*(3), 246–256.

Wesson, C., Skiba, R., Sevcik, B., King, R. P., & Deno, S. (1984). The effects of technically adequate instructional data on achievement. *Remedial and Special Education, 5*(5), 17–22.

W.E.T. v. Mitchell, 49 IDELR 130 M.D. N.C. (2008)

Wickstrom, K. F., Jones, K. M., La Fleur, L. H., & Witt, B. P. (1998). An analysis of treatment integrity in school-based behavioral consultation. *School Psychology Quarterly, 13*(2), 141–154.

Wigfield, A., & Eccles, J. S. (1994). Children's competence beliefs, achievement values, and general self-esteem: Change across elementary and middle school. *Journal of Early Adolescence, 14*(2), 107–138.

Windram, H., Scierka, B., & Silberglitt, B. (2007). Response to intervention at the secondary level: Two districts' models of implementation. *Communiqué, 35*(5), 43–45.

Wormeli, R. (2006). *Fair isn't always equal: Assessing & grading in the differentiated classroom.* Portland, ME: Stenhouse.

Wormeli, R. (2007). *Differentiation: From planning to practice, grades 6–12.* Portland, ME: Stenhouse.

Yeh, S. S. (2007). The cost-effectiveness of five policies for improving student achievement. *American Journal of Evaluation, 28*(4), 416–436.

Yeh, S. S. (2009). Class size reduction or rapid formative assessment? A comparison of cost-effectiveness. *Educational Research Review, 4*(1), 7–15.

Ysseldyke, J. E., Thurlow, M. L., Mecklenburg, C., & Graden, J. (1984). Opportunity to learn for regular and special education students during reading instruction. *Remedial and Special Education, 5*(1), 29–37.

Index

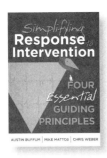

Simplifying Response to Intervention: Four Essential Guiding Principles

Austin Buffum, Mike Mattos, and Chris Weber

The sequel to *Pyramid Response to Intervention* advocates that effective RTI begins by asking the right questions to create a fundamentally effective learning environment for every student. Understand why paperwork-heavy, compliance-oriented, test-score-driven approaches fail. Then learn how to create an RTI model that works. **BKF506**

Pyramid Response to Intervention: RTI, PLCs, and How to Respond When Kids Don't Learn

Austin Buffum, Mike Mattos, and Chris Weber
Foreword by Richard DuFour

Accessible language and compelling stories illustrate how RTI is most effective when built on the Professional Learning Communities at Work™ model. Written by award-winning educators, this book details three tiers of interventions—from basic to intensive—and includes implementation ideas. **BKF251**

Power Tools for Adolescent Literacy: Strategies for Learning

Jan Rozzelle and Carol Scearce

Power Tools for Adolescent Literacy integrates key strategies from Dr. Robert Marzano's meta-analysis and research from top literacy experts in a comprehensive collection of best practices and powerful literacy tools for middle and high school teachers. **BKF261**

Closing the RTI Gap: Why Poverty and Culture Count

Donna Walker Tileston

Understand why RTI is so important and how to achieve successful implementation in your school. Get a clear understanding of poverty and culture, and learn how RTI can close achievement gaps related to these issues. Examine the critical planning phase of RTI, and preview common pitfalls of implementation. **BKF330**

Raising the Bar and Closing the Gap: Whatever It Takes

Richard DuFour, Rebecca DuFour, Robert Eaker, and Gayle Karhanek

This sequel to the best-selling *Whatever It Takes: How Professional Learning Communities Respond When Kids Don't Learn* expands on original ideas and presses further with new insights. Foundational concepts combine with real-life examples of schools throughout North America that have gone from traditional cultures to PLCs. **BKF378**

a division of
Solution Tree

Visit solution-tree.com or call 800.733.6786 to order.